SENTENCING

Selected Titles in ABC-CLIO's
CONTEMPORARY
WORLD ISSUES
Series

For a complete list of titles in this series, please visit
www.abc-clio.com.

Books in the Contemporary World Issues series address vital issues in today's society such as genetic engineering, pollution, and biodiversity. Written by professional writers, scholars, and nonacademic experts, these books are authoritative, clearly written, up-to-date, and objective. They provide a good starting point for research by high school and college students, scholars, and general readers as well as by legislators, businesspeople, activists, and others.

Each book, carefully organized and easy to use, contains an overview of the subject, a detailed chronology, biographical sketches, facts and data and/or documents and other primary-source material, a directory of organizations and agencies, annotated lists of print and nonprint resources, and an index.

Readers of books in the Contemporary World Issues series will find the information they need in order to have a better understanding of the social, political, environmental, and economic issues facing the world today.

SENTENCING

A Reference Handbook

Dean John Champion

**CONTEMPORARY
WORLD ISSUES**

A B C ☰ C L I O

Santa Barbara, California
Denver, Colorado
Oxford, England

Library of Congress Cataloging-in-Publication Data
Champion, Dean J.
    Sentencing : a reference handbook / Dean John Champion.
        p.   cm. — (Contemporary world issues)
    Includes bibliographical references and index.
    ISBN 978-1-59884-087-2 (hard copy : alk. paper) — ISBN 978-1-59884-088-9 (ebook)   1. Sentences (Criminal procedure)—United States.   2. Sentences (Criminal procedure)—United States—Cases.   3. Sentences (Criminal procedure).   I. Title.
    KF9685.C48 2007
    345.73'0772—dc22
                                                    2007007412

12   11   10   09   08   10 9 8 7 6 5 4 3 2 1

ABC-CLIO, Inc.
130 Cremona Drive, P.O. Box 1911
Santa Barbara, California 93116-1911

This book is also available on the World Wide Web as an ebook.
Visit www.abc-clio.com for details.

This book is printed on acid-free paper ∞

Manufactured in the United States of America.

Contents

Preface

Sentencing: A Reference Handbook examines the sentencing process in detail. Chapter 1 defines sentencing and its goals. Sentencing is the application of one or more punishments/sanctions following a criminal conviction. These punishments include fines and/or incarceration, or placement under the supervision of probation officers. The Sentencing Reform Act of 1984 restated a number of sentencing objectives that have guided sentencing judges in their leniency or harshness toward convicted defendants. Some of those objectives have been made explicit by various states and local jurisdictions in past years, while others have been implicitly incorporated into prevailing sentencing guidelines. Some of the more important functions and goals of sentencing are (1) to promote respect for the law, (2) to reflect the seriousness of the offense, (3) to provide just punishment for the offense, (4) to deter the defendant from future criminal conduct, (5) to protect the public from the convicted offender, and (6) to provide the convicted defendant with education and/or vocational training or other rehabilitative relief. The purposes of sentencing include punishment or retribution, deterrence, custodial monitoring or incapacitation, and rehabilitation. Four different types of sentencing schemes will be described: indeterminate, determinate, presumptive or guidelines-based, and mandatory. The differences between state and federal sentencing policies will be examined. A history of sentencing in the United States is presented as well.

Accused persons have established, constitutional rights under the law, which are examined here. The sentencing process often involves a formal sentencing hearing in which both convicted offenders and victims have the opportunity to influence the sentencing decision. This process is examined in detail. Both victim and offender input are crucial during sentencing hearings. Convicted offenders may choose to accept responsibility for their actions and thus attempt to minimize their sentences, while victims can explain to the court how their lives have been harmed by the offender's actions, in an effort to enhance punishment. Judges must weigh these factors and give them proper acknowledgment. Consideration is given to both aggravating and mitigating circumstances to enhance or minimize the punishments contemplated by judges when imposing sentences. Once sentences have been imposed, however, they may be appealed. Thus the appeals process is examined. Both legal and extralegal factors emerge as key considerations in the sentencing process. Some critics of the U.S. sentencing system say that it is racist and deprives certain persons of their full entitlement to legal rights according to socioeconomic factors. These factors will be discussed.

Chapter 2 is a discussion of some of the problems, controversies, and solutions to sentencing problems. Judicial decisionmaking about the types of sentences to be imposed is not always clear-cut. Every trial is different from the next, and sentencing offenders is not as easy as it appears at first glance. Sentencing is a major concern for those advocating justice reforms. The federal government and most states have passed new sentencing legislation in response to criticisms that present sentencing practices are discriminatory according to gender, race or ethnic background, and socioeconomic status. Over the years citizen discontent with existing sentencing laws and particular sensationalized crimes have caused state and federal legislators to change sentencing laws. It is believed that such changes will correct existing legal defects associated with sentencing practices and create a sentencing pattern based more upon just deserts. Thus proportionality of sentencing is a desired long-term objective of most sentencing schemes. Those who commit more serious offenses should receive harsher sentences.

But what is ideally visualized as the right sentencing scenario seldom materializes. There are continuing and pervasive problems with all sentencing schemes in virtually all jurisdictions. Many persons are wrongfully convicted, and many are overpenalized. Some guilty persons escape punishment. Although the exact figures of how many such persons pass through the legal system annually are unknown, there are sufficient documented occurrences of these cases that serious questions continue to be raised about our existing sentencing laws and the adequacy of our legal system.

Several key issues relating to sentencing policies at the state and federal levels will be examined. Should convicted persons receive probation or incarceration? Jail and prison overcrowding exists at unprecedented levels, and overcrowding problems are increasing rather than diminishing. It is strategically impossible to lock up everyone, and thus, some attention needs to be given to which offenders deserve incarceration the most. That is where selective incapacitation has been proposed. But the matter of false positives and false negatives arises. Some persons are predicted to be dangerous but in fact will not be dangerous if released to probation. Other offenders are predicted not to be dangerous, but once they are released on probation they commit heinous crimes or harm others. Clearly our prediction schemes are imperfect and are in need of revision and improvement.

The public blames judges and parole boards for abuses of discretion and faulty decision-making. But there are pressures upon these key figures and boards to minimize or abbreviate incarceration. Furthermore, offenders believe that they are entitled to some type of rehabilitation so that they may eventually be able to reintegrate themselves back into society. To what extent are jails and prisons providing effective rehabilitation and treatment for such persons? Only about 20 percent of all inmates in U.S. prisons and jails have vocational and educational opportunities. Contrary to popular belief, most prisoners do not perform prison labor. Thus many of these offenders are simply warehoused without any meaningful rehabilitation or improvement occurring. Recidivism and program effectiveness are closely intertwined, therefore, and various issues related to recidivism rates will be considered.

Chapter 3 examines the sentencing systems in fifteen other countries. This international perspective exposes many of the similarities and differences among the many industrialized countries of the world. While this chapter is not comprehensive, it is nevertheless representative of the sentencing schemes of most other world countries. It provides readers with a clearer idea of how the U.S. sentencing system and justice process work and how it compares with justice schemes used by other countries in punishing their criminals.

Chapter 4 is a chronology of key events in U.S. sentencing history. It is worth noting that many sentencing schemes have been appealed to the U.S. Supreme Court, where their constitutionality has been questioned. Each era of a U.S. Supreme Court is frequently cited by a reference to the presiding chief justice, such as the "Warren Court" or the "Burger Court." Particular landmark cases in sentencing issues are often defined by the justices who decide these cases, either for or against defendants.

Chapter 5 presents biographical sketches of key persons who have influenced the sentencing process in the United States. Some of these key figures are from Ireland and England, inasmuch as their innovations were presented at an international conference in Cincinnati, Ohio, in 1870 at the first meeting of the National Prison Association, which later became the widely known American Correctional Association; in 2006 it had a membership in excess of 33,000. These key figures, who have shaped our sentencing schemes over time, also include various chief justices of the U.S. Supreme Court, where final decisions about the constitutionality of various sentencing practices have been determined.

Chapter 6 is an examination of facts and data pertaining to sentenced persons in the United States. Profiles of those presently sentenced in U.S. prisons and jails are described. What are their ethnic/racial and gender characteristics? What types of crimes have they committed? Offenders on probation and parole are also profiled. These profiles give readers a good idea of the types of persons who are among us in our neighborhoods and cities. In addition, average sentence lengths give us an appreciation for how much justice is employed in the punishment process. State and federal sentencing patterns are compared, and sentencing trends are examined and discussed. This chapter also identifies and briefs approximately thirty leading U.S. Supreme Court cases pertaining to sentencing, including the constitutionality of the U.S. Sentencing Guidelines, sex offender sentencing laws, reconvictions and resentencing, acceptance of responsibility during sentencing hearings, and the presentation of aggravating and mitigating circumstances that weigh heavily in sentencing decisions by judges. These cases are presented chronologically and contain precise citations so that students may locate complete cases in legal volumes for further reading and study.

Chapter 7 is an annotated directory of organizations, associations, and agencies that relate to the sentencing process. Every attempt has been made to include relevant organizations that have a vested interest in sentencing, both from the prosecution side and the defense perspective. All indigent defendants are entitled to representation by competent counsel. Therefore organizations such as public defender agencies are presented. Based on our previous examination of world sentencing schemes, the United Nations has become involved in U.S. sentencing issues repeatedly, especially in issues relating to the death penalty and its administration. Amnesty International and the American Civil Liberties Union have also been involved in a concerted effort to ensure and protect the rights of both accused and convicted persons

Chapter 8 lists both print and nonprint resources pertaining to sentencing. These include bibliographical materials dealing with various sentencing issues and problems, annotated print resources pertaining to factual sentencing information, and nonprint resources such as films and documentaries that would enhance our understanding of the sentencing process.

Finally, a glossary of key terms used in sentencing offenders is presented. Terms used in the sentencing process are clearly defined. The glossary is reasonably comprehensive, although more extensive compendiums of terms exist and are cited for further student reading.

1

Background and History

Introduction

Judicial decision-making about the types of sentences to impose is not always a clear-cut matter. Every trial is different from every other, and the sentencing of offenders is not as easy as it appears at first glance. This chapter defines sentencing and describes the sentencing process. Sentencing is a major concern of those who advocate for judicial reform. The federal government and most states have passed new sentencing legislation in response to criticisms that present sentencing practices are discriminatory according to gender, race, or ethnic background, or according to socioeconomic status (Delone and Wilmot 2004). Four different types of sentencing schemes will be described: indeterminate, determinate, presumptive or guidelines-based, and mandatory. A brief history of sentencing in the United States is also presented.

Most major felony cases and some minor misdemeanor cases require probation officers to prepare presentence investigation reports (PSIs) about convicted offenders who are about to be sentenced. Such reports include information about the offender, the nature of the crime(s), the offender's employment history and prior criminal record (if any), the offender's family, the offender's educational background, and a statement from victims about how they were affected by the offender's actions. That information is eventually delivered to judges in a succinct report that is useful in determining the most appropriate sentence.

An important part of the sentencing process is the sentencing hearing, which is the opportunity for judges to weigh any aggravating or mitigating circumstances that might influence the

1

severity of the sentence. Both the offender and the offender's supporters speak out in his or her behalf, and victims also contribute information about how they were affected. After hearing from those parties, the judge pronounces the sentence prescribed by law. Sentencing options available to judges differ among jurisdictions. At the judge's discretion, in most cases, sentences may involve either probation with conditions or incarceration in a prison or a jail for a period of months or years, or both.

Sentencing Defined

Sentencing is the imposition of a punishment on an offender following conviction for a criminal offense. Judges impose sentences, which may involve incarceration in a prison or jail, or they may involve placement in community corrections facilities. Those allowed to remain free in the community are called probationers (Beyer, Grisso, and Young 1997). The U.S. district courts and state criminal courts vary in the amount of probation used. Approximately 70 percent of all sentenced offenders nationally are placed on probation. Federal probationers are supervised by the U.S. Probation Office, while state probationers are supervised by state probation officers, who often work out of county probation offices. There are many types of sentencing schemes, which are described below.

Goals of Sentencing

Some of the more important goals of sentencing are the following: (1) to promote respect for the law, (2) to reflect the seriousness of the offense, (3) to provide just punishment for the offense, (4) to deter the defendant from future criminal conduct, (5) to protect the public from the convicted offender, and (6) to provide the convicted offender with educational or vocational training, or other rehabilitative assistance. The purposes of sentencing include punishment or retribution, deterrence, custodial monitoring or incapacitation, and rehabilitation.

Promote Respect for the Law

When offenders are sentenced, judges send a message to the criminal community. If the sentence is too lenient, the message is that offenders will not be punished harshly. Many offenders may therefore engage in further criminal conduct, believing that even if they are subsequently apprehended the punishment will be mild. Judges attempt to promote respect for the law by imposing appropriate sentences that are proportional to the crime(s) committed. Their intended message is that if the law is violated, violators will be sanctioned. Ideally, such a view promotes respect for the law and functions as a deterrent to would-be criminals (Weidner, Frase, and Pardoe 2004).

Reflect the Seriousness of the Offense

One objective of sentencing is to match the sentence with the seriousness of the offense. More serious crimes deserve harsher punishments. Violent criminals are usually punished more severely than property offenders, because violent crimes often result in serious bodily injury or death. Property can be replaced, whereas life cannot. Thus punishments should be proportional to the seriousness of the crime.

Provide Just Punishment for the Offense

Sentencing policies in most jurisdictions in the United States have shifted in recent years to reflect the justice model, which is a legitimization of the power of the state to administer sanctions. The justice model emphasizes punishment as a primary objective of sentencing, the abolition of parole, the abandonment of the rehabilitative ideal, and determinate sentencing (Aas 2004).

Deter the Defendant from Future Criminal Conduct

Not only is sentencing designed as a punishment fitting to the crime, but it is also designed to function as a deterrent to future criminal activity. At least two major provisions have been designed to equate offense seriousness with the harshness of the penalty. One is esclated santions. As offenders reoffend, their penalties or sentence lengths increase, even if the same offenses are repeated in later, separate crimes. The most significant legislation has been the establishment of habitual offender or repeat offender laws, whereby those convicted of three or more felonies are sentenced to life imprisonment. California has a "Three Strikes and You're Out!" law, enacted in 1994, under which repeat offenders are sentenced to life without parole. That get-tough action was designed to deter violent recidivists, such as robbers and murderers. The thinking was that if repeat violent offenders have not learned their lesson by the time they are convicted of their third violent offense, they should be locked up permanently (Bruce et al. 1928).

Protect the Public from the Convicted Offender

Incarcerating convicted offenders is the most direct way of protecting the public from them. If they are locked up, they cannot commit crimes against fellow citizens. Longer sentences generally mean longer periods during which criminals cannot victimize society. Some persons believe that all criminals should be locked up for some period of time, in order to insulate a vulnerable public from their criminal activities (Ulmer and Johnson 2004).

Provide the Convicted Offender with Educational or Vocational Training, or Other Rehabilitative Assistance

This is the rehabilitative function of sentencing. Rehabilitation has always been a fundamental goal of sentencing. A prevailing belief is that some attempt should be made to reform criminals while they are incarcerated. We should not merely warehouse offenders; rather, educational and vocational programs should be offered to help those who are interested in helping themselves. It is better to provide some services for those who will use them than to withhold rehabilitative services because of those who will not (Klug 2001).

Purposes of Sentencing

The purposes of sentencing are: (1) retribution, (2) deterrence and prevention, (3) just deserts and justice, (4) incapacitation and control, and (5) rehabilitation and reintegration.

Retribution

Any sentence imposed for a criminal offense is designed to exact retribution for crimes committed. Perpetrators must be punished in some way in order to comply with criminal law. Punishments include jail or prison time, fines, or both. Proportionality is sought so that the greater the offense, the greater the punishment.

Deterrence and Prevention

When offenders see other offenders punished for their crimes and given harsh sentences, an element of deterrence is introduced wherein potential criminals are deterred from committing crimes because of the penalties they may suffer if caught. To some extent, at least, some crime is prevented and some criminals are deterred because of the sentences that others receive. If potential offenders refrain from committing crimes because of the painfulness of prospective punishments, then some deterrence and prevention has been accomplished.

Just Desserts and Justice

The judiciary attempt to match sentences imposed to the nature and seriousness of conviction offenses. Citizens are satisfied whenever criminals are punished in ways that equate with the seriousness of their crime. The public is dissatisfied whenever criminals receive lenient sentences that do not seem justified in view of the crime. Prosecutors seek penalties that satisfy the law, both technically and morally.

Incapacitation and Control

Whether criminals are sexual predators, embezzlers, murderers, or petty thieves, citizens wish to be protected from them. Thus, placing criminals in some type of confinement facility such as a jail or prison effectively removes them from society. But, because of chronic jail and prison overcrowding, not all convicted offenders can be incarcerated. Therefore alternative methods, such as probation, are used to supervise and control these criminals. Probation is a sentence in lieu of incarceration. For particularly low-risk offenders, probation permits offenders to remain in their communities, hold jobs, and support their families. They are supervised by probation officers and must comply with various program conditions. For offenders already serving prison terms, their terms of incarceration may be abbreviated through the use of parole. Parole is similar to probation in that parolees are supervised by parole officers and must comply with various program conditions for a fixed period of time.

Rehabilitation and Reintegration

Corrections programs are supposed to correct the behavior of offenders and make them into law-abiding citizens, respectful of the rights of others. However, two-thirds or more of all convicted offenders commit new offenses. The offending rate varies according to the type of offense and other variables. There is sufficient recidivism among criminals, however, to indicate that true rehabilitation does not occur in a majority of cases. Much effort is expended at the local, state, and federal levels to ensure that offenders receive vocational and educational training to maximize their chances for rehabilitation and reintegration. There are many reintegrative programs available to criminals of all types, including vocational-educational curricula, individual and group counseling, and a variety of social services. Offenders are encouraged to participate in these programs, whether they are offered in jails, prisons, or in the community. One indicator that rehabilitation does occur is the amount of remorse expressed by convicted offenders and their acceptance of responsibility for their criminal acts.

Types of Sentencing Schemes

During the last several decades, sentencing practices in most states have undergone transformation. There is disagreement, however, about the number and types of sentencing systems currently used by the states. Furthermore, new sentencing schemes continue to be proposed. The following types of sentencing schemes are used in most jurisdictions: (1) indeterminate sentencing, (2) determinate sentencing, (3) presumptive sentencing, and (4) mandatory sentencing. Beyond those four categories, other hybrid sentencing schemes have been devised.

Indeterminate Sentencing

For many decades the most frequently used form of sentencing was indeterminate sentencing. Indeterminate sentencing involves setting explicit upper and lower limits on the amount of time to be served by the offender, with one's early-release date (from either prison or jail) determined by a parole board. The judge may sentence an offender to "one to ten years," or "not more than five years," and a parole board determines when the offender may be released within the limits of those time intervals. In the "one- to ten-year" sentence, an inmate may be released early by a parole board after serving at least one year of the sentence. Alternatively, the parole board may release the inmate after two or three years. Early release is often based upon an inmate's institutional behavior. Good behavior is rewarded with early release, while bad conduct may result in an inmate's having to serve the full ten-year sentence. At the end of the sentence, however, the jurisdiction must release the inmate, as all of the sentence will have been served (U.S. Sentencing Commission 2006).

Determinate Sentencing

Determinate sentencing denotes a fixed term of incarceration that must be served in full, less any "good time" earned while in prison. Good time is a reduction in the time served, amounting to a certain number of days per month for each month served. If inmates obey the rules and stay out of trouble, they accumulate good-time credit that accelerates their release. In states using determinate sentencing, parole boards have no discretion in determining an inmate's early release. In 2005 there were twenty-six states that used determinate sentencing. There were thirty-five states using both indeterminate and determinate sentencing in 2005 (ibid. 2003).

Three types of good-time credit may be accumulated by inmates: (1) statutory good time, whereby inmates acquire good time by serving time without problems or incidents, (2) earned good time, in which inmates acquire good time by good behavior, or participation in education or self-improvement programs and work programs, and (3) meritorious good time, wherein good-time credit is earned by exceptional acts or services. Inmates may earn all three types of good time during their imprisonment. For example, Nebraska authorizes statutory good time of 7.5 days per month, up to half of the maximum term reduction, in addition to earned days of 7.5 days per month served, totaling 15 days per month per 30 days served. In North Dakota, 5 days of statutory good time are permitted per month; up to 2 additional days per month may be granted for extraordinary acts by inmates, and 5 days per month of earned good time (given for performance at work, school, and in treatment programs). All must comply to earn good time. For example, if an inmate chooses to enroll in a GED program, he/she may earn good-time credit, but it cannot be earned simply by serving time in prison. The inmate must enroll or comply with the rules for earned good-time credit accumulations; thus, all inmates must comply with the work, school, or treatment program requirements, if they want to earn good-time credit. All inmates are given the highest possible amount of good time to be earned upon entrance; if they become noncompliant, however, they receive an "incident report" (write-up), and the Adjustment Committee sanctions loss of good time (Champion 2008).

There are several variations on good-time accumulation. New Hampshire adds 150 days to one's minimum sentence; those days are reduced by earning 12.5 days per month for exemplary conduct; failure to earn this good time means that the inmate must serve additional time beyond the minimum sentence. In Ohio, 1 day of statutory good time per month up to a total sentence reduction of 3 percent may be accumulated, while 1 day per month of earned good time can be accumulated. The Federal Bureau of Prisons permits up to 54 days per year of statutory good time. Fifty-four days a year constitute approximately 15 percent of one's total sentence, and that fits the federal sentencing model in which offenders are expected to serve at least 85 percent of their sentence before becoming eligible for parole. The federal government has encouraged individual states to adopt truth-in-sentencing provisions whereby incarcerated offenders must serve most of their original sentences before being considered eligible for parole. Various states have adopted these truth-in-sentencing provisions in their sentencing schemes in exchange for federal grant money for correctional improvements.

Presumptive Sentencing

Presumptive or guidelines-based sentencing is a specific sentence, usually expressed as a range of months, for each and every offense or offense class. The sentence must be imposed in all unexceptional cases, but when there are mitigating or aggravating circumstances, judges are permitted some latitude in shortening or lengthening sentences within specific boundaries.

Aggravating circumstances are those factors that may increase the severity of punishment. Some of the factors considered by judges to be aggravating include the following: (1) whether the crime involved death or serious bodily injury to one or more victims, (2) whether the crime was committed while the offender was out on bail facing other criminal charges, (3) whether the offender was on probation, parole, or work release at the time that the crime was committed, (4) whether the offender was a recidivist who had been punished for several previous offenses, (5) whether the offender was the leader in the commission of the offense involving two or more offenders, (6) whether the offense involved more than one victim or was a violent crime, (7) whether the offender treated the victim(s) with extreme cruelty during the commission of the offense, and (8) whether the offender used a dangerous weapon in the commission of the crime and the risk to human life was high.

Whenever PSI reports or sentencing hearings disclose one or more aggravating circumstances about the offender or crime committed, judges are likely to intensify the punishment imposed. That might mean a longer sentence, incarceration instead of probation, or a sentence served in a maximum-security prison rather than a minimum- or medium-security institution. Mitigating circumstances may influence judges to be lenient with offenders and place them on probation rather than in jail or prison. For example, a sentence of a year or less may be imposed rather than a five-year term.

Mitigating circumstances are those factors considered by the sentencing judge to reduce the crime's severity. Some of the more frequently cited mitigating factors in the commission of crimes might be the following: (1) the offender did not cause serious bodily injury during the commission of the crime, (2) the convicted defendant did not contemplate that the crime would inflict serious bodily injury, (3) the offender acted under duress or extreme provocation, (4) the offender's conduct was possibly justified under the circumstances, (5) the offender was suffering from mental incapacitation or some physical condition that significantly diminished culpability, (6) the offender cooperated with authorities in apprehending other participants in the crime or in making restitution to the victims for losses suffered, (7) the offender committed the crime out of the need to secure basic necessities, and (8) the offender did not have a previous criminal record.

Judges weigh the mitigating and aggravating circumstances involved in an offender's conviction offense. If the aggravating circumstances outweigh the mitigating ones, the judge is justified in intensifying the severity of the sentence. However, if the mitigating circumstances predominate, the judge may exhibit greater leniency. Judges have considerable discretionary power when sentencing offenders. How particular circumstances may be evaluated, however, is highly individual. Some judges may impose especially harsh sentences even though there may be extensive mitigating circumstances, simply because they don't like, say, child sexual abusers. In addition, judges also consider the risk or danger posed by particular offenders.

If judges contemplate placing convicted offenders on probation and permitting them the freedom to move about within the community, they may want to have some objective criteria to assist them in their probation decision. One example of sentencing guidelines would be those created by the U.S. Sentencing Commission that went into effect in October 1987. Table 1.1 is the U.S.

TABLE 1.1
Sentencing (months of imprisonment)

	Offense Level	I (0 or 1)	II (2 or 3)	III (4, 5, 6)	IV (7, 8, 9)	V (10, 11, 12)	VI (13 or more)
	1	0–6	0–6	0–6	0–6	0–6	0–6
	2	0–6	0–6	0–6	0–6	0–6	1–7
	3	0–6	0–6	0–6	0–6	2–8	3–9
	4	0–6	0–6	0–6	2–8	4–10	6–12
Zone A	5	0–6	0–6	1–7	4–10	6–12	9–15
	6	0–6	1–7	2–8	6–12	9–15	12–18
	7	0–6	2–8	4–10	8–14	12–18	15–21
	8	0–6	4–10	6–12	10–16	15–21	18–24
Zone B	9	4–10	6–12	8–14	12–18	18–24	21–27
	10	6–12	8–14	10–16	15–21	21–27	24–30
Zone C	11	8–14	10–16	12–18	18–24	24–30	27–33
	12	10–16	12–18	15–21	21–27	27–33	30–37
	13	12–18	15–21	18–24	24–30	30–37	33–41
	14	15–21	18–24	21–27	27–33	33–41	37–46
	15	18–24	21–27	24–30	30–37	37–46	41–51

continues

TABLE 1.1 *(continued)*

	Offense Level	I (0 or 1)	II (2 or 3)	III (4, 5, 6)	IV (7, 8, 9)	V (10, 11, 12)	VI (13 or more)
	16	21–27	24–30	27–33	33–41	41–51	46–57
	17	24–30	27–33	30–37	37–46	46–57	51–63
	18	27–33	30–37	33–41	41–51	51–63	57–71
	19	30–37	33–41	37–46	46–57	57–71	63–78
	20	33–41	37–46	41–51	51–63	63–78	70–87
	21	37–46	41–51	46–57	57–71	70–87	77–96
	22	41–51	46–57	51–63	63–78	77–96	84–105
	23	46–57	51–63	57–71	70–87	84–105	92–115
	24	51–63	57–71	63–78	77–96	92–115	100–125
	25	57–71	63–78	70–87	84–105	100–125	110–137
	26	63–78	70–87	78–97	92–115	110–137	120–150
	27	70–87	78–97	87–108	100–125	120–150	130–162
Zone D	28	78–97	87–108	97–121	110–137	130–162	140–175
	29	87–108	97–121	108–135	121–151	140–175	151–188
	30	97–121	108–135	121–151	135–168	151–188	168–210
	31	108–135	121–151	135–168	151–188	168–210	188–235
	32	121–151	135–168	151–188	168–210	188–235	210–262
	33	135–168	151–188	168–210	188–235	210–262	235–293
	34	151–188	168–210	188–235	210–262	235–293	262–327
	35	168–210	188–235	210–262	235–293	262–327	292–365
	36	188–235	210–262	235–293	262–327	292–365	324–405
	37	210–262	235–293	262–327	292–365	324–405	360–life
	38	235–293	262–327	292–365	324–405	360–life	360–life
	39	262–327	292–365	324–405	360–life	360–life	360–life
	40	292–365	324–405	360–life	360–life	360–life	360–life
	41	324–405	360–life	360–life	360–life	360–life	360–life
	42	360–life	360–life	360–life	360–life	360–life	360–life
	43	life	life	life	life	life	life

Source: Federal Public and Community Defenders. Lucien B. Campbell and Henry J. Bemporad, eds. 2002. "An Introduction to Federal Guideline Sentencing."

sentencing table. Across the top of the table are criminal history categories, ranging from I to VI. Those with no prior records are in Category I, while those with extensive criminal records are in Category VI. Various factors determine an offender's placement in a particular category, such as the seriousness of previous crimes, the chronicity of offending, age, and mental state (Piquero and Davis 2004).

Down the left-hand side of the grid are offense levels, ranging from 1 to 43. These represent a crime's seriousness. All crimes are scored, and the more serious the crime, the higher the score. Notice that the higher the score, the longer the recommended time served. The point where a criminal's offense level and criminal history intersect defines the range of months that judges will use for sentencing. In a 30- to 40-month scenario, for instance, 35 months would be the presumptive sentence, or the middle-range sentence imposed, absent any mitigating or aggravating circumstances. An upward departure from 35 to 40 months would occur, for example, if someone showed extreme cruelty in the commission of an offense, or was a gang leader. A downward departure from 35 to 30 months, say, might occur if the offender cooperated with police and helped them to capture others involved in the crime.

In Table 1.1 four zones are shown, Zones A through D. These zones represent a sentenced offender's eligibility for probation or some other type of punishment. For instance, Zone A sentencing ranges include "0" months, which means that, at the judge's discretion, probation might be imposed. Thus, probation-eligible offenders sentenced in U.S. district courts would be eligible for probation if their sentence falls within Zone A. Zones B through D suggest other sentencing options. Zone B, for instance, may also include probation, but with home confinement or electronic monitoring. Persons whose sentences fall in Zone C must serve at least half of their sentence in prison. Those in Zone D must serve their maximum sentence in prison within the range of the guidelines. Under present federal law, federal prisoners may accrue 54 days per year against their maximum sentences as good-time credit, the equivalent of a 15 percent sentence reduction for every year served.

Presumptive sentencing has the following aims: (1) to establish penalties commensurate with the harm caused by the criminal activity, (2) to produce a fairer system of justice, (3) to reduce the typical severity of penalties, (4) to incarcerate only the most serious offenders, (5) to reduce the discretionary power of judges and parole authorities, (6) to allow special sentences for offenders when circumstances are clearly exceptional, (7) to eliminate early-release procedures for inmates, and (8) to make participation in treatment or rehabilitative programs completely voluntary by inmates, with no effect on their terms of incarceration (Champion 2008).

By 2005, 95 percent of the states had reformed their sentencing laws so that an offender's parole eligibility had been either eliminated or made more difficult. Accompanying those reforms were changes modifying the amount of good time that inmates can earn and how good time should be calculated. Therefore, while the certainty of incarceration has increased under determinate sentencing, the sentences served are often shorter than those resulting from indeterminate sentencing (U.S. Sentencing Commission 2003).

Mandatory Sentencing

Mandatory sentencing is the imposition of an incarcerative sentence of a specified length, for certain crimes or certain categories of offenders, in which no option of probation, suspended sentence, or immediate parole eligibility exists. California, Hawaii, Illinois, Kentucky, and Michigan are a few of the many states that have enacted mandatory sentencing provisions for certain offenses (Van Zyl Smit and Ashworth 2004). For instance, Michigan imposes a two-year additional sentence of flat time, whereby offenders must serve two full additional years, without relief from parole, if they use a dangerous weapon during the commission of a felony. In Kentucky, those convicted of being habitual offenders are sentenced to life without parole in prison for violating the state's Habitual Offender Statute. Usually, mandatory sentences including life imprisonment are prescribed for those who use dangerous weapons during the commission of a crime, habitual offenders with three or more prior felony convictions, and major drug dealers. But some critics question whether any significant deterrent value results from mandatory sentencing laws, inasmuch as attorneys and judges find numerous ways to circumvent them to suit their own purposes (Crow 2004).

The History of Sentencing in the United States

U.S. sentencing practices have been derived mostly from the sentencing practices of other countries. The system of punishments used during the American colonial period was patterned after English penal methods, largely because most colonists had emigrated from England. However, there were several important differences. England continued to execute large numbers of misfits and political and religious nonconformists because of their labor supply excesses, while the American colonies reserved execution for only the most serious offenders. However, the colonists continued using the pillory, flogging, mutilation, branding, and even banishment as corporal solutions to crime and as deterrents to criminal conduct (Roy 2004).

One colonial punishment was the ducking stool: offenders were placed in a chair at the end of a long lever and dunked in a nearby pond until they almost drowned. These offenders were often town gossips or wife beaters. Branding irons were also used on both serious criminals and petty offenders. Thieves were branded with a "T," drunkards with a "D."

Such punishments continued to be used in the colonies until William Penn, the Quaker founder of Pennsylvania, commenced correctional reforms in 1682. Under the Great Law of Pennsylvania, Penn abolished corporal punishment and gradually introduced fines and incarceration in facilities known as jails, named after their British counterpart, the jail (pronounced the same). Penn commissioned each county in Pennsylvania to establish jails to accommodate offenders. Local constables or sheriffs were appointed to administer these county jails.

The sheriff concept emerged in the aftermath of the Norman Conquest of 1066. William the Conqueror introduced the feudal system, which lasted for several centuries. During that time, English counties known as shires were administered by reeves or political appointees. Reeves collected the taxes, kept the peace, and operated gaols on behalf of the king. Thus every shire had a reeve or peace officer, and eventually those terms were combined into the word *sheriff* (shire-reeve). Today sheriffs are the chief law enforcement officers of U.S. counties in most states.

Penn's ideas about correctional reform were unpopular with Pennsylvania citizens, and when Penn died in 1718 his colony quickly reverted to the use of corporal punishment. Pillories were re-established, and floggings and lashings were reinstituted. Every colony practiced such punishment methods for many decades preceding the Revolutionary War.

Many early jails and prisons in the United States were designed to exploit prisoners through forced labor. Profits from prison labor were frequently diverted to wealthy interests in the private sector. Prisoners were given only sufficient food to survive and to work (Ribeaud and Manzoni 2004).

Historians and penologists have devised date categories to correspond with and emphasize notable reforms or penal developments. For example, Frank Schmalleger and John Smykla (2001) have identified nine stages of penal development:

> *Penitentiary Era* (1790–1825): Construction of at least thirty state prisons, as well as large jails in Philadelphia and other large cities
>
> *Mass Prison Era* (1825–1876): At least thirty-five more prisons were constructed, mainly as warehouses for criminals; little thought was given to rehabilitation or reintegration
>
> *Reformatory Era* (1876–1890): Invention of reformatories in various jurisdictions; emphasis was placed on rehabilitating prisoners and teaching them marketable skills
>
> *Industrial Era* (1890–1935): Characterized by the use of prison labor to manufacture cheap goods for public consumption
>
> *Punitive Era* (1935–1945): Emphasis on maximum-security prisons with a focus upon inmate isolation and control
>
> *Treatment Era* (1945–1967): Greater differentiation among prisoners according to their needs; attention given to different types of prisoners who could be treated through individual or group therapy, counseling, or vocational and educational training
>
> *Community-Based Era* (1967–1980): Emphasis on community corrections and the use of community resources to meet the social, economic, and psychological needs of less serious offenders; focus upon community reintegration
>
> *Warehousing Era* (1980–1995): Focus of prisons upon containment and control of large numbers of inmates; overcrowded conditions and limited access to programs and services for rehabilitation
>
> *Just Desserts Era* (1995–present): Due process is emphasized, as well as deserved punishment, as states and the federal government seek to equate the punishment with the seriousness of the crime

Sentences for offenders in early U.S. district courts were served in their entirety. Early release from prison was unknown;

however, between 1790 and 1815, the federal inmate population grew appreciably, and prison officials were faced with serious prison overcrowding. Soon federal district judges were permitting prison administrators to grant prisoners early release through parole, a European innovation. Parole was used simply to make room in prisons for new and more dangerous prisoners. Sometimes prison administrators made those decisions on their own without court approval. State prisons and local jails were both experiencing overcrowding problems during this period, despite the fact that by 1840 the national inmate population was only 4,000. Thirty years later, in 1870, the national inmate population had grown to 33,000, which meant that there were about 83 inmates for every 100,000 persons in the United States. Prison and jail construction had not kept pace with the growing inmate population (Rappaport 2003).

The National Prison Association was founded in 1870, with Rutherford B. Hayes (later U.S. president) its first president. Its name was subsequently changed to the American Prison Association. By 1954, as its membership increased, it had been renamed the American Correctional Association (ACA). By 2006 the ACA had a membership of more than 35,000, more than triple the 10,000 members enrolled in 1992. Members represent a cross-section of many corrections-related professions, including correctional officers, teachers, prison and jail administrators, probation/parole officers, and court personnel. When originally formulated, the goals of the ACA were: (1) to provide technical assistance to correctional institutions, (2) to provide training and publications to any interested agency, (3) to work toward establishing a national correctional philosophy, and (4) to design and implement high correctional standards and services (American Correctional Association 2006).

Probation and parole were established as nonincarcerative strategies for managing offenders during the early 1800s. Evidence of the early use of parole is found in the 1820s, while probation was used informally during the 1830s in selected jurisdictions. By 1944, all states had parole. Parole is the early release of inmates from incarcerative sentences originally imposed by judges. The parole decision is usually, though not always, made by parole boards consisting of prison administrators, other correctional personnel, and prison psychiatrists or group counselors. Probation is a sentence in lieu of incarceration. Offenders are assigned to probation officers or to community programs in which they must comply with several stringent conditions. Probationers are responsible to judges for their conduct during their probation period, while parolees are accountable to the parole board (Aos, Roman, and Beckman 2006).

During the late 1700s and early 1800s, English judges increasingly exercised their discretion in numerous criminal cases by granting convicted offenders judicial reprieves. Under English common law, judicial reprieves suspend the incarcerative sentences of convicted offenders. These reprieves were demonstrations of judicial leniency, especially in cases in which offenders had no prior criminal record and had committed only minor offenses, and in which punishments were deemed excessive by the courts. Judges believed that, in certain cases, incarceration would serve no useful purpose. Although no accurate records are available about how many convicted offenders actually received judicial reprieves in English courts during this period, the practice of granting such reprieves was adopted by some judges in the United States.

Judges in Massachusetts courts during the early 1800s typically used their discretionary powers to suspend the incarcerative sentences of some offenders. Jail and prison overcrowding no doubt spurred their interest in devising options to incarceration. One of the more innovative judges of that period was Boston municipal judge Peter Oxenbridge Thatcher. Judge Thatcher used judicial leniency when sentencing offenders. He also sentenced some offenders to be released on their own recognizance (ROR), either before or after their criminal charges had been adjudicated. Thatcher's ROR decisions amounted to an indefinite suspension of their incarcerative sentences. Thatcher believed that such sentences would encourage convicted offenders to practice good behavior and refrain from committing new crimes.

Although judicial reprieves and suspensions of incarcerative sentences for indefinite periods continued throughout the nineteenth century, the U.S. Supreme Court declared the practice unconstitutional in 1916. The Supreme Court at the time believed that such discretion among judges infringed upon the "separation of powers" principle by contravening the powers of the legislative and executive branches to write laws and ensure their enforcement. However, during the 1830s, when releases on an offender's own recognizance and judicial reprieves flourished, the stage was set for the work of another Boston correctional pioneer.

The sentence of probation in the United States was probably conceived in 1841 by the successful cobbler and philanthropist

John Augustus, although historical references to the phenomenon may be found in writings as early as 437–422 BC. Of course, the actions of Judge Thatcher have been regarded by some scholars as probation, inasmuch as he sentenced convicted offenders to release on their own recognizance rather than jail. However, John Augustus is most often credited with pioneering probation in the United States, although no statutes existed at the time to label it or prescribe how it should be used.

The Temperance Movement against alcohol provided the right climate for the use of probation. Augustus attempted to rehabilitate alcoholics and to assist those arrested for alcohol-related offenses. Appearing in a Boston municipal court one morning to observe offenders charged and sentenced for various crimes, Augustus intervened on behalf of a man charged with being a "common drunkard" (Augustus 1852). Instead of seeing the convicted offender placed in the Boston House of Corrections, Augustus volunteered to supervise the man for a three-week period and personally guaranteed his reappearance later. Knowing Augustus's reputation for philanthropy and trusting his motives, the judge agreed with the proposal. When Augustus returned three weeks later with the drunkard, the judge was so impressed with the man's improved behavior that he fined him only one cent plus court costs, which were less than $4.00. The judge also suspended the six-month jail term. Between 1841 and 1859, the year in which Augustus died, nearly 2,000 men and women were spared incarceration because of Augustus's intervention and supervision (Champion 1989).

Augustus attracted several other philanthropic volunteers to perform similar probation services. These volunteers worked with juvenile offenders as well as with adults. However, few records were kept about the dispositions of juveniles. Thus, the precise number of those who benefited from the work of Augustus and his volunteers is unknown. In all likelihood, several thousand youths were probably supervised effectively as informal probationers.

A new era of correctional reform was introduced with the establishment of the American Correctional Association (originally known as the National Prison Association) in 1870. Subsequently, in 1876, Elmira State Reformatory in Elmira, New York, was established. Elmira Reformatory was innovative in that it experimented with certain new rehabilitative philosophies espoused by various penologists, including its first superintendent, Zebulon Reed Brockway (1827–1920). Brockway began his correctional career as a clerk and guard at the Wethersheld, Connecticut, Prison in 1848. Later he moved to New York to become superintendent of the Albany Municipal and County Almshouse, the first county hospital for the mentally ill and insane. His experience included superintendencies of prisons and houses of correction at various sites in New York and Michigan. Brockway was critical of the harsh methods employed by the establishments he headed, and he envisioned better and more effective treatments for prisoners. He had his chance in 1876, when he was selected to head the Elmira Reformatory.

Elmira was touted as the new penology, employing the latest, state-of-the-art scientific advances in correctional methods. Penologists from Scotland and Ireland—Captain Alexander Maconochie and Sir Walter Crofton—were instrumental in bringing about changes in European correctional methods during the period when Elmira was established in the early 1870s. These men influenced American corrections by introducing the mark system, whereby prisoners could accumulate good-time credits to be applied against their original sentences. Thus, through hard work and industry, prisoners could shorten their original sentences, which earlier had to be served in their entirety.

Elmira was truly a reformatory. Concurrent with penal developments in Great Britain and other UK countries, prisoners were channeled into productive activities of an educational or vocational nature, in which their good behavior and productivity could earn them time off for good behavior. Thus, parole and indeterminate sentences became distinguishing features of Elmira. Brockway established a board of managers to oversee the parole or early-release process. He employed a three-grade system wherein all new inmates were placed in the middle grade. If inmates earned perfect marks in school, work, and deportment for six straight months, they were advanced to the first grade, which gave them extra privileges. Another six months of good marks would earn them parole at the discretion of the board of managers. However, if they received unsatisfactory marks, they would be demoted to the third grade, being outfitted with a red suit and required to march in lockstep, with a loss of privileges relating to correspondence and visitation.

Individualized treatment was also practiced. Actually, Zebulon Brockway attempted to classify and segregate prisoners in meaningful ways in order to improve the quality of their individualized assistance. In fact, Brockway is credited with establishing the first modern classification process for inmates. As a part of the classification procedure, Brockway interviewed each new inmate. Questions were asked about each inmate's social, economic, psychological, biological, and moral makeup. On the basis of the interviews, Brockway would determine each inmate's subjective defect or limitation, whatever that might be. The defect would then be used as the means of individualizing offender programming. Also, Brockway would place each inmate in a particular grade, with specific work and school assignments. He also took cranial measurements and conducted research into criminal types. Special programs were devised for what he termed mental defectives. Inmate progress was monitored constantly, and Brockway continued to reclassify offenders as they progressed in their respective programs. The long-range impact of such classification is illustrated by the creation of a special training class for mental defectives that commenced in 1913. About 37 percent of all Elmira inmates were considered mental defectives and placed in menial jobs, such as janitorial duties, mending clothes, and shelling peas. A few years later, in 1917, inmates were administered IQ tests and other psychological measures in an attempt to improve work and educational programs for them.

Brockway also hired several teachers and used some of his more literate inmates to teach other prisoners to read. Elementary classes were conducted six nights a week. For advanced students, courses in bookkeeping, geography, physiology, and other disciplines were taught by professors from nearby schools, such as the Elmira Women's College. An instructor from the Michigan State Normal School was hired as the moral director in 1878, and he began teaching courses in psychology and ethics. Subsequently, history and literature were added to the Elmira curriculum. Elmira Reformatory actually began a summer school program in 1882, and in 1883, Elmira installed a printing press and began to publish *The Summary,* an eight-page weekly digest of world and local news. This digest became the world's first prison newspaper. Brockway used the paper as a propaganda device to promote Elmira and its diverse programs. Subsequently, Brockway routinely printed 3,000 copies of his annual reports and 1,500 copies of *The Summary* weekly. These were distributed to various influential persons around the state.

Use of the military model at Elmira was prevalent, as prisoners were trained in close-order drill, wore military uniforms, and paraded about with wooden rifles. This was regarded as one means of instilling discipline in inmates and reforming them. Historians view Elmira Reformatory as introducing the first individualization of prisoner treatment and the large-scale use of indeterminate sentencing. The influence of Maconochie and especially Crofton is apparent here. Crofton invented indeterminate sentencing by establishing various work stages whereby prisoners could progress, thus shortening their original sentences.

Brockway, who left Elmira in 1900, was suspected of misconduct in his administration, although little evidence was discovered to substantiate those accusations. Two investigations of Brockway's methods yielded contradictory findings. The second investigation exonerated Brockway, although the first resulted in formal charges of cruel and inhuman punishment of inmates. Brockway dismissed the allegations as meaningless, claiming that his harmless parental discipline of inmates had been grossly misrepresented.

Inmate overcrowding was a major problem contributing to ineffective programming at Elmira. When Elmira was originally constructed, 504 cells were created. However, more inmates were sent to Elmira than were being paroled. By 1886, and again in 1892, substantial additions were made to Elmira's facilities to enable it to house 1,296 inmates, although by the late 1890s there were approximately 1,500 prisoners being accommodated there. No prison administrator, regardless of how well intentioned, could operate a rehabilitative program successfully under such overcrowded conditions.

Subsequently the New York legislature approved a second reformatory, the Eastern New York Reformatory at Napanoch, which was opened in 1900. The first inmates at Eastern were transferred from Elmira. These were the older and stronger inmates. Thus Eastern became known as a repository for hard-core recidivists, parole violators, troublemakers, and incorrigibles, while Elmira accepted and concentrated on younger criminals with better prospects for reform. Over the next century Elmira underwent numerous structural and operational changes. Renamed the Elmira Correctional and Reception Center in 1970, the facility continues to offer industrial, vocational, academic, and other diverse programming for inmates, who average thirty-five years of age. Subsequently services to treat substance abusers were established, together with a shock incarceration program for new offenders. (Shock incarceration occurs whenever a judge sentences an offender to a lengthy jail or prison term of one year or longer, but within 30, 60, 90, or 120 days of being confined, the offender is brought back from jail or prison before the judge and is resentenced or placed on probation.)

Rehabilitation was not a poor concept theoretically. In fact, it remains one of correction's continuing goals as a part of general prison reform. But prison overcrowding results in significant changes in prison operating policies, and criminal justice procedures must change to accommodate growing numbers of inmates. Of course, forces external to prison have always been at work to shape prison policies. For example, economic fluctuations over time have worked to modify the growth and development of prison industries. And prison industries, including the labor generated by inmates, provide training and development opportunities for prisoners that are closely connected with and facilitate rehabilitation.

Many prisons have reported greater inmate idleness and violence as a result of overcrowding in recent years. Furthermore, many prisons are experiencing declining staff-to-prisoner ratios. Accordingly, the quality of programs offered to inmates suffers as prison capacities are exceeded through higher conviction rates and changes in sentencing and parole policies. Although the link between prison population growth and program quality is unclear, overcrowding does seem to adversely influence prison practices and policies.

There was no federal prison system until 1891, when Congress passed the Three Prisons Act. That act authorized the construction of a prison in Fort Leavenworth, Kansas, opened in 1895; a prison in Atlanta, Georgia, opened in 1902; and a prison at McNeil Island, Washington, opened in 1909. When the prison at Fort Leavenworth was constructed, it was intended for military prisoners. Under another act of Congress in 1895, a U.S. Penitentiary (USP) was authorized for construction about 2 miles from the military prison at Fort Leavenworth. The labor of military prisoners from Fort Leavenworth was used to construct what is now USP Leavenworth. When a portion of this new prison was completed in 1903, 418 federal prisoners were housed at the new prison site in a large facility that now serves as the laundry building. USP Leavenworth was eventually opened in 1906. All of the other federal prisoners from Fort Leavenworth were housed in the new USP Leavenworth, and the military prison there was returned to the War Department. The first warden at USP Leavenworth was James W. French.

These and subsequent federal prisons were originally under the supervision of the superintendent of prisons and prisoners, whose title was subsequently changed to superintendent of prisons. The first superintendent of prisons was R. V. LaDow, who served from 1908 to 1915. Successively, the next superintendents included Francis H. Duehay (1915–1920), Denver S. Dickerson (1920–1921), Heber H. Votaw (1921–1925), Luther C. White (1925–1926), Albert H. Conner (1927–1929), and, finally, Sanford Bates (1929–1930).

No central authority existed to administer these facilities until Congress created the Federal Bureau of Prisons in 1930. Under the direction of the attorney general of the United States, the Bureau of Prisons was established to manage and regulate all federal penal and correctional institutions, to provide suitable quarters, subsistence, and discipline for all persons charged with or convicted of federal crimes, and to provide technical assistance to state and local governments in the improvement of their own correctional facilities. The first director of the new Federal Bureau of Prisons was Sanford Bates (1884–1972), who retained that post from 1930 to 1937. When the Federal Bureau of Prisons was established, there were eleven federal prisons in existence.

At present a director oversees each of five U.S. regions, in which all federal correctional institutions are located. These regional directors are headquartered in Atlanta, Dallas, Kansas City, Philadelphia, and San Francisco. Harley G. Lappin has been the director of the Federal Bureau of Prisons since 2003.

Because of prison overcrowding and other factors, the federal prison system has not always been able to accommodate adequately all prisoners in its charge. Thus, contractual arrangements are frequently made between the federal government and state and local corrections departments to house a portion of the federal prisoner overflow. Early challenges by prisoners to the constitutionality of such contracting have upheld the right of the federal government to make such arrangements with the states. In 1876 the U.S. Supreme Court declared that, as long as a state permits a federal prisoner to remain in its prison and does not object to his detention, he is rightfully detained in custody under a sentence lawfully passed (*Ex parte Karstendick* 1876). States also have the right to deny the use of their jails and prisons for housing of those convicted of federal crimes if they so desire (*Ex parte Shores* 1912). In 2006 there were 145 federal correctional institutions, ranging from penitentiaries and prison camps to detention centers, medical centers, and low-security facilities (U.S. Department of Justice 2006).

The Sentencing Process

Almost every serious felony conviction is followed by a sentencing hearing. This hearing is usually scheduled six to eight weeks following conviction. A sentencing hearing is a formal proceeding in which the sentencing judge hears pleadings and arguments from both the prosecution and defense either to impose the maximum sentence under law or to show leniency. The sentencing hearing is arguably the most critical stage in the criminal justice process. Sentencing hearings may be conducted exclusively by the judge or with a jury. In murder cases in which the death penalty may be imposed, juries find defendants guilty in a first phase, deliberating at the conclusion of the trial. Then the same juries must convene again, in a second phase, the sentencing hearing, to determine whether the death penalty should be imposed.

Sentencing hearings are usually held in the same courtroom in which the convicted offender's trial was conducted. Defense counsel may present friends and relatives of the offender who can testify about the offender's past, his good qualities, and his likelihood of behaving in a law-abiding fashion in the future. The defense attempts to influence the judge to hand down a light sentence, and friends and family members may be called in to offer favorable remarks about the offender. However, the prosecution may call the victims as witnesses against the offender, as well as relatives and friends who can give testimony about why the judge should impose a heavy sentence.

Besides hearing orally from the defense and prosecution, letters and other documents may be introduced. Additionally, psychiatrists may provide testimony, either favorable or adverse to offenders. However, their information is not always accurate. It has been found, for instance, that mental health professionals have erred in various ways when giving testimony in sentencing hearings. These errors have included: (1) inadequate reliance on base rates, (2) failure to consider context, (3) susceptibility to illusory correlation, (4) failure to define the severity of violence, (5) overreliance on clinical interviews, (6) misapplication of psychological testing, (7) exaggerated implications of antisocial personality disorder, (8) ignorance of the effects of aging, (9) misuse of behavior patterns, (10) neglect of preventive measures, (11) insufficient data, and (12) failure to express the risk estimate in probabilistic terms (Cunningham and Reidy 1999). Unfortunately, we have no way of estimating the incidence of such errors in testimony given by such experts. Despite the possibility of errors, however, sentencing hearings do permit ample opportunity for both sides to present inculpatory and exculpatory information to the judge from a variety of sources.

Judges also request a presentence investigation. A presentence investigation is a thorough background check of a convicted offender by a probation officer, usually at the direction of the sentencing judge. This background check includes a description of the offense; the educational, familial, and social background of the offender; an indication of any prior record; a report of any prior juvenile offending; and other relevant information. Presentence investigations almost always involve the preparation of presentence investigation reports (PSIs). Those documents, usually prepared by probation officers at court request or order, are submitted to the judge during the interval between the conviction and sentencing hearing. Thus an additional written statement, evaluation, and recommendation are parts of the documentation that judges consider when imposing sentences.

The presentence investigation report is an informational document prepared by a probation officer containing the following personal data about convicted offenders, the conviction offense(s), and other relevant data:

1. Name
2. Address
3. Prior record, including offenses and dates
4. Date and place of birth
5. Crime(s) or conviction offense and date of offense
6. Offender's version of conviction offense
7. Offender's employment history
8. Offender's known addiction to or dependency on drugs or alcohol or controlled substances of any kind
9. Statutory penalties for the conviction offense
10. Marital status
11. Personal and family data
12. Name of spouse and children, if any
13. Educational history

14. Any special vocational training or specialized work experience
15. Mental or emotional stability
16. Military service, if any, and disposition
17. Financial condition, including assets and liabilities
18. Probation officer's personal evaluation of the offender
19. Sentencing data
20. Alternative plans made by the defendant if placed on probation
21. Physical description
22. Prosecution version of conviction offense
23. Victim impact statement prepared by victim, if any
24. Codefendant information, if codefendant is involved
25. Recommendation about sentencing from probation officer
26. Name of prosecutor
27. Name of defense attorney
28. Presiding judge
29. Jurisdiction in which offense occurred
30. Case docket number and other identifying numbers (e.g., Social Security, driver's license)
31. Plea
32. Disposition or sentence
33. Location of probation or custody

Presentence investigation reports are written summaries of information obtained by the probation officer through interviews with the defendant and an investigation of the defendant's background. An alternative definition is that PSI reports are narrative summaries of an offender's criminal and noncriminal history, used to aid the judge in determining the most appropriate sentence. These documents are often partially structured, in that they require probation officers to fill in standard information about defendants. PSIs also contain summaries or accounts in narrative form highlighting certain information about defendants and containing sentencing recommendations from probation officers. In some instances, space is available for the defendant's personal account of the crime and why it was committed.

Regardless of whether convictions are obtained through plea bargaining or trial, a presentence investigation (PSI) is often conducted upon instructions from the court. This investigation is sometimes waived, however, in the case of negotiated guilty pleas, because an agreement has already been reached between the prosecution and defense concerning the case disposition and nature of the sentence to be imposed.

No standard format exists among the states for PSI report preparation. The PSI report was adopted formally by the Administrative Office of the U.S. Courts in 1943. Since then, the PSI has been revised several times. The 1984 version reflects changes in correctional law that have occurred in recent decades. Prior to 1943, informal reports about offenders were often prepared for judges by court personnel. Although the U.S. Probation Office represents federal interests and not necessarily those of particular states, their PSI report functions are very similar to the general functions of PSI reports in most states. The PSI report for the U.S. district courts and the U.S. Probation Office serves at least five important functions: (1) to aid the court in determining the appropriate sentence for offenders, (2) to aid probation officers in their supervisory efforts during probation or parole, (3) to assist the Federal Bureau of Prisons and any state prison facility in the classification, institutional programming, and release planning for inmates, (4) to furnish the U.S. Parole Commission and other parole agencies with information about the offender pertinent to a parole decision, and (5) to serve as a source of information for research.

Providing information for offender sentencing is the primary function of a PSI. It continues to be an important tool, inasmuch as judges want to be fair and impose sentences fitting the crime. If there are mitigating or aggravating circumstances that should be considered, those factors appear in the report submitted to the judge. Aiding probation officers in their supervisory efforts is another important report objective, because rehabilitative programs can thereby be individualized for offenders. If vocational training or medical help is needed, the report may suggest that. If the offender has a history of mental illness, psychological counseling or medical treatment may be recommended. This information is also helpful to ancillary personnel who work in community-based probation programs and supervise offenders with special problems, such as drug or alcohol dependencies. PSIs assist prisons and other detention facilities in their efforts to classify inmates appropriately. Inmates with special problems or who are handicapped physically or mentally may be diverted to special prison facilities or to housing in which their needs can be addressed by professionals. Inmates with contagious diseases or viruses such as AIDS can be isolated from others for health purposes.

The fourth function of federal PSIs regards parole. In jurisdictions in which parole boards determine an inmate's early release potential, PSIs are often consulted as background data. Decisions about early release are often contingent upon the recommendation of the probation officer contained in the report. For instance, if the prospective parolee is a sex offender, it is important for the parole board to understand the likelihood that the parolee may reoffend. Finally, criminologists and others are interested in studying those sentenced to various terms of incarceration or probation. Background characteristics, socioeconomic information, and other relevant data assist researchers in developing explanations for criminal conduct. Also, the research efforts of criminologists and those interested in criminal justice may be helpful in influencing the future design of prisons or jails. Special needs areas can be identified and programs devised that will assist offenders in dealing with their problems. Because most inmates will eventually be paroled, research through an examination of PSIs may help corrections professionals to devise more effective adaptation and reintegration mechanisms, permitting inmates to make a smoother transition back into the community.

The Administrative Office of the U.S. Courts uses standardized PSIs that include five core categories which must be addressed in the body of the report: (1) the offense, including the prosecution version, the defendant's version, statements of witnesses, codefendant information, and a victim impact statement, (2) prior record, including juvenile adjudications and adult offenses, (3) personal and family data, including parents and siblings, marital status, education, health, physical and mental condition, and financial assets and liabilities, (4) evaluation, including the probation officer's assessment, parole guideline data, sentencing data, and any special sentencing provisions, and (5) recommendation, including the rationale for the recommendation and voluntary surrender or whether the offender should be transported to the correctional institution on his own or should be transported by U.S. marshals.

When requested by federal district judges, PSIs are usually prepared within a sixty-day period from the time of the request. Although there is no standard PSI format among states, most PSIs contain similar information. Presentence investigation reports are usually prepared by probation officers. Although his was much more informally prepared than modern PSIs, John Augustus has been credited with drafting the first one in 1841. It is now estimated that more than a million PSI reports are prepared by probation officers annually in the United States (Norman and Wadman 2000).

The specific duties of probation officers relating directly to PSI report preparation include the following: (1) probation officers prepare presentence investigation reports at the request of judges, (2) probation officers classify and categorize offenders, (3) probation officers recommend sentences for convicted offenders, (4) probation officers work closely with the courts to determine the best supervisory arrangement for probationer-clients, and (5) probation officers are a resource for information about any extralegal factors that might affect the sentencing decision.

There are at least three legal approaches to PSI report preparation. In forty-three states, PSI report preparation is mandatory for all felony offense convictions. Other factors may initiate PSI report preparation in those jurisdictions, such as when incarceration of a year or longer is a possible sentence; when the offender is under twenty-one; and when the defendant is a first-time offender. In nine states, statutes provide for mandatory PSI report preparation in any felony case in which probation is a possible consideration. When probation is not a consideration, PSI report preparation is optional or discretionary with particular judges. Finally, in seventeen states a PSI report is totally discretionary with the presiding judge.

The offender sentencing memorandum is an essential component of PSI reports. Sentencing memorandums are a written account of how and why the crime occurred, including the offender's explanation and apology. This memorandum is especially crucial in most sentencing decisions, since the offender uses the occasion to accept responsibility for the crime. That is an obligatory component and must be written convincingly. If judges believe that offenders have honestly taken upon themselves the responsibility for their actions and are ready to accept the consequences, they may impose a more lenient sentence.

Many U.S. jurisdictions today request that victims of crimes submit their own versions of the offense as a victim impact statement. The victim impact statement is a statement made by the victim and addressed to the judge for consideration in sentencing. It includes a description of the financial, social, psychological, and physical harm inflicted upon the victim. It also includes a statement concerning the victim's feelings about the crime, the offender, and a proposed sentence. Victim participation in sentencing is increasingly encouraged, and a victim impact statement is given similar weight to the offender's version of events. While victim participation in sentencing raises certain ethical, moral, and legal questions, indications are that victim impact statements are used with increasing frequency and appended to PSI reports in various jurisdictions. In capital punishment cases in which the death penalty may be imposed, for example, victim impact evidence has increased the use of the death penalty for some crimes.

Victim impact statements may be in the form of a written attachment to a PSI report. Victims may also make a speech or verbal declaration during the offender's sentencing hearing. That is ordinarily a prepared document read by one or more victims at the time that offenders are sentenced. The admission of the victim impact statements is controversial. Defense attorneys may feel that such statements are inflammatory and detract from objective sentencing considerations. Victim impact statements may also intensify sentencing disparities in certain jurisdictions with sentencing schemes that rely more heavily upon subjective judicial impressions, as opposed to those jurisdictions in which more objective sentencing criteria are used—such as mandatory sentencing procedures or guidelines-based sentencing schemes. Proponents of victim impact statements believe that such statements personalize the sentencing process by showing that real people were harmed by the criminal. Also, victim's rights advocates contend that victims have a moral right to influence the punishment decision. In recent years, the U.S. Supreme Court has ruled that victim impact statements are constitutional in *Payne v. Tennessee* (1991).

PSI reports have an impact on judicial sentencing decisions, and the contents of PSI reports furnish judges with a detailed account of an offender's prior record. Socioeconomic, gender, and racial or ethnic differences may, to varying degrees, have a pervasive effect on judicial attitudes and sentencing, although many judges believe themselves to be fair and impartial. Most will weigh one's prior record heavily, however, when imposing a prison term or nonincarcerative alternative. Good predictors of sentence type and sentence length include case facts; offender characteristics such as age, educational level, and employment history; and prior record of other criminal activity. Crime seriousness and victim injury also figure prominently when judges calculate the most appropriate sentence.

Judges have considerable discretion under most sentencing schemes. Mandatory sentences must be imposed on offenders for specific conviction offenses, although prosecutors decide in advance which crimes will or will not be prosecuted. Judges see only the conviction offense rather than other charges that have been dropped. The fairest state of affairs for convicted offenders is for judges to have a knowledge of both the bad and the good information about offenders and their crimes. Information unfavorable to offenders is often expressed as aggravating circumstances, while favorable information consists of mitigating circumstances. All of these circumstances are detailed in the PSI report.

Today, all states and the federal government continue to experiment with different variations of sentencing schemes. Mississippi, for instance, changed its sentencing scheme at least ten times between 1990 and 2006. Each time a sentencing change is made, offenders sentenced under the new version are bound by the sentencing policies of that version. Subsequent sentencing changes in Mississippi leave previously sentenced offenders unaffected under most circumstances. Almost every state and the federal government are prompted to change the present sentencing scheme, however, largely because of high recidivism rates among probationers and parolees. But it seems that no matter what new sentencing scheme is adopted, the recidivism rate remains at 65 to 70 percent—meaning that at least 65 to 70 percent of offenders placed on probation or parole will commit new offenses. Despite those discouraging statistics, each jurisdiction is intent on revising sentencing policies in an effort to find the right solution to the recidivism problem.

Summary

Sentencing is the imposition of a punishment on an offender resulting from a conviction for a criminal offense. The sentence may involve incarceration, a fine, or both. The severity of the sentence is dependent upon the nature of the offense and other factors. The purposes of sentencing include deterrence and crime prevention, revenge or retribution, rehabilitation and reintegration, just deserts, due process, justice, and crime control.

Several popular sentencing schemes have been and continue to be used in the United States. These include indeterminate sentencing, in which offenders are sentenced to a range of years with a stipulated minimum and maximum sentence. A parole board determines possible early release. Determinate sentencing has replaced indeterminate sentencing in many jurisdictions, however, whereby early release can be obtained through an accumulation of good-time credits. These are credits applied toward the maximum sentence, divided into statutory, earned, and meritorious good time.

Presumptive or guidelines-based sentencing is now increasingly used, inasmuch as it places various restrictions or limits on judicial sentencing discretion. Another sentencing variation is mandatory sentencing. Mandatory sentences are prescribed for those who use dangerous weapons during the commission of a crime. They also are applied to chronic or repeat offenders, or recidivists. Some states have enacted habitual offender laws—three-strikes-and-you're-out provisions—to impose life imprisonment on those with three or more felony convictions. Today most states have hybrid sentencing schemes, including sentencing provisions different from all of the schemes described in this chapter. It is even not uncommon for states to change their sentencing schemes back to earlier versions in the quest to reduce recidivism.

References

Aas, K. F. 2004. "Sentencing Transparency in the Information Age." *Journal of Scandinavian Studies in Criminology and Crime Prevention* 5:48–61.

American Correctional Association. 2006. *2006 Directory, Adult and Juvenile.* Lanham, MD: American Correctional Association.

Aos, Steve, John Roman, and Marlene Beckman. 2006. "Understanding Cost Effectiveness of Probation and Parole: A Toolbox for Community Corrections Practitioners." Unpublished paper presented at the annual meeting of the American Probation and Parole Association, Chicago, IL.

Augustus, John. 1852. *A Report of the Labors of John Augustus for the Last Ten Years: In Aid of the Unfortunate.* New York: Wright and Hasty.

Austin, James, et al. 1995. *National Assessment of Structured Sentencing.* Washington, DC: U.S. Bureau of Justice Statistics.

Beyer, Marty, Thomas Grisso, and Malcolm Young. 1997. *More than Meets the Eye: Rethinking Assessment, Competency, and Sentencing for a Harsher Era of Juvenile Justice.* Washington, DC: American Bar Association Juvenile Justice Center.

Bruce, A. A., et al. 1928. *Parole and the Indeterminate Sentence.* Springfield, IL: Illinois Parole Board.

Champion, Dean J. 1989. *The U.S. Sentencing Guidelines: Implications for Criminal Justice.* New York: Praeger.

Champion, Dean John. Forthcoming, 2008. *Probation, Parole, and Community Corrections.* Upper Saddle River, NJ: Pearson Education/Prentice Hall.

Crow, Matthew. 2004. "The Impact of Sentencing Guidelines Policy Reform: Florida's 1994 Sentencing Guidelines." Unpublished paper presented at the annual meeting of the American Society of Criminology, November, Nashville, TN.

Cunningham, Mark D., and Thomas J. Reidy. 1999. "Don't Confuse Me with the Facts: Common Errors in Violence Risk Assessment at Capital Sentencing." *Criminal Justice and Behavior* 26:20–43.

DeLone, Miriam, and Keith A. Wilmot. 2004. "Minnesota Sentencing Guidelines Revisited: Does Race Matter for Native American Offenders?" Unpublished paper presented at the annual meeting of the American Society of Criminology, November, Nashville, TN.

Ex parte Karstendick. 1876. 93 U.S. 396.

Ex parte Shores. 1912. 195 F. 627.

Federal Bureau of Prisons. 2002. *A History of the Federal Bureau of Prisons.* Washington, DC: Office of the Solicitor General.

Irwin, John. 2005. "A Dialogue on Sentencing Reform." Unpublished paper presented at the annual meeting of the Academy of Criminal Justice Sciences, March, Chicago, IL.

Klug, Elizabeth A. 2001. "Geographical Disparities among Trying and Sentencing Juveniles." *Corrections Today* 63:100–107.

Norman, Michael D., and Robert C. Wadman. 2000. "Utah Presentence Investigation Reports: User Perceptions of Quality and Effectiveness." *Federal Probation* 64:7–12.

Payne v. Tennessee. 1991. 501 U.S. 808.

Piquero, N. L., and J. L. Davis. 2004. "Extralegal Factors and the Sentencing of Organizational Defendants: An Examination of the Federal Sentencing Guidelines." *Journal of Criminal Justice* 32:643–654.

Rappaport, Aaron J. 2003. "Unprincipled Punishment: The U.S. Sentencing Commission's Troubling Silence about the Purposes of Punishment." *Buffalo Criminal Law Review* 6:1043–1122.

Ribeaud, Dennis, and Patrik Manzoni. 2004. "The Relationship between Defendant's Social Attributes, Psychiatric Assessment, and Sentencing." *International Journal of Law and Psychiatry* 27:375–386.

Roy, Dina. 2004. "Age Disparity in Criminal Court Sentencing." Unpublished paper presented at the annual meeting of the American Society of Criminology, November, Nashville, TN.

Schmalleger, Frank, and John Ortiz Smykla. 2001. *Corrections in the 21st Century.* New York: Glencoe McGraw-Hill.

Ulmer, Jeffrey T., and Brian Johnson. 2004. "Sentencing in Context: A Multilevel Analysis." *Criminology* 42:137–177.

U.S. Department of Justice. 2006. *State and Federal Corrections Statistics.* Washington, DC: U.S. Department of Justice.

U.S. Sentencing Commission. 2003. *Downward Departures from the Federal Sentencing Guidelines.* Washington, DC: U.S. Sentencing Commission, 2003.

U.S. Sentencing Commission. 2006. *United States Sentencing Commission Guidelines Manual.* Washington, DC: U.S. Sentencing Commission.

Van Zyl Smit, D., and A. Ashworth. 2004. "Disproportionate Sentences as Human Rights Violations." *Modern Law Review* 67:541–560.

Weidner, R. R., R. Frase, and I. Pardoe. 2004. "Explaining Sentence Severity in Large Urban Counties: A Multilevel Analysis of Contextual and Case-level Factors." *Prison Journal* 84:184–207.

Wilmot, Keith Alan. 2002. *Prosecutorial Discretion and Real Offense Sentencing under the Federal Sentencing Guidelines: An Analysis of Relevant Conduct.* Ann Arbor, MI: University Microfilms International.

2

Problems, Controversies, and Solutions

Introduction

This chapter examines several sentencing issues. Whenever a defendant is convicted of a crime, a judge determines the sentence. The sentence may involve incarceration, probation in lieu of incarceration, a fine, or several other types of sentences, sometimes known as hybrid sentences. A hybrid sentence may be intermittent jail confinement, such as serving one's time on weekends in order to permit convicted offenders to support their families by working during the workweek. Or sometimes a judge will impose jail as a condition of probation, in which case an offender must spend a certain number of days or months in jail, followed by a probationary term.

The first part of this chapter questions whether incarceration is the best sentencing option for particular offenders. While get-tough policies toward crime suggest that much of the general public feels that all persons who commit crimes should be locked up, incarceration is not necessarily the best option for all lawbreakers. Furthermore, there is simply insufficient jail and prison space to confine all persons who deserve confinement. Therefore, judicial discretion is necessary to discern which offenders should be incarcerated and which should receive alternative sentences.

Jail and prison overcrowding is pervasive, and the problem is growing worse. Jail and prison construction simply cannot keep pace with the growing numbers of offenders. Increasingly, community corrections are being relied upon to supervise offenders in their communities. That option, however, raises safety issues among the general public. A delicate balance must be attained, therefore, between the public's need for safety and an offender's potential to be rehabilitated. It is difficult for most offenders to become rehabilitated or reintegrated into their communities if they are locked up. Supervised freedom in the community maximizes rehabilitation opportunities and augments the reintegrative efforts of probation and parole departments, loosely grouped under the umbrella term *community corrections*. There is a constant tension, however, between public safety and offender freedom of access to community services and rehabilitation.

If offenders have been confined in a jail or prison for a more or less lengthy period, they are eventually paroled or freed in some way. Estimates suggest that some 99 percent of all imprisoned persons will eventually be released from confinement to reenter their communities. Parole boards in many jurisdictions function like judges, in that early-release decisions are made according to varying criteria. Both judges and parole boards attempt to ascertain which offenders pose the least risk to public safety and ought to be freed into the community. Various forms of prediction are used, therefore, to make behavioral forecasts of which offenders will be most likely to remain law-abiding if released.

Unfortunately, the perfect prediction instrument for such forecasts has not yet been created. There are pervasive flaws with most judicial and parole board decision-making. Despite intensive efforts to develop objective parole criteria or behavioral indicators for judges to use, some 65–70 percent of all released offenders will commit new offenses within three years of release. It is for this reason alone that sentencing schemes have been changed in every jurisdiction, to limit judicial and parole board discretion. A disgruntled public holds these persons accountable for offender/client failures. However, judges and parole boards may have little to do with determining who succeeds on probation or parole because so many interventions have been attempted. No matter what is done, recidivism rates have remained fairly constant at the 65 percent mark for many decades. It is little wonder, therefore, that some jurisdictions experiment with different sentencing schemes and good-time credits in an effort to reduce recidivism. But no matter what is done, recidivism rates remain high.

In the case of offenders deemed dangerous, or who may pose societal risks, judges and parole boards may decide that they should remain confined. Many of those persons will never reoffend and would be law-abiding if released into society. Because of the imprecision of our instruments that forecast one's dangerousness, we simply lack the ability to make accurate behavioral forecasts. We don't have the ability to know who those persons are, but they are referred to as "false positives," or persons believed to pose risks to society who in fact do not. Then, of course, there are those who are freed by judges into probation programs or community corrections and inmates who are granted early release, who go on to engage in new criminal conduct. Such persons are known as "false negatives." The goal is to minimize both false positives and false negatives, but at present there are no means to make perfect behavioral predictions. Thus, some persons are placed in prisons or jails for more or less lengthy periods under a condition known as selective incapacitation. That is an important issue, which will be addressed here.

Some offenders are convicted wrongfully. For whatever reason, each year some innocent persons are convicted of crimes they have not committed, and occasionally the criminal justice system realizes its mistake and sets them free. But many such persons are not identified and serve their sentences despite their innocence. Various civil rights organizations, such as the American Civil Liberties Union, attempt to identify such persons and assist them in gaining their freedom.

The judiciary and parole boards have been targeted here for examination, inasmuch as they seemingly abuse their discretionary authority. A brief glimpse at discretionary abuse on the part of judges and parole boards will be provided, as well as a look at preconviction programs such as pretrial diversion and alternative dispute resolution. These are controversial measures because they assume defendant guilt without benefit of a trial. But their use in the criminal justice system alleviates crowded court dockets and frequently results in civil resolution of otherwise criminal matters. Accompanying such programs are attempts by various agencies to predict offender risk. Risk instrumentation has been developed and continuously refined, but, as has been stated, serious problems persist.

Another dimension of sentencing is dealing with those with mental illnesses, serious diseases, drug or alcohol dependencies, and other addictions. Such special-needs offenders pose problems for judges and parole boards. Various categories of offenders will be briefly examined, as will the types of problems they pose for decision-makers and the issue of recidivism. How is recidivism conceptualized or measured? How is it used to measure program effectiveness? This chapter concludes with a discussion of the appeals process. Once offenders have been sentenced, what are their options to challenge their sentences? Most offenders have little success in contesting their convictions. But, nevertheless, they may exercise their right to appeal.

Sentencing Issues

The following sentencing issues will be examined here: (1) whether to grant probation or to incarcerate offenders, (2) the growing problem of jail and prison overcrowding, (3) the tension between the need for public safety and offender rehabilitative and reintegrative needs, (4) selective incapacitation and the matter of false positives and false negatives, (5) wrongful convictions, (6) judicial and parole board discretionary abuses, (7) punishments without convictions, and (8) predicting offender risk.

Probation or Incarceration?

Whether offenders should be placed on probation or incarcerated is often a difficult judicial decision. Probation officers might recommend probation to judges when filing a PSI report for some convicted offender, although the court may disregard the recommendation. The just desserts philosophy is a dominant theme in U.S. corrections today, and judges appear to be influenced by that philosophy, as is reflected in the sentences they impose. Generally, their interest is in imposing sentences that suit the seriousness of the offense (Shane-Dubow et al., 1998).

Jail and Prison Overcrowding

Overcrowded jail and prison conditions affect judicial sentencing decisions. Judges have many sentencing options, including incarceration or non–jail/prison penalties such as fines, probation, community service, restitution to victims, halfway houses, treatment, or some combination of the above. It is precisely this broad range of discretionary options associated with the judicial role, as well as the independence of other actors in the criminal justice system, that has led to jail and prison overcrowding becoming the most pressing problem facing the criminal justice system today.

There have been drastic changes in the sentencing policies of most states and the federal government (Grimes and Rogers 1999). As increasing numbers of jurisdictions adopt tougher sentencing policies and implement sentencing schemes that keep offenders behind bars for longer periods, overcrowding worsens. In many instances, judges have no choice but to impose incarceration for specified durations because of mandatory terms for certain offenses; often they have little latitude in such cases. For example, the discretion of federal court judges to impose probation as an alternative to incarceration was drastically curtailed when the U.S. sentencing guidelines were implemented in 1987 (Conaboy 1997). The preguidelines use of probation applied to more than 60 percent of all convicted federal offenders. In the postguidelines aftermath, fewer than 15 percent of all convicted federal offenders are granted probation at the discretion of federal judges, leading to still greater overcrowding. An emerging dilemma is that proportionately larger numbers of nonviolent federal offenders are now being incarcerated, when it is quite likely that they might do well in community programs (Irwin, Schiraldi, and Ziedenberg 1999).

The failure of incarceration—or the various nonincarcerative alternatives—to rehabilitate offenders successfully may not necessarily be the fault of those particular programs, but rather the nature of the clients served by those programs. While most prisons and some jails have programs to assist inmates to develop new vocational skills and to counsel them, the effectiveness of such programs is questionable. Understaffing is a chronic problem often attributed to lack of funding. and the equipment used in prison technical education programs is often outdated. Furthermore, if inmates earn an educational certificate it often bears the name of the prison facility, and employers may be deterred from hiring persons with prison records. Many of these institutions, in fact, are principally concerned with the custody and control of their inmate populations, and rehabilitation is a somewhat remote consideration.

One important reason that rehabilitation is less effective in prison and jail settings is the chronic overcrowding. In some instances the overcrowding in prisons approaches the level of "cruel and unusual punishment," at which point court intervention is required (Welsh 1995). Thus there may be an extensive array of vocational and educational programs within various prison settings, but overcrowding means that not all inmates can take advantage of them. Furthermore, having too many inmates in classes makes both teaching and learning more difficult (Call and Cole 1996).

Offender Needs or Public Safety?

As courts move toward the greater use of felony probation, judicial concern is increasingly focused upon determining which offenders should be incarcerated and which should not. Therefore, in recent years several investigators have attempted to devise schemes that would permit judges and other officials to predict a convicted defendant's dangerousness, or level of danger, to society. Obviously, this concern is directed toward preserving public safety and minimizing public risk.

Most states have laws permitting officials to detain criminal defendants on the basis of the defendant's perceived dangerousness. The legal test used is called the dangerous-tendency test, which is the propensity of a person to inflict injury (*Frazier v. Stone* 1974). Dangerousness is interpreted differently depending upon the jurisdiction. In twenty-one states, for example, *dangerousness* is defined as a history of prior criminal involvement. That history may include a prior conviction, probation or parole status at the time of arrest, or a pending charge when the defendant was arrested. In seven states the type of crime with which the offender is charged defines dangerousness, and in twenty-three states judicial discretion determines dangerousness. However, many offenders, even those convicted of numerous offenses, are nonviolent and not dangerous. Some persons believe that we tend to overincarcerate those types of offenders, even though they can function normally within their own communities, under close supervision, as an alternative to confinement (Vitiello 1997).

Selective Incapacitation: False Positives and False Negatives

Selective incapacitation means incarcerating only those offenders deemed to be high risks to public safety. The term is applied to certain high-risk offenders and is designed to reduce the crime rate by incapacitating only those most likely to recidivate.

Obviously, selective incapacitation is discriminatory in its application, and the ethics and fairness of predictive sentencing are frequently called into question. Professionals who deal with violent persons on a regular basis, mental health professionals and psychiatrists, also question the accuracy of dangerousness indices, especially when such devices are used for justifying preventive detention. There are simply too many variables that can interfere with accurate prediction of individual behavior. If we factor in drug abuse, substance abuse, or some other chemical dependency, prediction attempts become increasingly unreliable (Auerbahn 2002).

In Washington, for instance, specific types of offenders have been targeted for special punishment following their sentences. Washington State's legislature passed the Sexual Predatory Act in 1990, which allows for the civil commitment of sex offenders in a mental health facility if they are deemed to pose a future danger to others. Identifying a specific offender aggregate for more extensive punishment when those persons have served their full terms raises questions about the fairness of those extended terms, even though they are served in mental hospitals and not prisons. Similarities have been drawn between the treatment of habitual sex offenders and habitual drunken drivers: one view is that we have created a special category of offender from which there is no escape. The only real predictor to be inferred based on current knowledge, however, is that patients with a history of sexually violent behavior are at a high risk of committing future acts of that nature (McGrath, Cumming, and Holt 2002). In many cases, unfortunately, the law selects inappropriate candidates for more extensive treatment in mental hospitals. Inappropriate candidates for treatment include a majority of sex offenders who do not need treatment or hospitalization because they are very unlikely to commit new sex offenses in the future. Often, they are first-time sex offenders without any history of prior sexual misconduct. Their offense was more situational rather than arising from some deep-seated disposition to commit a sex crime that should be dealt with through extensive counseling, hospitalization, or other aggressive treatment. The use of preventive detention for these types of offenders raises both moral and legal questions.

In the case of false positives and false negatives, similar moral and legal questions arise. When a false positive is denied parole, the issue raised is the continuing confinement of an otherwise harmless person. When a false negative is granted parole and commits a new, serious offense, the public is outraged, the parole board is embarrassed, and the integrity of test developers and the validity of prediction instruments are called into question. Judges who impose probation instead of incarceration, or incarceration instead of probation, may be subjected to similar attacks on similar grounds. Numerical scales therefore are often used as more objective criteria for probation or parole decision-making. It is not necessarily the case that these scales are superior to personal judgments by judges or parole boards, but reference to numbers seems to objectify an early-release or probation-granting decision, in comparison to the use of visual appraisals of offenders and subjective interpretations of their backgrounds.

Wrongful Convictions

The U.S. criminal justice system is not perfect. While no conclusive data are available, it is clear that more than a few innocent persons are convicted of serious crimes. This same problem holds true in other countries as well, such as Canada, France, England, and Australia. There are many reasons for a wrongful conviction. Sometimes there is extensive circumstantial evidence implicating the accused: a defendant may have had the motive, means, and opportunity to commit the crime and may not have a reasonable alibi. Sometimes not being able to explain where one was at a particular time, coupled with other seemingly incriminating factors, may make a defendant appear guilty in the eyes of jurors.

Some aggressive prosecutors may threaten or intimidate certain defendants, using the possibility of charging them with crimes that carry stringent penalties, such as long sentences of incarceration or the death penalty. Although it is wrong and unethical to engage in such prosecutorial misconduct, some prosecutors threaten and overwhelm certain defendants with extremely serious charges that have little or no basis in fact. A gray area exists within which prosecutors have great latitude in their charging decisions. Most skillful prosecutors can present only incriminating or inculpatory information to grand juries about criminal suspects, withholding exculpatory information. And it is well known that indictments against virtually anyone can be obtained, depending upon the prosecutor's wishes.

Cases against many suspects never come to trial. This is because the plea bargaining process today circumvents trials in more than 90 percent of all criminal cases. After being initially overwhelmed by very serious charges, defendants and their attorneys may be approached by "generous" prosecutors who wish to save the government the time and expense of a protracted trial. A compromise is thus offered, such as a lesser charge. If the defendant pleads guilty to the lesser charge, probation may be offered instead of the jail or prison time that might be imposed if a jury trial were held and the suspect convicted. Many defense attorneys urge their clients to accept these "generous" offers from prosecutors, especially if the client has a prior criminal record or appears guilty on the basis of circumstantial evidence. Thus many defendants relinquish their right to a jury trial, as well as other important constitutional rights, in an effort to avoid the possibility of potentially serious punishment.

Then there are the cases in which innocent defendants do go to trial and are convicted simply because they look guilty to the jury, which the state has overwhelmed with extensive circumstantial evidence. These innocent convicted persons may spend a great deal of time seeking appeals of their cases by higher courts, but they must face the powerful presumption that the original trial court verdict was correct. That is an extremely difficult presumption to overcome, especially if there is little or no hard evidence to substantiate one's claim of innocence.

In recent years there has been greater news media attention focused upon very serious cases, particularly death penalty cases, in which modern technology has been used to determine innocence (Davis 2005). Evidence in most serious criminal cases is carefully preserved for many years following the crime, in anticipation of the appeals that will follow. During the 1990s DNA typing was increasingly used as evidence against suspects, but its use has also led authorities to rule out certain persons as suspects. By 2005 many of those serving lengthy prison sentences or on death row throughout the United States were demanding re-examination of the blood evidence originally used to convict them (Burnett 2005). In the case of a 1975 convicted black rapist with Type A negative blood, it may turn out that there is no DNA match for that offender. In fact, increasing numbers of law enforcement agencies and correctional institutions are collecting blood specimens from suspects or convicted offenders and typing those specimens according to unique DNA patterns. On re-examination, it may turn out that, not only was the black defendant wrongfully convicted in 1975, but that another convicted rapist, presently serving time for another crime, is a perfect DNA match for the crime in question. Often a confrontation of the actual perpetrator with DNA evidence may elicit a confession. While prosecutors are reluctant to admit their mistakes, appellate courts have been persuaded by such DNA evidence, and wrongful convictions have been overturned (Boller 2005).

In 2005, only 37 percent of all wrongfully convicted persons received state compensation for the months or years they had spent in prison. Only twenty states had mechanisms in place and institutional pathways for seeking compensation for wrongful imprisonment or conviction (Scheck and Neufeld 2002), and not all of those states had uniform reimbursement provisions. For instance, in 2005, Ohio capped awards to wrongfully convicted offenders at $25,000 per year of incarceration, while the federal government capped such awards at $100,000 per year. Also by 2005, 119 persons had been set free from death rows throughout the United States and classified as not guilty. They were granted full pardons on the basis of evidence conclusively showing their innocence; they had all charges against them dropped by the prosecution, or they were acquitted of the charges that had originally placed them on death row (Death Penalty Information Center 2005).

Judicial and Parole Board Abuse of Discretion

Judicial discretion in sentencing is often criticized, in that judges make decisions primarily on extralegal factors rather than on legal ones. Legal factors include prior record, the seriousness of the current offense, age, and acceptance of responsibility. Extralegal factors refer to race or ethnicity, gender, socioeconomic status, and attitude. Sentencing disparities attributable to race, gender, socioeconomic status, and other extralegal factors have plagued judges for years. Attempts have been made by commissions and state legislatures to create greater sentencing consistency and to bind judges to nonarbitrary standards. Sentencing guidelines have been created in most jurisdictions to standardize the punishments for various offenses. However, it has been questioned whether structured sentencing guidelines will eliminate disparities in judicial decision-making. Experiments with various types of sentencing reforms have evidenced some success in improving judicial fairness (Irwin 2005).

Early release from prison, under appropriate supervision, implies an agreement of trust between the state and the offender. In many instances, this trust instills a degree of self-confidence in the offender that yields the desired law-abiding results. Then again, it is claimed that parole is a failure, although critics cannot say for certain whether the problem rests with parole itself or with the abuse of discretion on the part of parole-granting bodies. Deterrence and crime control actually extend beyond parole board decision-making. Probation officer supervisory practices within the community play an important part in controlling offender behavior. Furthermore, probation officers can be of assistance in linking their clients with necessary community services, such as psychological counseling and programming, vocational/technical and educational programs, and other services.

Punishments without Conviction: Alternative Dispute Resolution and Pretrial Diversion

In cases involving minor criminal offenses, one option used increasingly by the prosecution is alternative dispute resolution (ADR). ADR is a community-based, informal dispute settlement between offenders and their victims. Most often targeted for participation in these programs are misdemeanants. A growing number of ADR programs are being implemented throughout the nation. With their early roots in the Midwest, victim-offender reconciliation or ADR programs now exist in more than a hundred U.S. jurisdictions; also, there are 54 in Norway, 40 in France, 25 in Canada, 25 in Germany, 18 in England, 20 in Finland, and 8 in Belgium (Griffiths and Bazemore 1999).

ADR is also known as restorative justice. ADR involves the direct participation of the victim and offender, with the aim of mutual accommodation for both parties. The emphasis of ADR is upon restitution rather than punishment. There are lower costs associated with it than with trials, and criminal stigmatization is avoided. However, it is sometimes difficult to decide which cases are best arbitrated through ADR and which should be formally resolved through trial. This should not be interpreted as meaning that juveniles are excluded from ADR. In a growing number of jurisdictions, many criminal cases are being diverted from the criminal justice system through ADR. ADR is a relatively new phenomenon, but it is increasingly recognized as a means whereby differences between criminals and their victims may be resolved through a conciliation, mediation, or arbitration process. Restitution or victim compensation also makes such programs easier for victims to accept.

Another version of alternative dispute resolution is the victim-offender reconciliation program (VORP). Victim-offender reconciliation is a specific form of conflict resolution between the victim and the offender. Face-to-face encounter is the essence of this process. The primary aims of VORPs are (1) to make offenders accountable for their wrongs against victims, (2) to reduce recidivism among participating offenders, and (3) to heighten the responsibility of offenders through victim compensation and repayment for damages (Roy and Brown 1992).

Officially, VORP was established in Kitchener, Ontario, in 1974, and it was subsequently replicated as PACT, or Prisoner and Community Together, in northern Indiana near Elkhart. Subsequent replications in various jurisdictions have created different varieties of ADR, each spawning embellishments, additions, or program deletions deemed more or less important by the particular jurisdiction. The Genessee County (Batavia), New York, Sheriff's Department, for example, established a VORP in 1983, followed by programs in Valparaiso, Indiana; Quincy, Massachusetts; and Minneapolis, Minnesota, in 1985. In Quincy the program was named EARN-IT, and it was operated through the Probation Department. More than twenty-five states have one version of VORP or another (Umbreit, Coates, and Vos 2002). Both juvenile and adult offenders have been involved in this project over the years.

Pretrial diversion is a procedure whereby criminal defendants are either diverted to a community-based agency for treatment or assigned to a counselor for social or psychiatric assistance. Pretrial diversion may involve education, job training, counseling, or some type of psychological or physical therapy. Diversion is the official halting or suspension of legal proceedings against a criminal defendant or juvenile after a recorded justice system entry, and possible referral of that person to a treatment or care program administered by a nonjustice agency or private agency. Technically diversion is not true probation, in that the alleged offender has not been convicted of a crime. The thrust of diversion is toward an informal administrative effort to determine (1) whether nonjudicial processing is warranted, (2) whether treatment is warranted, (3) if treatment is warranted, which treatment to use, and (4) whether charges against the defendant should be dropped or reinstated (National Association of Pretrial Services Agencies 1995).

Diversion is intended for first offenders who have not committed serious crimes. It is similar to probation because offenders must comply with specific conditions established by the court. Successful completion of those conditions usually leads to a dismissal of charges against the defendant. A totality of circumstances assessment of each offender's crime is made by the prosecutor and the court, and a decision about diversion is made. Each case is considered on its own merits. Those charged with driving while intoxicated, for example, may be diverted to attend Alcoholics Anonymous meetings or special classes for drunken drivers as a part of their diversion. Often diverted defendants must pay monthly fees or user fees during the diversion period to help defray expenses incurred by the public or private agencies who monitor them.

Diversion originated in the United States through the early juvenile courts in Chicago and New York in the late 1800s. There were determined efforts by religious groups and reformers to keep children from imprisonment of any kind, since at the time children over eight years of age were considered eligible for adult court processing. Cook County, Illinois, implemented a diversion program for youthful offenders in 1899 (Doeren and Hageman 1982). The underlying philosophy of diversion is community reintegration and rehabilitation, whereby offenders avoid the stigma of incarceration and the public notoriety accompanying appearances and trials. In most state courts in which diversion is condoned, diversion does not entirely remove offenders from court processing, since the court usually must approve prosecutorial recommendations for diversion. Because these approvals are often conducted in less publicized hearings, a divertee's crimes are less likely to be scrutinized publicly. When an offender completes a diversion program successfully, one of two things happens. First, the offender's arrest record pertaining to that offense is erased through an expungement and the prosecution is terminated. If that should not occur, however, the second, optional result is a downgrading of the original criminal charge to a lesser offense and a resulting conviction. For instance, a first offender charged with felony theft may have the offense downgraded to misdemeanor theft following successful completion of the diversion program. Either way, though, for offenders who are granted diversion, such programs are win-win situations.

Predicting Offender Dangerousness or Risk

Three basic categories of risk classifications have been identified (Morris and Miller 1985):

1. *Anamnestic prediction.* This is a prediction of offender behavior based on past circumstances. If circumstances are similar in the future, it is thought likely that the offender will behave in the same way. For example, a presentence investigation report may show that an offender was alcohol and drug dependent, unemployed, inclined toward violence because of previous assault incidents, and poorly educated. Recidivists convicted of new crimes may exhibit present circumstances similar to those that prevailed when they were convicted of their earlier offense. Thus judges and others might rely heavily upon the situational similarity of past and present circumstances to measure offender risk. However, if some offenders have made a significant effort between convictions to obtain additional education or training, or if they are no longer alcohol or drug dependent, other types of behavioral forecasts will have to be made, because circumstances have changed.

2. *Actuarial prediction.* This type of prediction is based upon the characteristics of offenders as a class, similar to others being considered for probation, parole, or inmate classification. It is believed, for example, that those persons who exhibit characteristics similar to those of their general class of offenders will behave in ways similar to the other members of that particular class. In effect, this is an aggregate predictive tool.

3. *Clinical prediction.* This type of prediction is based upon the predictor's professional training and experience working directly with the offender. The belief is that the offender will behave in a particular way, based upon extensive diagnostic examinations conducted by psychiatrists and psychologists. The subjectivity inherent in clinical predictions is apparent, and the skills of the as-

sessor are paramount. However, such predictions are more expensive, since each clinical prediction is individualized. Both anamnestic and actuarial prediction make use of situational factors and the general characteristics of offenders in forecasting their future risk. Interestingly, the highest degrees of validity are associated with actuarial and anamnestic predictions, and they are considered very reliable. Predictors in clinical predictions are usually psychiatrists or psychologists with extensive clinical training and experience with deviant conduct and criminal behavior.

Judges and especially probation officers are also interested in behavioral prediction. A presentence investigation report prepared for an offender sometimes contains a recommendation for some form of probation or incarceration. That recommendation is based on the probation officer's belief concerning how good a candidate the offender will be for probation. This is behavioral prediction. Prediction means an assessment of some expected future behavior, including criminal acts, arrests, or convictions. Predictions of future criminal behavior date back to biblical times, although our concern here is with contemporary developments and current prediction and assessment devices. Assessments of offender risk have been devised by most departments of corrections throughout the United States. Iowa, Kansas, and Massachusetts are only a few of the states that have devised such instruments. Several important and desirable characteristics of these instruments have been outlined. They include the following:

1. The model should be predictively valid.
2. The model should reflect reality.
3. The model should be designed for a dynamic system and not remain fixed over time.
4. The model should serve practical purposes.
5. The model should not be a substitute for good thinking or responsible judgment.
6. The model should be both qualitative and quantitative (Rans 1984).

In theory, parole boards apply a consistent set of standards to prisoners who have committed similar offenses. When the board departs from those standards—especially when parole is possible for an offender but denied—a written rationale is provided for both the prisoner and appellate authorities. And an inmate has the right to appeal the decision of the parole board to a higher authority, such as the National Appeals Board (U.S. Code 2007). Consistency is highly desirable in the application of any parole criteria. Many inmate lawsuits involve allegations of inconsistent application of parole eligibility guidelines. Present efforts to develop classification schemes for predicting offender behavior remain at best an unstable business. This criticism applies to both adult and juvenile risk assessment measures as currently applied. Risk assessment devices developed and used in one state are often not applicable to offenders in other states.

There are two important questions in designing any instrument for predicting future criminal conduct: (1) what factors are most relevant in such predictions and (2) what weight should be given to each of those factors? We don't know the answers for certain. In fact, one recurring criticism of prediction studies and the development of risk assessment instruments is that much work is needed on the definition and measurement of criteria. This does not mean that all of the current instruments are worthless as predictors of success on probation or parole. But it does suggest that the measures are imperfect. Therefore, it may be premature to rely exclusively on instrument scores to decide who goes to prison and who receives probation. In many jurisdictions, however, risk assessment scores are used precisely for that purpose (Robinson 2002).

Special Types of Offenders

Special needs offenders include physically, mentally, psychologically, or socially impaired offenders who require extraordinary care and supervision. Sometimes elderly offenders are classified as special-needs offenders to the extent that they might require special diets, medicines, or environments. Mental retardation, illiteracy, and physical disabilities are some of the many kinds of problems associated with special needs offenders. Regarding the provisions necessary for special needs offenders, several major problems have been identified, including lack of access to adequate mental health services, inadequate information and training among court and corrections personnel, and insufficient interagency coordination and cooperation.

Special needs offenders may require (1) mental health counseling, (2) substance abuse treatment, (3) parenting and family services, (4) employment planning, education, and vocational counseling, and (5) health screenings, treatment, and referrals. Such services seem offender-relevant, since a lack of education and drug abuse are two of the major obstacles to finding employment (Dennehy 2006).

Special-needs offenders who have a mental illness or some other type of mental condition are of particular concern. No one knows how many mentally ill inmates there are in prisons and jails throughout the United States. Mentally ill or retarded inmates present correctional officials with problems similar to those resulting from drug and alcohol dependency. Frequently, inadequate staffing makes diagnoses of inmates and their problems difficult. Because jails are designed for short-term confinement, they cannot adequately treat inmates with serious mental disturbances or deficiencies. Suicides in jails and prisons have frequently been linked to the mental condition of inmates unable to cope with confinement. Mentally ill inmates also exhibit a high degree of socially disruptive behavior. This behavior occurs not only during confinement but also later, when the inmates are discharged. Offenders who are mentally ill are incarcerated in greater numbers than other offenders. Also, mentally ill inmates tend to mask their limitations and are highly susceptible to prison culture and inmate manipulation. These offenders are often unresponsive to the rehabilitation programs traditionally available to inmates. They present correctional officers with unusual discipline problems (Carr, Collins, and Leary 2006).

Another category of special-needs offenders is sex offenders, including child sexual abusers. Sometimes these offenders are grouped with criminals who are mentally ill and receiving special services, while some feel that they should receive no unusual consideration. Since many sex offenses are committed against victims known by the offender as a friend or family member, a large number of such incidents are never reported to the police. Thus no one really knows how many sex offenders there are in the United States at any given time.

Sex offenders are persons who commit a sexual act prohibited by law. Fairly common types of sex offenders include rapists and prostitutes, although sex offenses may include voyeurism, exhibitionism, child sexual molestation, incest, date rape, and marital rape. The list is not exhaustive. Child sexual abusers are adults who involve minors in virtually any kind of sexual activity, ranging from sexual intercourse with children to photographing them in lewd poses. Although the precise figure is unknown, it is believed that some 2 million children are sexually victimized annually. It is also estimated that 90 percent of all child sexual abuse cases are never prosecuted, although that situation appears to be changing (Kruttschnitt, Uggen, and Shelton 2000). Public interest in and awareness of sex offenders is based on the belief that most convicted sex offenders will commit new sex offenses when released. Regardless of the diverse motives of sex offenders, there is general agreement among professionals that these offenders need some form of counseling or therapy. Many jurisdictions currently operate sex therapy programs designed to rehabilitate sex offenders, depending upon the nature of their crime.

Drug and alcohol abuse are highly correlated with criminal conduct (Deschenes, Turner, and Clear 1992). Large numbers of pretrial detainees are characterized as having drug or alcohol dependencies. Offenders with such dependencies present several problems for correctional personnel. Often, for example, jails are not equipped to handle their withdrawal symptoms, especially if they are confined for long periods. Also, the symptoms themselves are frequently dealt with, rather than the social and psychological causes for the dependency. Thus when offenders go through alcohol detoxification programs or are treated for drug addiction, they leave those programs and are placed back into the same circumstances that caused the drug or alcohol dependency originally.

A growing problem in corrections is AIDS/HIV, or acquired immune deficiency syndrome/human immunodeficiency virus. Estimates are that by 1997 there were more than 3 million AIDS/HIV cases in the United States, and that the number of AIDS cases was doubling about every 8 to 10 months (Office of Justice Programs 2001). AIDS is particularly prevalent among jail and prison inmates. Prisoners living in close quarters are highly susceptible to the AIDS virus because of the likelihood of anal-genital or oral-genital contact. Although there has been much improvement in creating greater AIDS awareness among inmates through educational programs, the fact is that AIDS education in incarcerative settings has not slowed the spread of the disease appreciably. Interestingly, female inmates in state and federal prisons have a higher infection rate than men. Some 2.2 percent of men were AIDS infected in 1997, compared with 3.5 percent of all female inmates (Office of Justice Programs, 1991).

It follows that if AIDS is prevalent and increasing among jail and prison inmates, it is prevalent and increasing among probationers and parolees as well. Thus AIDS has become a primary topic of concern among probation and parole officers and their agencies. In view of the multifarious circumstances under which AIDS has been transmitted in recent years—including saliva or blood residue contacted by dentists and other health professionals—probation and parole officers have perceived their own risk of becoming infected with the AIDS virus accidentally. Many probationers and parolees are former drug offenders. Drug-dependent clients represent a special danger, since AIDS is known to be easily transmitted when drug addicts share needles. And it is widely known that some crimes have been perpetrated by offenders wielding needles or other objects they claim to have been infected with AIDS. Thus supervising probation and parole officers must be on their guard to protect themselves from becoming infected.

Another category of special-needs offender is the gang member. Gangs are defined as self-formed associations of peers, united by mutual interest, with identifiable leadership and internal organization, that act collectively or individually to achieve specific purposes, including the conduct of illegal activity and control of a particular territory, facility, or enterprise. They may count as members either adults or juveniles. In 2002 there were more than 800,000 active gang members in 29,000 youth gangs throughout the United States, both on the streets and in U.S. prisons and jails (Wilson 2000). Many gangs are involved in illicit activities, such as dealing drugs or transporting firearms, and many gang members are smart enough not to get caught taking drugs while serving time in probation or while on parole. Supervising officers often regard their interventions with gang members as unproductive, since it is difficult to overcome the influence of gang membership: identification with a gang and involvement in delinquent activities are highly compelling (Bjerregaard 2002). Virtually every city with a population of 250,000 or more has reported the presence of gangs. Furthermore, there have been significant increases in gang membership in suburban and rural areas of the United States; the number of gang members in those areas increased by 50 percent between 1996 and

2002. It is difficult to understand why youth gangs form and perpetuate themselves over time, however: gangs emerge, grow, dissolve, and disappear for reasons that are poorly understood.

Offenders with physical handicaps constitute a growing but often neglected population. Some offenders are confined to wheelchairs, and therefore special facilities must be constructed to accommodate their access to probation or parole offices or community-based sites. Other offenders have hearing or speech impairments that limit them in various ways.

Physically challenged offenders often require greater attention from their supervising officers. Acquiring and maintaining employment may be difficult for them, and many probation and parole officers become brokers between their own agencies and community businesses that are encouraged to employ some of these people. Community volunteers have been increasingly helpful in assisting probation and parole agencies with physically handicapped clients.

Recidivism and Sentencing Effectiveness

There is a great deal of controversy over the definition of *recidivism*. A conventional definition is that recidivism is the commission of a new crime after conviction for an earlier offense. Many investigations of this phenomenon have been conducted, although no consensus exists about the meaning of the term. Criminologists and others can recite lengthy lists of characteristics that describe recidivists, but describing recidivists and using those characteristics as effective predictors of recidivism are two different matters.

Several problems have been identified relating to recidivism and its measurement. Some of the more common ones are listed here:

1. The time interval between commencing a probation or parole program and recidivating is different from one study to the next. Some standards use 6 months, while others use a year, two years, or five years.
2. There are at least fourteen different meanings of the term *recidivism*. The differences lead to confusion.
3. Recidivism is often dichotomized rather than graduated. Thus, it is said that people either recidivate or they

don't. No flexibility exists to allow for degrees of seriousness of the offense.

4. Recidivism rates are influenced by many factors, such as the intensity of supervised probation or parole, the number of face-to-face visits between POs and their clients, and even the rate of prison construction.
5. Recidivism rates may be indicative of program failure rather than client failure.
6. Recidivism rates include only officially reported violations of the law; self-reported information indicates that rates of recidivism may actually be higher than the reported rates indicate.
7. Considerable client variation exists, as well as many programmatic variations. Recidivism varies with the client population under investigation.
8. Policy shifts in local and state governments may change how recidivism is used or defined, as well as the amount of recidivism observed in given jurisdictions (Maltz and McCleary 1977).

We know, or at least we believe we know, that recidivists tend to be male, black, young, less well educated, and with lengthy prior records. In fact, having a lengthy prior record appears to be most consistently related to recidivism. Therefore, should we make it official judicial or parole board policy not to grant probation or parole to younger, less educated, black men with lengthy prior records? No. These are aggregate characteristics that do not easily lend themselves to individualized probation or parole decision-making.

One continuing problem is that while these and other characteristics describe the general category of recidivists, they are also found among many nonrecidivists. Thus, based upon relevant information about offenders, prediction measures must be devised and tested to improve their validity. A related problem is determining whether recidivism has occurred. This means that some degree of agreement needs be established concerning what does and does not constitute recidivism.

Existing measures of recidivism complicate rather than simplify the term's definition. It is important to pay attention to how recidivism is conceptualized in the research literature, because probation or parole program success is measured by recidivism rates. A general standard has emerged among professionals that a failure rate above 30 percent means that a probation or parole program is ineffective. But ineffective in what sense? Reducing crime? Rehabilitating offenders? Both?

Recidivism means program failure—or does it? There are a wide variety of probation and parole programs available to the courts and corrections officials for many different kinds of offenders. One common problem faced by all programs is that observers have trouble matching the right program with the right client. We have much descriptive information about recidivists. Numerous evaluative studies are conducted annually of various offender programs, and virtually all strategies for dealing with offenders have been examined and re-examined. No matter the cure proposed, however, the illness remains. Treatments are rarely simple, and therefore their evaluations are always complicated. Probationers or parolees who violate one or more terms of their probation or parole—regardless of the type of program—are considered recidivists.

Sentencing Appeals and the Appeals Process

Once defendants have been convicted of a crime, they are entitled to at least one appeal to a higher court. The primary purpose of an appeal is to correct a wrong that may have been committed. These wrongs may be mistakes by police, the prosecution, or the court. Errors may have occurred that influence the trial outcome. Appeals are intended to correct those mistakes and errors.

A secondary purpose of an appeal is to render judgment about one or more issues that will influence future cases. Thus, when an appellate court hears a case from a lower trial court, their decision becomes a precedent for subsequent similar cases. That is the doctrine of *stare decisis,* meaning that once a higher court has ruled a particular way on an issue, lower courts are bound to make rulings consistent with that finding. However, trial court judges do have some discretion in deciding whether particular cases resemble previous cases in which appellate courts have ruled. Thus trial court judges may decide that, although a subsequent case is similar in various respects to previous cases already decided by higher courts, there may be enough differences to require a separate finding.

All death sentences are automatically appealed. The appellate process for any case, capital or otherwise, begins by filing an appeal with the most immediate appellate court above the trial court level. In capital cases originating in state courts, state remedies must be pursued on appeal before the federal system is accessed. For instance, a person convicted of murder in California and sentenced to death must direct an appeal first to the Court of Criminal Appeals. If there is an unfavorable ruling by that appellate court, the offender may direct an appeal to the California Supreme Court. If the ruling by that court is also unfavorable to the offender, a direct appeal for relief may be made to the U.S. Supreme Court.

Appellants are persons who initiate appeals; appellees are those who have prevailed in the trial court and argue against reversing the decision of the lower court. Those convicted of capital crimes and sentenced to death are appellants. In most instances, the state is the appellee. There are many grounds upon which to base appeals. Furthermore, appeals in most death penalty cases cause those cases to drag out over a period of ten to fifteen years before appellants are finally executed.

Appeals may be directed to appellate courts on diverse grounds. Appellants may raise questions before appellate courts about how they were originally arrested and processed. They may challenge the admissibility of certain evidence used to convict them. They may claim incompetent or ineffective assistance of counsel. They may challenge the sentence imposed by the judge. Almost every one of these challenges may be included within the scope of a habeas corpus petition.

Habeas corpus means, literally, "produce the body." A habeas corpus petition challenges three things: (1) the fact of confinement, (2) the length of confinement, and/or (3) the nature of the confinement. The fact of confinement involves every event that led to the present circumstances of the appellant (Westervelt and Cook 2004). If the appellant is on death row resulting from a capital offense conviction, any aspect of the justice process leading to that offender's placement on death row is a potential habeas corpus target.

Appeals of any kind, especially death penalty appeals, consume a great deal of time. On the average, it takes about ten to eleven years for inmates on death row to exhaust the appeals process. In some instances, appeals have dragged out for fifteen years (Maguire and Pastore 2005). One reason for the length of the appeals process is that prisoners are permitted to file new petitions with state or federal courts, under a variety of theories. While habeas corpus is the most frequently used appeal, there is almost no limit to the number of issues that may be raised by inmates and their counsel that can result in a conviction or sentence being overturned.

If an offender's case is reviewed by the U.S. Supreme Court and the Court rules in the offender's favor, the case is often reargued at a new trial. When second or third trials occur, however, the results are almost always the same as those of the first trial. In fact, some evidence exists to show that sentencing judges may abuse their sentencing discretion and punish those offenders with harsher penalties than earlier prescribed (Williams 1995). But the U.S. Supreme Court has usually condoned harsher sentences by judges, especially in cases in which judges have provided a logical, written rationale for the harsher sentence. Increased sentences have survived constitutional challenges as violations of double jeopardy, equal protection, and due process.

Appeals are launched by appellants, or those who lose their cases in the trial court. Most frequently, appellants are convicted offenders. They must first file a notice of appeal—a written statement of the appellant's intent to file an appeal with a higher court. Such notices are required within a fixed period following an offender's conviction. A copy of the court record or complete transcript of proceedings is forwarded to the appellate court for review. Also, a brief is filed with the appellate court, outlining the principal arguments for the appeal. These arguments may pertain to particular judicial rulings believed to be incorrect. Appellants are required to list the issues that are the substance of the appeal. If the appellant believes that thirty mistakes were committed by the trial judge, or if the prosecutor was believed to have made prejudicial remarks to the jury where such remarks are prohibited, or if the police did not advise the offender of the Miranda rights upon arrest, all of these mistakes or errors should be listed in the legal brief. These errors or mistakes are considered appealable issues. An offender's first appeal should contain all of the relevant issues, since it is unlikely that courts will consider further appeals over omitted issues.

In response, appellees may file briefs as well, defending why they believe that there were no procedural irregularities or errors committed. These arguments are intended to counter allegations of irregularities raised by appellants. Thus the groundwork is provided for argument later before the appellate court. Most states and the federal government have criminal appellate courts, in which offenders direct their appeals. These appellate courts frequently consist of three-judge panels who will hear the legal arguments and decide whether the trial court was in error. Rulings by appellate courts that overturn a lower trial court are rare, however. One reason is that appellate courts assume that whatever occurred during the offender's trial was correct, and that the criminal conviction was valid. That is a difficult presumption for appellants to overcome. They often must present overwhelming evidence of prosecutorial misconduct or judicial indiscretion in order to convince an appellate court to reverse or set aside their conviction. And if a conviction is reversed, that decision does not absolve the offender of criminal liability. A new trial may be ordered, or a sentencing decision may be modified to be consistent with a higher court ruling.

Presenting the case for the appellant is the defense attorney in most criminal cases, while the district attorney or state prosecutor (the U.S. attorney or assistant U.S. attorney in federal courts) will offer the government's position in the matter to be argued. The dispute process is in the form of oral argument. Once the appellate court has heard the oral arguments from both sides and has consulted the trial transcript, it will render an opinion. An opinion is a written decision about the issue(s) argued, and a holding as to which side—appellant or appellee—prevails. If the appellate court holds in favor of the appellant, and if the appellant is a convicted offender, the case is reversed and remanded back to the trial court with instructions for modifying the original decision. When the ruling favors the government, the appellate court is said to affirm the holding or judgment against the appellant/offender. When the case against the offender has been affirmed by an appellate court, the offender may then direct an appeal to the next higher appellate court. In state courts, this higher appellate court is the state supreme court or court of last resort within the state judicial system. If the state supreme court affirms the conviction, the offender may direct an appeal to the U.S. Supreme Court.

In some opinions by appellate courts, not all of the appellate judges agree about the decision rendered. The minority view is sometimes summarized in a dissenting opinion. Legal historians value dissenting opinions, because they believe that the policy changes of appellate courts may be predicted over time. That is especially true if those rendering dissenting opinions are younger judges on appellate panels. However, the fact is that these minority or dissenting opinions have no impact on the appeal outcome. The majority opinion is the governing opinion in the case and is the more important. Appellate judges who write the majority opinion also outline the legal rationale for their opinion. Such opinions are more or less lengthy. The ultimate court deciding the fate of appellants is the U.S. Supreme Court, or the court of last resort.

Summary

Some of the problems and controversies surrounding sentencing policies in the United States are exacerbated by prison and jail overcrowding. It is an impossible task for states and the federal government to keep pace with the growing number of incarcerated offenders. In lieu of incarceration, therefore, corrections have turned to community supervision of offenders as a viable and effective alternative. Professionals contend that many offenders do not need to be incarcerated, but get-tough proponents suggest that all persons who break the law should be punished, and they may equate punishment with incarceration.

A tension exists, therefore, between citizens who have legitimate fears of offenders living among them and the need to allow offenders some freedom to seek and hold jobs to support themselves and their families and to become rehabilitated and reintegrated. Public relations efforts have been useful in most jurisdictions in convincing citizens of the advantages of successful reintegration and its correlation with lower crime rates. It is not now, and it has never been, the intention of corrections to set free dangerous criminals.

In an effort to be more selective regarding who gets probation and parole, judges and parole boards have devised various means of assessing risk and the potential for dangerous conduct. Measures of risk and needs have been devised as a means of making behavioral forecasts. However, those forecasts have proved faulty and are continuously being revised and improved. No perfect prediction instrument exists, and it is likely that we will never develop such an instrument. In the meantime, many persons, because of characteristics they share with chronic recidivists, are kept in prisons and jails, while others who may be dangerous are permitted their freedom.

Mistakes are made, to be sure. Some of the offenders placed in prison or jail will never reoffend. These are known as false positives. By the same token, some who are deemed safe and unlikely to pose a risk do become dangerous and harm others. Those are known as false negatives. The criminal justice system is intent upon reducing the number of false positives and false negatives. It is believed that only those deserving incarceration should receive it, through selective incapacitation, and that those committing the most serious offenses should receive the longest sentences. Selective incapacitation has been criticized, however, in many circles, largely because of faulty prediction instruments.

Several types of prediction have been used to forecast risk. These include actuarial prediction, anamnestic prediction, and clinical prediction. For all practical purposes, little difference in effectiveness exists among them, and all have similar degrees of predictive utility. But clinical prediction is the most expensive, inasmuch as it requires one-on-one evaluations by psychiatrists and psychologists. Actuarial and anamnestic prediction seem to forecast with equal effectiveness.

A vexing problem is that wrongful convictions against defendants are sometimes obtained, although it is unknown how often such travesties of justice occur. Various organizations work to prevent wrongful conviction and to free those who can demonstrate their innocence. Judicial discretion often influences the nature of criminal proceedings against particular criminal defendants, and wrongful convictions may ensue as the result of an abuse of that discretion. Whenever such abuses of discretion are detected, they are investigated. By the same token, parole boards sometimes release dangerous offenders who eventually commit new crimes. Those discretionary abuses are also investigated. One reaction on the part of the citizenry, expressed through the actions of legislators, is to change sentencing laws to curb the discretionary powers of judges and parole boards. However, despite the changes made over several decades, there is a continuing pattern of recidivism among those on probation and parole that is alarmingly high. It is consistently the case that at least 65 percent of all probationers and parolees will reoffend within three years, regardless of the interventions attempted on their behalf. This high recidivism rate frustrates both the public and politicians.

Some persons are chronic recidivists, meaning that they make their living from crime as career criminals, or are persistent violent offenders intent on harming or exploiting others. Recidivism may be variously defined, depending upon the term's use in the research literature. It may refer to reincarcerations, rearrests, reconvictions, technical program violations for those on probation or parole, or several other actions. But reconvictions are the most reliable indicator of recidivism used at present.

For many offenders, especially those who commit minor offenses or who are first-time offenders, civil alternatives to criminal trial may exist. Two civil means of processing offenders include alternative dispute resolution (ADR) and pretrial diversion. ADR is victim-offender reconciliation wherein the two parties attempt to resolve their differences through a third-party arbiter. Their aim is to reach an amicable solution whereby property is restored, medical bills are paid, and some form of restitution is exacted. Those who successfully complete ADR may succeed in having the records of their arrests expunged. For pretrial divertees, the intent is that they remain law-abiding for a period of time. If they are successful in complying with the terms and conditions of their diversion program, they are likely to have the criminal charges against them dismissed. Their records may even be expunged. These programs, however, assume guilt without the benefit of trial, and critics insist that in order for the criminal justice system to be fair to all, everyone is entitled to a day in court. However, many ADR participants and pretrial divertees like things as they are and wish that civil rights groups would not interfere.

Many persons charged with and convicted of crimes have special needs; they are designated as special-needs offenders. These include the mentally ill, sex offenders or child sexual abusers, those with communicable diseases such as HIV/AIDS or tuberculosis, drug- or alcohol-dependent offenders and those with other dependencies, and handicapped persons or those with physical disabilities. These offenders pose various kinds of supervisory problems for probation and parole officers, and even for correctional officers who must interact with them closely.

Whenever persons are sentenced for any type of crime, they have the right to appeal their sentences, usually to higher courts or appellate courts. Each state has its own appellate court system, and the federal court process is organized similarly. Pursuing appeals is costly and time-consuming, but some appealable issues eventually reach the court of last resort or the U.S. Supreme Court. Various grounds are used to launch appeals from trial courts, the most common being habeas corpus, wherein the fact, nature, and length of confinement are challenged.

References

Auerbahn, Kathleen. 2002. "Selective Incapacitation, Three Strikes, and the Problem of Aging Prison Populations: Using Simulation Modeling to See the Future." *Criminology and Public Policy* 1:353–388.

Bjerregaard, Beth. 2002. "Self-definitions of Gang Membership and Involvement in Delinquent Activities." *Youth and Society* 34:31–54.

Boller, Kelley G. 2005. "Wrongful Convictions: Theoretical Explanations for the Differing Perceptions of Criminal Justice Actors." Unpublished paper presented at the annual meeting of the Academy of Criminal Justice Sciences, Chicago, IL.

Burnett, Cathleen. 2005. "Restorative Justice and Wrongful Capital Convictions." *Journal of Contemporary Criminal Justice* 21:272–289.

Call, Jack E., and Richard Cole. 1996. "Assessing the Possible Impact of the Violent Crime Control Act of 1994 on Prison and Jail Overcrowding Suits." *Prison Journal* 76:92–106.

Carr, Brent A., Linda Collins, and Pam Leary. 2006. "Mental Health Diversion Program: Diverting Persons with Mental Impairments out of the Traditional Criminal Court Process." Unpublished paper presented at the annual meeting of the American Probation and Parole Association, Chicago, IL.

Conaboy, Richard P. 1997. "The United States Sentencing Commission: A New Component in the Federal Criminal Justice System." *Federal Probation* 61:58–62.

Davis, Jacqueline. 2005. "Texas Landmark Cases: An Analysis and Comparison of *Ruiz v. Estelle* and *Morales v. Turman*." Unpublished paper presented at the annual meeting of the Academy of Criminal Justice Sciences, Chicago, IL.

Death Penalty Information Center. 2005. *Innocence and the Crisis in the American Death Penalty.* Washington, DC: Death Penalty Information Center.

Dennehy, Kathleen M. 2006. *Massachusetts Correctional Institution MCI.* Milford, MA: DOC Central Headquarters.

Deschenes, Elizabeth, Susan Turner, and Todd Clear. 1992. "The Effectiveness of ISP for Different Types of Drug Offenders." Unpublished paper presented at the annual meeting of the American Society of Criminology, New Orleans, LA.

Doeren, Stephen E., and Mary J. Hageman. 1982. *Community Corrections.* Cincinnati, OH: Anderson.

Frazier v. Stone. 1974. 515 S.W.2d 766.

Griffiths, Curt Taylor, and Gordon Bazemore, eds. 1999. "Restorative Justice." *International Review of Victimology* 6:261–405.

Grimes, Paul W., and Kevin E. Rogers. 1999. "Truth-in-sentencing, Law Enforcement, and Inmate Population Growth." *Journal of Socio-Economics* 28:745–757.

Irwin, John. 2005. "A Dialogue on Sentencing Reform." Unpublished paper presented at the annual meeting of the Academy of Criminal Justice Sciences, Chicago, IL.

Irwin, John, Vincent Schiraldi, and Jason Ziedenberg. 1999. *America's One Million Nonviolent Prisoners.* Washington, DC: Justice Policy Institute.

Kruttschnitt, Candace, Christopher Uggen, and Kelly Shelton. 2000. "Predictors of Desistance among Sex Offenders: The Interaction of Formal and Informal Social Controls." *Justice Quarterly* 17:61–87.

Maguire, Kathleen, and Ann L. Pastore. 2005. *Sourcebook of Criminal Justice Statistics 2004.* Albany, NY: Hindelang Criminal Justice Research Center.

Maltz, Michael D., and R. McCleary. 1977. "The Mathematics of Behavioral Change: Recidivism and Construct Validity." *Evaluation Quarterly* 1:421–438.

McGrath, Robert J., Georgia Cumming, and John Holt. 2002. "Collaboration among Sex Offender Treatment Providers and Probation and Parole Officers: The Beliefs and Behaviors of Treatment Providers." *Sexual Abuse: A Journal of Research and Treatment* 14:49–65.

Morris, Norval, and Marc Miller. 1985. "Predictions of Dangerousness." In *Crime and Justice: An Annual Review of Research, Vol. 6.* Michael Tonry and Norval Morris, eds. Chicago: University of Chicago Press.

National Association of Pretrial Services Agencies. 1995. *Performance Standards and Goals for Pretrial Release and Diversion.* Frankfort, KY: National Association of Pretrial Services Agencies.

Office of Justice Programs. 2001. *Rates of HIV Infection and AIDS-related Deaths.* Washington, DC: Office of Justice Programs.

Rans, Laurel L. 1984. "The Validity of Models to Predict Violence in Community and Prison Settings." *Corrections Today* 46:50–63.

Robinson, Gwen. 2002. "Exploring Risk Management in Probation Practice: Contemporary Developments in England and Wales." *Punishment and Society* 4:5–25.

Roy, Sudipto, and Michael Brown. 1992. "Victim-offender Reconciliation Project for Adults and Juveniles: A Comparative Study in Elkhart County, Indiana." Unpublished paper presented at the annual meeting of the American Society of Criminology, San Francisco, CA.

Scheck, Barry, and Peter Neufeld. 2002. "Toward the Formation of Innocence Commissions in America." *Judicature* 86:98–105.

Shane-Dubow, Sandra, et al. 1998. "Structured Sentencing in the U.S.: An Experiment in Modeling Judicial Discretion." *Law and Policy* 20:231–382.

Umbreit, Mark S., Robert B. Coates, and Betty Vos. 2002. "Restorative Justice Circles: The Impact of Community Involvement." *APPA Perspectives* 26:36–40.

U.S. Code. 2007. Title 18, Sec. 4215.

Vitiello, Michael. 1997. "Three Strikes: Can We Return to Rationality?" *Journal of Criminal Law and Criminology* 87:395–481.

Welsh, Wayne N. 1995. *Counties in Court: Jail Overcrowding and Court-ordered Reform.* Philadelphia: Temple University Press.

Westervelt, Saundra D., and Kimberly J. Cook. 2004. "Life after Death: Life Histories of Innocents Released from Death Row." Unpublished paper presented at the annual meeting of the American Society of Criminology, Nashville, TN.

Williams, Jimmy J. 1995. "Type of Counsel and the Outcome of Criminal Appeals: A Research Note." *American Journal of Criminal Justice* 19:275–285.

Wilson, John J. 2000. *1998 National Youth Gang Survey.* Washington, DC: National Youth Gang Center.

3

Worldwide Perspective

Introduction

Sentencing in the United States is unique among the nations of the world. There are obvious parallels to other nations, such as sentencing goals, including deterrence, retribution, rehabilitation and reintegration, punishment, just deserts and justice, and crime control. But how other nations sentence their offenders varies widely. One explanation for these sentencing variations is that crime is often defined differently elsewhere. Greater or lesser emphasis may be placed on rehabilitation, and some countries lack the resources and skills to construct and operate sophisticated prisons and rehabilitation centers. Their facilities, therefore, are more primitive confinement institutions. Still other countries have very liberal policies toward most offenders, permitting them frequent opportunities to leave confinement to visit with families and interact with others.

This chapter focuses on the sentencing practices in a select number of countries. The countries chosen for inclusion here were targeted because of their differences from U.S. sentencing policies and practices. The sentencing schemes of each country presented here are best understood in the sociopolitical environment of the country itself. Thus some preliminary factual information about each country is provided, including its political structure, judicial apparatus and functioning, and the nature and frequency of crimes most often committed. Where applicable, assumptions are noted that partially explain the reasons for the types of punishments imposed. Also discussed are how offenders are treated following sentencing and the types of systems in place to meet their individual needs or to provide necessary counseling and vocational/technical education.

How Do Other Countries Sentence Their Offenders?

It is important to understand the government in a country to appreciate the type of sentencing scheme it adopts to punish offenders. Like the United States, each country defines its own crimes, although there are vast differences in the types of crimes and the names given to them. Specialized courts are designated to deal with various categories of crime, and in that respect there is some similarity to U.S. court practices. Indeed, several countries have elaborate court systems similar in complexity to that of the United States. Also, some acts defined as criminal and treated harshly elsewhere would not be considered crimes in the United States.

Sentencing Schemes and Practices in Other Countries

Australia

Australia, a British Commonwealth nation, is composed of Queensland, Western Australia, Tasmania, New South Wales, Victoria, and South Australia. Within each state are shires, the equivalent of U.S. counties, and within each state, local communities may pass their own laws and ordinances, such as traffic enforcement and public order laws (Biles 2005).

Crimes in Australia are defined as any conduct prohibited by law that may result in punishment (Australian Institute of Criminology 2005a). Crimes may be felonies, misdemeanors, or minor offenses, with most being indictable or nonindictable. Indictable offenses, like U.S. felonies, are tried in superior courts; some may require juries. The vast majority of Australian offending, however, involves nonindictable offenses that are heard and decided in magistrate's local courts.

The minimum age of criminal responsibility is seven years. Persons under age seven are not accountable. Persons age sixteen or older can be tried in an adult court, but there is considerable variation among the states regarding juvenile court jurisdiction, with some states having a ten-to-seventeen age range, while others have an eight-to-seventeen or a seven-to-sixteen age range. Any youth over the age of seven who is charged with homicide, however, may be tried in adult court. In some rare instances, youths over the age of seven but under the age of eighteen can be tried in adult court for rape or treason (ibid. 2006a).

All suspects have the right to defend themselves, or to have an attorney appointed for them if they are indigent. A legal aid commission oversees assignment of public defenders to indigents. Guilty pleas are accepted, and judges may dispense with trials and impose sentences whenever guilty pleas are entered. The most serious cases are heard in court, where an accused is entitled to a twelve-member jury trial. Plea bargaining is a form of charge bargaining, in which some charges against suspects are dropped in exchange for a guilty plea (ibid.). Defendants may or may not be entitled to bail. Most defendants are granted bail, however. Those charged with murder, robbery, or rape may be held without bail and are remanded until trial.

The court system of Australia is hierarchical, headed by the High Court of Australia. Each state and territory has a supreme court. There are intermediate appellate courts, and in heavily populated areas there are district courts and criminal courts. Rural areas have county courts. Magistrate's courts exist in each community. Approximately 90 percent of all criminal cases are heard and decided in magistrate's courts. Presentence investigation reports are prepared by probation officers in more serious cases, and victim impact statements may be appended to those reports: there is significant victim involvement in the sentencing process. Probation officers have a great deal of influence in offender sentencing, because they prepare presentence investigation reports and make sentencing recommendations. Probation is used frequently as a punishment (Commonwealth of Australia 2006).

Prisons in Australia are under the control of each state or territory. There are no federal penitentiaries. In 2004 there were 24,171 persons in prison. Men make up some 93 percent of all inmates. There were 55,000 clients on probation or parole in 2005 (Department of Corrective Services 2006).

The range of penalties for crimes includes fines, probation, and incarceration, depending upon the seriousness of the crime and other factors. Judges may also impose home confinement, community service, restitution, and almost every other type of intermediate punishment available to convicted offenders in the

United States. Probation orders are also much like those in the United States. There is no death penalty, however. Inmates in prisons fall into the following categories: 42 percent are violent offenders, 15 percent are drug offenders, and 40 percent are property offenders. All prisoners have vocational and educational opportunities while confined. Counseling programs are offered, including drug treatment programs. There are several security levels in prison, and inmates may earn privileges and less secure confinement through good conduct. Furloughs are permitted after prisoners have served a portion of their sentence with a good conduct report. Furloughs are weekend leaves for inmates, enabling them to rejoin their families and look for work. The goals of the criminal justice system are retribution, incapacitation, rehabilitation, and crime prevention or deterrence. Restorative justice is used, particularly among Aborigines.

Parole is also used. Inmates become eligible for parole after serving two-thirds of their maximum sentence. In 2005, there were approximately 220,000 persons under probation or parole supervision. Many treatment programs are offered, including individual counseling, group work, and family counseling. Coordination is emphasized, together with accurate record-keeping, documentation, and individual evaluation and progress reports (Australian Institute of Criminology 2005b).

Canada

Canada is a federalist country consisting of ten provinces and two territories. The criminal code, created in 1892, has been revised regularly. Parole was established in 1959 through the Parole Act, and the National Parole Board was created. Each province has established its own parole board.

Bail will be granted if someone is charged with a crime that brings with it a prison sentence of five years or less, and if a police officer has no reasonable grounds to believe that (1) continued detention is necessary in the public interest, (2) the accused is unlikely to attend a subsequent trial if released, and (3) the issue of release is of such a serious nature that it should be dealt with by a justice of the peace. The minimum age of criminal responsibility is twelve for all provinces and territories. The age of adult criminal responsibility is eighteen in all provinces.

Crimes consist of the following: (1) summary offenses, which are the least serious crimes (for example, public disturbance and traffic violations), (2) indictable offenses, or the most serious crimes (such as murder, rape, and robbery), involving confinement in a penitentiary for a minimum of two years, and (3) hybrid offenses, which are dual offenses that may be prosecuted either as summary or indictable offenses. Summary offenses are violations of localized ordinances. Following arrest, suspects must be brought before a justice of the peace within twenty-four hours. Pretrial detention is used infrequently. Determining bail can take up to eight days, and the amount of bail is set by the justice of the peace.

Persons accused of crimes are entitled to counsel and the full range of rights. Indigent defendants are provided with court-appointed counsel. Police officers often serve as prosecutors, but private citizens may also function as prosecutors under certain circumstances. Trials are for indictable offenses, although defendants are given the choice of a jury or bench trial, and diversion is an alternative to trial for the least serious offenses. Alternative dispute resolution and restorative justice programs are also used. Only about 10 percent of all criminal cases each year are heard before a judge and jury (Cohen and Longtin 2004).

The court system consists of the Supreme Court of Canada, which hears appeals for both summary and indictable offense convictions. A Court of Appeal hears summary and indictable offense conviction appeals. District and county courts and a provincial courts-criminal division hear all summary offense cases. Each province has three levels of trial court. The highest is the superior court of criminal jurisdiction. This court has jurisdiction over all indictable offense cases. The second type of court is the court of criminal jurisdiction. That court has jurisdiction over all indictable offenses except for the most serious. The third court is the summary conviction court. Youth courts are provided for juveniles.

When defendants are convicted, trial judges impose a sentence. Judges must follow maximum, minimum, and fixed penalty guidelines provided by statute for all offense categories. Sentencing may occur at the time of conviction, and all convictions may be appealed. Judges consider the mental status of defendants when imposing sentences.

The range of penalties in Canada includes life imprisonment (there is no death penalty), deprivation of liberty for a period of years or months, control of freedom (through probation), verbal warnings and admonitions, community service orders, and restitution and compensation (Canada Correctional Services 2005).

Probation is used for most crimes. Probationers are required to abide by various conditions set by the court, and those conditions are enforced by local probation departments. Community residential centers exist in most urban jurisdictions. The aims of probation are rehabilitation, community reintegration, and self-improvement. These aims are accomplished by an interconnected network of social and vocational services, including counseling, vocational/educational training, and other treatments. Community service orders are frequently imposed and involve a fixed number of community service hours. Incarceration in prison is a last resort. Offenders who serve probationary terms and are convicted of new offenses may be resentenced to probation, and there may be five or six probation sentences before those persons are actually imprisoned. The thrust of the criminal justice system is on offender rehabilitation and reintegration.

Federal penitentiaries hold federal prisoners sentenced to two or more years. Offenders serving shorter sentences are placed in provincial prisons. Vocational, educational, and counseling opportunities are provided. Prison industries train inmates in skills such as laundry, shoe manufacture, clothing manufacture, farming, and machine operation. Inmates lacking education are encouraged to work toward a G.E.D. or high school diploma, and inmates are encouraged to take college courses where offered.

Parole is granted once offenders have served one-sixth of their sentence. All parole actions are at the discretion of a parole board, and both federal and provincial inmates may be released on full or day parole. Another type of parole is through the Mandatory Release Program. This provides for the release of inmates who have served two-thirds of their prison time and who have exhibited good behavior. But those released must remain in their communities under the supervision of parole officers until their original sentence expires. Parole officers assist parolees in finding employment, in obtaining housing, and in solving personal problems.

Some provinces have Temporary Absence programs. Inmates may be released on furloughs of up to 15 days. These leaves are preparole programs and assist inmates to locate work and housing and support their families and dependents. Under mandatory release, parolees are not responsible to parole boards, but they are accountable to their parole officers.

Probation services are operated through the Adult Corrections Services. In 2005 there were more than 130,000 persons on probation. A total of 166,000 persons were under some form of correctional service supervision, and about 10 percent of those were women. Some 1,200 parolees were under supervision in the various provinces in 2005 (Saskatchewan Corrections and Public Safety 2005).

Costa Rica

Costa Rica is a constitutional democracy. Crimes in Costa Rica are classified either as (1) *delitos* (crimes against life or family, sex crimes, property damage, human rights crimes, drug trafficking, robbery, burglary, and aggravated assault), or (2) misdemeanors or contravention offenses (crimes against public safety, minor property offending, and minor physical injury). *Delitos* crimes carry penalties of fines and/or imprisonment for periods of one year or longer, while misdemeanor punishments are for periods of less than one year (Giralt 2004).

The age of criminal responsibility is eighteen years, with the exception of persons who are close to the legal age (that is, sixteen to seventeen) and who have committed heinous crimes. Youths over twelve and under eighteen who have committed one or more crimes are sent to rehabilitative facilities. The focus is entirely upon rehabilitation of a vocational or educational nature. For those under age twelve no punitive action is taken; social agencies accept responsibility for their welfare.

The most frequently committed crimes in Costa Rica are robbery and larceny. Victim's assistance agencies have been established to care for crime victims (Bureau of Democracy, Human Rights, and Labor 2002). Criminal suspects may be held for twenty-four hours before charges must be filed. Judges decide to detain or release suspects (Williams 2003).

All those arrested have the right to an attorney, and indigent defendants have counsel appointed for them. The Justice Department conducts all interrogations, and confessions are admissible against suspects. All persons accused of a crime have rights: they are brought before a fact-finding authority, where an initial questioning period is conducted. Cases with merit proceed to the next level, where the *ministerio publico,* or prosecutor, conducts an official prosecution. Evidence is gathered, and witnesses are obtained. There is no plea bargaining, and accused persons may not accept lighter sentences in exchange for testimony against others or for confessions. However, judges may impose lighter sentences on convicted offenders if they believe that the information provided by them is noteworthy and leads to a successful prosecution of others. Pretrial detention exists. Bail depends on the offenses alleged, the person's prior criminal record, the reliability of the offender, and the impact on the community. About 85 percent of all persons charged with crimes are released on bail.

Not all cases result in trials. Pretrial diversion is granted to defendants upon a recommendation from prosecutors and with judicial approval. Of the 103,000 cases processed in 1999, for instance, about 26 percent were dismissed. Pretrial diversion was recommended in 5 percent of those cases, while the others resulted in minor penalties including home confinement and fines.

The court system is multileveled, the highest court being the Supreme Court, or Salas Corte Suprema de Justicia. Several courts of appeal hear appeals from lower courts. The lowest courts consist of Alcaldias, which handle misdemeanor cases in which punishments are of less than three years. The next higher courts are the Juzgados, or courts of First Instance. These deal with crimes in which penalties are for more than three years. The Tribunal Superior and the Supreme Tribunal are courts of appeal for lower courts as well as trial courts for felonies. In 2000 there were 103 Alcaldia courts, 84 Juzgados courts, 10 Tribunal Superior courts, and 1 Supreme Court.

When a defendant is found guilty, a judge or panel of judges imposes a sentence. Sentences are determined by the penal code. Sentencing hearings are conducted and involve input from social workers, clergy, psychologists, and other professionals. The range of penalties includes fines, imprisonment, and house arrest. Most crimes carry one- to twenty-five-year sentences, although longer sentences may be imposed. There is no death penalty. Fines are correlated with the offender's income, and offenders have 15 days to pay their fines or they will be imprisoned.

There were 2,500 to 4,000 persons in prisons and local jails in 2005. Costa Rica keeps no records of the characteristics of its inmate population. Inmates may earn time off for good behavior up to 50 percent of their maximum sentence. Determination of who should receive parole is through judicial referrals of cases to the Criminology Institute, where a criminological diagnosis of each inmate is made. For first offenders, early release may be earned after serving 6 months and receiving reports of good conduct. Judges may impose any program conditions as parole requirements. The report from the Criminology Institute is important and is like a presentence investigation report (United Nations 2000).

Inmates do not have to work while confined, although they are encouraged to do so. Vocational and educational training are provided and may prepare compliant inmates for community reintegration. Prisoners have access to group therapy sessions, anger management training, counseling, educational and vocational training, television sets, and radios, and they have the right to possess a certain amount of personal property. Conjugal and family visits are permitted on a regular basis. Medical care and religious services are provided.

Probation does not exist, although judges may suspend criminal proceedings against defendants. Divertees are placed on suspension for short periods, and their cases may be dismissed when their suspension period is complete (Costa Rica National Assembly 2005).

Great Britain

The government of Great Britain consists of the monarchy, Parliament, the House of Lords, and the House of Commons; laws are derived largely from common law. Defendants have a full range of rights, and indigent defendants have court-appointed counsel. Plea bargaining is an accepted practice, and about 50 percent of all criminal cases are concluded through guilty pleas (Phillips, Cox, and Pease 2004). The age of criminal responsibility is ten years, and children between the ages of ten and seventeen are brought before a youth court if charged with a criminal offense. Persons eighteen or older are under the jurisdiction of adult courts.

Crimes are classified into three categories: (1) summary offenses (for example, public intoxication, mischief, public disorder, and other nuisance offenses), (2) indictable offenses (such as rape, murder, robbery, and assault), and (3) hybrid offenses, the seriousness of which is determined by prosecutorial discretion. According to the 2004 *British Crime Survey*, a victimization report, there were 11.7 million crimes in that year (Nielson 2005).

Summary offenses are usually tried in magistrate's courts, while more serious offenses are tried in Crown Courts. There are approximately one hundred Crown Courts in different jurisdictions in Great Britain. Juries may hear the more serious cases, although bench trials are pervasive. Juries consist of twelve persons, and guilt must be established beyond a reasonable doubt. A conviction in a magistrate's court is appealable to the Crown Court. Appeals of convictions in Crown Courts are made to the Court of Appeal Criminal Division. In Crown Courts, guilty verdicts have sentences imposed by judges.

Sentencing hearings are preceded by an order for a presentence report, prepared by the Probation Service. Judges may follow presentence recommendations, or they may impose sentences at their discretion.

Punishments range from verbal warnings and fines to incarceration, depending upon the seriousness of the offense. More than 80 percent of all convictions result in fines. Community service orders or community work, and probation supervision, may also be ordered. Victim compensation or restitution orders may be imposed as well. About 20 percent of all defendants found guilty of indictable offenses are incarcerated. Such sentences may be suspended or begun immediately, at judicial discretion. There is no death penalty (British Home Office 2006).

Criminal proceedings are commenced with arrests and the filing of charges. Prosecutors may defer prosecution for up to 6 months, and they may discharge defendants at their discretion based on the defendant's conduct. Some offenses may be diverted to a mediation process. The aim of mediation is restitution or restoration.

A speedy trial provision exists wherein criminal defendants must be tried within 70 days of being charged with a crime. Bail is granted to those entitled to bail, but it may be denied to those considered a societal risk or who are likely to flee to avoid prosecution.

The range of penalties includes unconditional discharges, in which defendants are simply fined. Incarceration may be imposed for more serious criminal convictions. Early release may be granted to certain inmates, and a parole board grants or denies parole. All conditional prison releasees are referred to as probationers. In 2005, 8 percent of all charges resulted in discharge or dismissal; 71 percent resulted in standard probation, 13 percent in community sentences (probation), and 7 percent in incarceration.

In 2005 there were 76,000 inmates; less than 10 percent were women. Inmates have various amenities, including television and radio. They receive regular health care, educational opportunities, vocational training, religious worship, and visitation privileges from family or friends.

Probation may be imposed in different ways, and inmates leaving prison or receiving a community sentence will be put on probation and supervised. Thus offenders are placed on probation whenever:

1. Judges sentence them to a community sentence, as an alternative to prison.
2. The parole board decides that the offender can be released short of serving the full term of imprisonment.
3. The offender is automatically released from prison after serving three-fourths of the original sentence.

Being on probation involves conditions. If one or more conditions are violated, violators face revocation of their probation and possible return to prison. Clients must report regularly to supervising probation officers and attend supervision sessions. If sessions are missed, a warning will be issued to the violator. Missing two or more sessions means that clients will be sent to court and possibly imprisoned. Other probation requirements include the following:

1. Completing community sentences successfully.
2. Completing alcohol or drug treatment programs.
3. Staying in a probation hostel.
4. Staying away from the area where the crime was committed.

Community sentences may include compulsory work, such as cleaning up local areas and removing graffiti, which may enable offenders to acquire new skills while repaying societal debts; community rehabilitation, which may involve regular meetings with probation officers to facilitate behavioral changes; and curfews, whereby offenders must stay indoors at certain times under a form of house arrest or home confinement. The aims of sentencing include protecting the public, punishing offenders, reducing crime, rehabilitating offenders, and repairing harm to society by means of restorative justice. Sentences by judges are influenced by the seriousness of the offense, one's remorsefulness, and the defendant's prior record.

In 2005 probation officers supervised approximately 250,000 offenders. About 70 percent of those probationers were serving community sentences and had not been imprisoned. Consistent with an emphasis upon rehabilitation is the use of better offender management methods, including home confinement and electronic monitoring.

In 2006 the Sentencing Guidelines Council set forth sentencing procedural guidelines for all courts. These are the National

Allocation Guidelines, which assist courts in dealing with all criminal cases. Their purpose is to provide judges with guidance in sentencing. Their creation suggests strong governmental interest in formalizing and systematizing the sentencing process (Sentencing Guidelines Council 2006).

France

The government of France is highly centralized. There are both criminal and civil justice systems serving twenty-two regions and 36,000 municipalities. Since 1994, France has established new criteria for different crime categories. The three major crime categories are as follows:

1. Contraventions: petty offenses associated with fines (for example, minor traffic offenses, breaches of bylaws, minor assaults, and noise offenses).
2. Delits: offenses of greater importance and possibly requiring confinement for periods ranging from a half-year to ten years and possible fines (for example, theft, manslaughter, assault, drug offenses, and driving while intoxicated).
3. Crimes: the most serious offenses, punishable by imprisonment of from ten years to life and possible fines (there is no death penalty in France) (for example, murder, rape, robbery, kidnapping, or abduction).

The French court system consists of the Police Court, which deals with summary offenses or minor violations of the law (such as reckless driving or public intoxication), and maximum fines of 25,000 francs or confinement of 2 months or less in a jail. The next higher court is the Correctional Court, with jurisdiction over all crimes involving a maximum punishment of ten years in prison. A third court is the Assize Court, in which life sentences may be imposed upon conviction. Juries of nine persons are used in the most serious cases. The numbers of jurors in these courts range from six to twelve, depending upon the jurisdiction. In 2006 there were more than 7,000 judges in France (Borricand 2006).

Serious criminal investigations are conducted by public prosecutors under the control of the Public Ministry. Accusations are made after investigation, once a suspect has been identified. Defendants are considered innocent until proven guilty, and all defendants are entitled to court-appointed counsel. Bail is optional according to the seriousness of the offense, and judges make bail decisions. The burden of proof is upon the state. If there is insufficient evidence against the accused, the case is dropped (Clavier 1997).

Plea bargaining does not exist in France. Persons accused of crimes cannot plead guilty. They may confess to crimes, but those confessions are used as evidence against them. When defendants are found guilty, judges impose sentences using broad sentencing powers. The death penalty does not exist, although life sentences may be imposed. All cases are individualized, depending on the evidence presented and the seriousness of the offense, offender attitudes, and other factors. All sentences may be appealed, and judges may impose probation at their discretion. For custodial sentences of up to five years, probation is used most frequently. Probation judges appoint persons to supervise probationers (*Juge de l'application des peines*), and probationary terms may be ordered for up to three years.

Community orders may also be imposed, especially for petty offenders. Such orders may involve service from 40 hours to 240 hours. In 2006 there were more than 40,000 community service orders issued. Fines are also imposed. Alternative punishments or creative sentencing is used for indigent defendants who cannot pay fines.

The probation system in France supervised more than 200,000 probationers in 2006. Probationers in France are expected to seek and maintain employment, support their families, seek counseling and other forms of assistance (depending upon the nature of their offense), and engage in productive vocational or educational training. if necessary. Their activities are closely monitored by probation officers who work under the jurisdiction of the judicial probation service. Volunteers work with various offenders by teaching literacy training (Bertrand 2006).

The prison population of France in 2005 was 60,000 inmates, and the average sentence length is 10 months. Prison labor is voluntary, but vocational and educational activities are provided for interested prisoners. About 20 percent of all prisoners cannot read or write. Prison authorities have the discretion to grant particular prisoners *semi-liberté*, whereby they are permitted to leave their prisons during daytime hours and work or study in their communities. Thus there is a heavy emphasis upon community reintegration. These measures are used to assist prisoners in avoiding job loss and to receive medical treatment, psychological counseling, or other types of assistance. Probation judges may also grant furloughs or short-term leaves to particular inmates, particularly those serving sentences of 12 months or less.

Parole in France commenced in 1885 as a means of reintegrating offenders back into society, and in 2005 approximately 7,000 paroles were granted. Parole and parole orders are granted by the *juge de l'application des peines,* if the sentence being served is less than ten years, or if the remaining time to be served is less than three years. Full judicial hearings are held, in which paroles are either granted or denied to parole-eligible offenders. Paroled offenders are supervised in a manner similar to those supervised by probation officers or social workers. Special conditions may accompany both probation and parole programs, including curfews, drug and alcohol monitoring, and residence searches. If parolees or probationers violate one or more conditions of their program, the program will be terminated and they will be imprisoned to serve their full terms. In some special cases, pardons may be granted by the president of France.

Ghana

The government of Ghana is a multiparty parliamentary government with a president and legislature. The legislature creates all civil and criminal laws (Winslow 2005). Statutory law governs most of Ghana (Ebbe 2005). The age of criminal responsibility is eighteen, and there are five degrees of offense: (1) capital offenses, in which the death penalty may be administered, for murder, treason, or piracy, (2) first-degree felonies, punishable by life imprisonment, for manslaughter, rape, and mutiny, (3) second-degree felonies, punishable by up to ten years in prison, for intentional harm to persons, perjury, and robbery, (4) misdemeanors, including assault, theft, and official corruption, and (5) public nuisance activities, meaning crimes punishable by either fines or various short terms of imprisonment. Corporal punishment is not permitted. No juveniles may be imprisoned, and no one under the age of eighteen may be executed, regardless of the nature of the offense (Office to Monitor and Combat Trafficking in Persons 2006).

Defendants have many legal rights, and indigent defendants have court-appointed counsel. Defendants may plead guilty, but such confessions or admissions do not mean that leniency will be granted by judges. The maximum penalty for the most serious offenses is death. Any person charged with a crime that may result in the death penalty is entitled to a trial before the High Court. For lesser offenses, including misdemeanors, cases are tried by magistrates in a summary fashion and fines are typically imposed. All other serious cases are tried in either a Circuit Court or the High Court. There is no plea bargaining, and there are no jury trials. Police officers who make arrests become the prosecutors and pursue cases against their arrestees. Police officers may also give testimony about the cases they prosecute.

Bail is available to all persons entitled to bail. The court system consists of (1) the Supreme Court, consisting of a chief justice and six other justices, (2) a Court of Appeal, having appellate jurisdiction over high courts and circuit courts, (3) high courts and circuit courts, which consist of from one to three judges who sit and decide cases, (4) district courts, which have jurisdiction to hear local cases, and (5) customary courts, or those located in the most rural regions.

Sentencing in Ghana is on the basis of judicial discretion, but sentencing decisions must be unanimous if more than one judge hears a case. The only persons having input in sentencing matters are professionals such as psychiatrists and social workers. Medical experts may also be consulted, as well as probation officers (Ministry of Justice 2006b). The range of punishments includes fines, community service, restitution, probation, and prison. Prison terms can be imposed from one year to life, although the death penalty may be administered for the most serious crimes. Most executions have been for treason, murder, or attempting to overthrow the government.

The number of persons under supervised probation is unknown. Offenders who are imprisoned can be released short of serving their full terms because of good behavior, and parole exists, with release based on good conduct. Inmates who participate in self-help programs, counseling, anger management, vocational or educational courses, and other rehabilitative services earn good-time credit against their maximum sentences (United Nations 2005). The prisons are notoriously overcrowded: in 2005, prisons designed to hold 7,500 inmates accommodated 15,000 (Bureau of Democracy, Human Rights, and Labor 2001).

Japan

Japan has a centralized federal system of government. The criminal justice system is accusatorial, and the judicial system consists of summary courts, family courts, district courts, and high courts, in which decisions can be appealed from district courts. Criminal appeals may be made to the Supreme Court, although most appeals involve constitutional issues. Summary courts are located in towns and cities and try cases punishable only by fines. High courts exist in all major cities, with similar jurisdiction over more serious cases. The criminal code has set minimum and maximum sentences for offenses in order to individualize punishments for different offenders. Judges conduct trials and are authorized to examine witnesses, call for evidence, and decide upon one's guilt. Judges may also suspend the sentences of those convicted, placing them on probation or ordering them to perform various types of service (Conant 2004).

There are three general categories of crime: (1) crimes against the state, (2) crimes against society, and (3) crimes against individuals. The age of criminal responsibility is twenty. Anyone under that age is considered a juvenile and subject to juvenile court jurisdiction.

Whenever police officers arrest offenders, prosecutors bring charges against them. All accused persons have rights, and indigent defendants are provided with court-appointed legal counsel. Speedy and public trials are provided. There is no plea bargaining. Confessions are accepted, but prosecutors must present evidence that establishes one's guilt in court. Suspects may be detained without bail, although bail is most frequently permitted in the less serious cases. The range of penalties includes death, imprisonment with labor, imprisonment without labor, fines, short-term detention (less than 30 days), and a variety of other penalties such as asset forfeiture. Judges may impose community punishments such as probation in various forms with a variety of conditions.

The Correction Bureau is responsible for administering Japan's prison system. There are three major types of prisons: (1) prisons for convicted inmates who are sentenced to imprisonment with or without labor, (2) juvenile prisons for convicted offenders under age twenty-six, with or without labor, and (3) detention houses for unconvicted offenders, such as those awaiting trial. The treatment of prisoners in Japanese prisons is oriented toward rehabilitation and reintegration or resocialization. Prison treatment programs are specifically tailored for each inmate, following a thorough classification process in which one's needs are determined or assessed. Prison labor, vocational training, educational course work, living guidance, counseling, learning social coping skills, and receiving various types of medical and mental health care are all addressed. There were 83,000 persons in Japanese prisons in 2005. Less than 10 percent of all inmates were females (National Center for Policy Analysis 2001).

Although estimates are somewhat unreliable, it is believed that there were more than 250,000 probationers and parolees in Japan in 2005. The responsibility for aftercare for those offenders resides with the jurisdiction of the Rehabilitation Bureau, which supports some 1,400 probation officers and more than 60,000 volunteer probation officers.

The volunteer probation system has been used in Japan since the 1980s. Volunteer probation officers are community volunteers selected from their communities to assist in probationer and parolee reintegration and rehabilitation. The ideal plan for the volunteer probation system is for each volunteer to supervise and work with up to five offenders, although most work with only two at any given time. They are given the responsibility of ensuring that these offenders do not reoffend, largely by offering them assistance and guidance as well as close supervision (Japan Rehabilitation Bureau, Ministry of Justice 2006b).

Prison inmates become eligible for parole after serving a portion of their sentence. Regional parole boards hear and decide cases, and whether to release certain offenders short of serving their maximum sentence. These parole boards may also revoke a parole program if one or more program conditions are violated. About 15 percent of all supervised offenders under the jurisdiction of the Rehabilitation Bureau are parolees. There is a very low recidivism rate among both probationers and parolees. Offenders must show a great deal of remorse and meet rigorous selective criteria before probation or parole is granted. Individualization of offender supervision and treatment contributes significantly to low recidivism.

Probationers and parolees are subject to periodic checks of their employment and home, and they are obligated to observe various behavioral requirements. All major cities have community residential centers. These residential centers offer offenders a variety of services, including educational and vocational training and job-seeking advice (Hashimoto 2004).

When probationers are initially sentenced to probation they must report to the probation office, where a professional probation officer interviews them and reviews their criminal history and problems. A special treatment plan is eventually established, and probation officers assign probationers to volunteer probation officers for supervision. Parole works similarly. Each community residential center can accommodate up to 100 offenders, with some variation among the different localities. More noncompliant probationers and parolees will be supervised by professional probation officers, who use more rigorous supervision methods. Japan's probation and parole systems utilize electronic monitoring and home confinement; they have used such individualized tracking and placement methods since the early 1990s.

The Netherlands
The Netherlands consists of the Netherlands, Aruba, and the Netherlands Antilles. A unitary governmental structure exists that is governed by laws embodied within the criminal or penal code and the Code of Criminal Procedure and Special Acts. The criminal justice system is modified regularly. A probation service was established in 1986, and that, too, is modified periodically (U.S. Department of State 2006).

Commission of a crime sets the criminal justice system in motion. When suspects are arrested, accusations are made. Trials are accusatorial processes, the purpose of which is to determine the truth about the crime, how it occurred, and who committed it. Only judges are permitted to ask questions of witnesses and suspects during trials. Prosecutors and defense counsels are permitted to ask a limited range of questions, although such questions are primarily supplementary. Cross-examination of witnesses is not permitted, and lower courts follow higher court precedents (Ministry of Internal Affairs 2006a).

Prosecutors have much power. They may keep cases from the courts and engage in conditional waivers, or what is known as "transaction." Conditional waivers involve informal disposition of cases, which may include minimally restrictive conditions. Transaction vests prosecutors with the authority to impose fines in cases in which maximum sentences are up to six years. Out-of-court monetary settlements, when they occur, conclude cases. Plea bargaining is prohibited, but guilty pleas are acceptable and may be used against defendants later in court. Prosecutors can hold suspects for several months before bringing formal charges against them. Their ability to interview and interrogate suspects is unlimited, but defense counsel are restricted in the number of contacts they have with their clients.

In 2005 the judiciary consisted of sixty-two cantonal courts, nineteen district courts, five courts of appeal, and a supreme court with twenty-four justices. Cantonal courts hear both civil and criminal cases; a single judge presides in such courts. District courts hear both civil and criminal matters, but in those courts there are panels of three judges who hear each case. Courts of appeal hear both civil and criminal cases decided in the lower district courts. All lower-court cases are subject to appeal, and once the Supreme Court has heard an appealed case the case is concluded (Aronowitz 2005).

The range of criminal penalties includes fines, suspended sentences, automatic release from prison after serving two-thirds of the maximum sentence, and community service. All prohibited acts are either crimes or felonies (*misdrijven*), or infractions or transgressions (*overtredingen*). Transgressions (misdemeanors) include traffic offenses and public order offenses.

The age of criminal responsibility in the Netherlands is twelve. Juveniles between ages twelve and eighteen are subject to juvenile criminal laws, and youths between ages sixteen and eighteen are tried in criminal courts when the cases involve murder, robbery, or rape. Juvenile law may be applicable to persons between the ages of eighteen and twenty-one on a case-by-case basis, according to prosecutorial discretion. All persons age twenty-one or older are subject to adult criminal penalties, regardless of the circumstances. The most serious crimes are punishable by imprisonment. There is no death penalty. The maximum punishment for the most serious offense is twenty years and/or a fine (Public and Cultural Affairs Press 2005).

Criminals are treated in different ways. Defendants convicted of murder or rape may be imprisoned and then sent to a mental institution. Sexual offenses bring time in a mental institution as a form of TBS (*ter beschikking stelling*). Sex offenders might spend an indeterminate amount of time in a mental hospital, even the remainder of their lives, should a committee believe that they pose a serious risk to society.

The rights of defendants in the Netherlands are different from those of U.S. citizens. Defendants may petition the court to dismiss a case if it is not brought to trial within a short time. All defendants are entitled to an attorney, and indigents have court-appointed counsel. Defendants have the right to remain silent and refrain from giving testimony.

Prosecutorial discretion determines which cases will be tried. Judges have no discretion over prosecutors or whom they decide to prosecute. One-third of all criminal cases go to trial, and two-thirds of all cases are concluded by prosecutors through transaction or dismissal. Cases tried in court have a high conviction rate of 85 percent. Defendants awaiting trial do not have an absolute right to bail, although few defendants are kept in pretrial confinement.

The range of punishments available to judges includes fines, imprisonment, detention, community service, and court-ordered treatment. The minimum incarcerative sentence is 1 day, and maximum sentences are fifteen years, or twenty years for murder. Life sentences may be imposed in the most serious cases. Other punishments may include property seizure and dispossession of certain rights, such as the right to hold particular jobs. Prison sentences of three or fewer years may be suspended, although judges cannot suspend sentences longer than three years. Those receiving suspended sentences may be placed on probation.

The inmate population in 2005 was 15,000. Supervised release has been offered to those inmates who have served two-thirds or more of their sentence. Supervision is believed fundamental for an inmate's successful reintegration into society. Prisons have work programs and educational facilities. More than 20,000 offenders have obtained early release from prison during the period 2000 to 2005, and about half of those offenders are under some form of supervision. Both electronic monitoring and home confinement are used, together with community service.

The probation service supervises many offenders who are convicted but freed without serving time in either jail or prison. Probation supervision is minimal, probation officers being largely brokers and educators. They provide networking services between their offender-clients and the business community for job placements. There were approximately 60,000 persons under some form of probation supervision in 2000 (van der Linden 2000).

Norway

Norway's government consists of three branches: legislative, judiciary, and executive. The national parliament, known as the Stortinget, passes all laws, both criminal and civil. The court system is autonomous, and courts act independently to make individualized decisions about defendants. All evidence submitted is allowed, and all information about crimes is considered relevant and given appropriate weight by the judiciary. Most judges are lay judges who may have no legal qualifications. Some judges, however, are professionally trained (Bygrave 1997).

All criminal laws have been codified into the penal code and the Criminal Procedure Act. The age of criminal responsibility is fifteen, with persons under fifteen under the jurisdiction of social welfare agencies. The aim is to rehabilitate youths. Vocational and educational opportunities, counseling, and other forms of assistance are provided.

Crimes are divided into felonies and misdemeanors. Felonies carry sentences of 3 months or longer in prison, while misdemeanors have lesser punishments. Incarceration is rarely used, since it is believed to be counterproductive to rehabilitation and reintegration. Misdemeanors have a maximum penalty of 3 months in jail, together with fines. In 2005 there were more than 450,000 reported crimes. A third of those offenses were misdemeanors, while the remainder were felonies.

Overseeing prosecution of all criminal offenses is the director general of public prosecutions, or *Riksadvokaten.* Approximately fifty-five public prosecutors are assigned to the various geographical jurisdictions. All public prosecutors are appointed by the king and must have sufficient legal training. When someone is accused of a crime, that person has the full range of rights, and all indigent persons are entitled to court-appointed counsel. Persons who plead guilty may have their cases concluded in courts of summary jurisdiction without a formal trial. Courts may or may not involve juries. Judges decide whether defendants are entitled to jury trials, and defendants are not entitled to be present during proceedings against them. All court judgments of guilt or innocence must be supported in writing, with a detailed rationale and supporting evidence. All convicted offenders have the right to appeal their convictions and sentences to higher courts (Central Administration of the Correctional Service 2006).

Alternatives to trials may involve fines, or *foreleggs,* and they are often assessed for traffic violations and other minor offenses. Prosecuting attorneys have considerable discretion and may decline to prosecute certain cases. In most cases involving youths under age eighteen, even though criminal responsibility attaches at age fifteen, municipal child welfare boards hear cases instead of the courts. Deferred prosecution or diversion is used in some cases. Some defendants may be required to perform community service or have counseling or other treatments, or they may be freed on the condition that they remain law-abiding. Half of all criminal cases go to trial. Restorative justice is also used, and such cases are referred to arbitration and conflict boards.

Courts determine sentences to be imposed upon conviction. Victim input weighs heavily in all sentencing, and penalties may include fines, social service, and/or imprisonment. Maximum sentences are twenty-one years in prison. Such sentences are imposed for murder, rape, and serious drug offenses. Suspended sentences are given to younger or first-time offenders, and fines usually accompany most sentences of imprisonment or sentence suspensions (Prison and Probation Department 2005).

Community service involves unpaid labor to the community performed by offenders for up to 360 hours. Such community service is imposed for crimes punishable by up to one year in prison. Community service punishment may also involve fines. Another punishment is detention, or *forvaring*, which is rarely used. Most persons sentenced to preventive detention are recidivists with a strong likelihood of reoffending.

Persons sentenced to prison may participate in rehabilitative programs including vocational and educational training. All levels of education are offered to prisoners. Prisoners have visitation privileges with their families, as well as the right to be outdoors for at least an hour a day. Prisoners who have served two-thirds of their sentence are entitled to apply for parole, which is often granted. Persons who have served 50 percent of their sentence may also apply for early release, although that is seldom granted.

Corrections is under the Corrections Service, which oversees the Prison and Probation Department. This department is the superior authority for the Prison Service and the Probation Service. The Prison Service is responsible for implementing custodial sentences and preventive detention. There is a strong rehabilitation emphasis for all inmates, and the Probation Service enforces community sanctions, such as community service orders, drunk-driving prevention programs, and early release and suspended sentence supervision. House arrest or home confinement is used. The goals of the Probation Service are to enforce reactions set by the prosecuting authority and by the courts, and to enable offenders to change their criminal behavior through reintegration and rehabilitation. In 2005 there were four halfway houses, twenty-one probation offices, and forty-two prisons under the Correctional Service authority. Estimates are that there are approximately 35,000 persons under the supervision of the Correctional Service. In 2001 there were 12,130 persons serving prison sentences and approximately 2,100 awaiting sentencing. Some 5,500 clients were serving community sentences (ibid. 2006).

Several offense-specific treatment programs include cognitive skills programs; offender substance abuse assistance and treatment; Choices, which assists persons in proper law-abiding decision-making; a Brotts-brytet (Stop Crime) program, aimed at crime prevention methods; a WIN program, which is a change program for women; a one-to-one program, which is a cognitive activity for use in both prisons and communities that relies heavily on counseling; ATV, which involves discussion groups for violent sex offenders; an anger management program; and a sexual offenders program. The recidivism rate is less than 30 percent.

Russia

Russia is a federative state with a president. Criminal laws are contained in the criminal code, the Criminal Procedure Code, the Criminal Punishment Execution Code, and the Law in the Justice System. Other specialized legal codes and compendiums exist.

The age of criminal responsibility in Russia is sixteen. Persons over fourteen years of age bear criminal responsibility only for murder, major bodily injury, rape, kidnapping, and other violent acts. Any act not included in the criminal code is not a crime. Crimes are classified according to whether they are major or minor. Major offenses are crimes such as rape, kidnapping, murder, treason, espionage, crimes against the justice system, and all other serious violent crimes. Minor crimes include offenses against property, such as theft or burglary, hooliganism, and offenses against public order. Another class of offense pertains to drugs. In 2005 there were more than 4 million crimes reported (Foreign Broadcast Information Service 2004; Nikiforov 2002).

Investigated criminal suspects are held in Special Isolation Facilities (SIZOs). SIZOs are pretrial detention facilities. Approximately 400,000 persons were held in SIZOs awaiting trial in 2005. All defendants have the right to be advised of the charges against them. They may present evidence on their own behalf and may be represented by counsel. Court-appointed counsel is made available to all indigent defendants, and defendants accused of less serious crimes may deposit money for bail. Only about 20 percent of all defendants were in pretrial detention in 2005. Judges decide upon sentences for convicted offenders, either through a jury or bench trial. The maximum punishment is the death penalty, and approximately sixty to seventy executions a year are conducted (Ministry of Internal Affairs 2006b).

For less serious offenses punishments include imprisonment for indeterminate terms, fines, reforming work in lieu of prison (community service), adverse publicity, dismissal from one's office or job, deprivation of the right to hold certain positions or perform certain activities, restitution of financial damages, and confiscation of property (asset forfeiture) (Bureau of Democracy, Human Rights, and Labor 2001). Nearly 2 million persons were held in Russian labor camps in 2005. About 5 percent of all prisoners in Russia are women. Labor camps engage prisoners in various vocational activities often related to agriculture, and all prisoners confined in labor camps must work. They are paid a minimum wage for the labor they perform. Prisoners may be given furloughs to visit families or obtain jobs, and they may be permitted to spend additional money on food or goods and to receive mail or parcels from their families. Parole exists, in that through an inmate's good work he or she may be released into the community under supervision. In 2005 some cities and towns in Russia were experimenting with restorative justice and community corrections programming (Penal Reform Internationale 2005).

South Africa

The criminal justice system of South Africa applies to a culturally diverse population. The Criminal Procedure Act of 1977 was enacted and amended several times subsequently. In 1991 each province was authorized on a provincial basis to impose a community sentence for offenders not considered to pose a risk to their community. The requirements for correctional supervision include the following:

1. The offender does not pose a threat to the community.
2. The offender has a fixed, verifiable address.
3. The offender has a means of support so as to be financially independent.

Pre-Trial Services (PTS) are used. The aim of PTS is to assist the courts in making bail decisions. Discretionary power to make bail decisions rests with magistrates, and PTS provides courts with detailed information about defendants. PTS actions help ensure that (1) dangerous suspects are less likely to be released on bail, (2) petty offenders are released on bail with warnings or granted affordable bail, (3) all accused persons are closely supervised while on bail, thus reducing the likelihood of witness intimidation or court delays caused by failure to appear, and (4) a decrease in the sheer number of prisoners awaiting trial occurs. Estimates are that without PTS, the number of prisoners held in South African prisons and jails would double (Shaw 1996).

A diversion program exists to divert low-risk offenders from the criminal justice system. The aims of diversion are these: (1) to prevent first offenders from prolonged or frequent encounters with the criminal justice system, (2) to promote conformity to the laws, and (3) to prevent persons from being imprisoned. Diversion is believed therapeutic as a rehabilitative action. It is restricted largely to persons ages fourteen to eighteen, although under special circumstances diversion may be granted to older or younger offenders. Victim-offender mediation and family group conferencing through restorative justice are also used.

Pursuant to an investigation of various parole systems in other countries by a South African delegation in 1992–1993, the Department of Correctional Services was charged with the supervision of parolees, under the authority of community corrections personnel (Department of Correctional Services 2005). A Correctional Supervision and Parole Board was established to determine (1) definite dates of parole release of convicted offenders, (2) the communities in which offenders should be placed, and (3) the parole conditions to be followed during the parole term. These requirements pertain to any convicted offenders sentenced to the following:

1. Imprisonment for corrective training, for which purpose they may be detained in prison for a period of two years and may not be placed on parole until they have served at least 12 months.
2. Imprisonment for the prevention of a crime, for which they may be detained in a prison for a period of five years and may not be placed on parole until at least two and a half years of the sentence have been served.
3. Life imprisonment: Such persons may not be placed on parole until they have served at least twenty-five years of the sentence, although a person who is age sixty-five may be placed on parole after having served at least fifteen years of the original sentence.

The Correctional Supervision and Parole Board makes both parole and parole revocation decisions. General conditions for persons serving terms on either probation or parole include the following:

1. Refraining from committing criminal offenses.
2. Complying with any reasonable instructions by the court.
3. Refraining from making any contact with particular persons.
4. Refraining from threatening any persons by word or action.

Differing levels of supervision for offenders are determined by offense seriousness. More serious offenders are supervised more intensively than less serious offenders. A classification system for all offenders is in the process of being devised. The classification system assesses risks posed by offenders and also their individual needs. Community officials are charged with supervising them and ensuring that they receive necessary rehabilitative and reintegrative services. The following supervision categories guide the nature of correctional supervision:

Maximum supervision cases: visited four times per month.
Medium supervision cases: visited twice per month.
Minimum supervision cases: visited once per month.

Both parole and probation may include house arrest; victim compensation; community service; correctional programming for treatment of drug/alcohol abuse and other problems; restrictions to one's community; fixed addresses; alcohol/drug monitoring; searches; and/or an obligation to seek and maintain employment (Wilkinson 1998).

Incarceration is used for those who pose the most serious community threats. In 2005 there were 239 correctional centers. The inmate population in 2005 was 155,800, with 3,200 of those inmates female. The death penalty was abolished in 1995. The number of parolees in 2005 was 31,300, while the number of probationers was 20,500 (Moatshe 2004).

South Korea

South Korea has a government consisting of an administration, a legislature, and a judicature. The criminal justice system is highly centralized, having been established by the Criminal Law of 1953 and continuously revised through 2005.

Three types of criminal offenses include the following: (1) crimes breaching a national interest, such as rebellion, (2) crimes breaching a social interest, such as arson, and (3) crimes breaching personal interests, such as larceny, robbery, murder, and drug offenses. Punishments are proportional to the type of crime committed. Crimes are further distinguished according to whether they are violent crimes or property crimes (Richards 2006).

The Supreme Public Prosecutor's Office prosecutes all criminal offenses. The age of criminal responsibility in South Korea is fourteen, although persons ranging in age from fourteen to twenty are specially treated under juvenile laws. A youth under age eighteen who is convicted of a criminal offense cannot be sentenced to capital punishment or life imprisonment. Since the early 1990s, South Korea has permitted greater citizen involvement in criminal matters, including sentencing. Victims are permitted to speak and give their punishment recommendations to judges, although judges decide upon the punishment.

Bail is granted for most defendants. Suspects enjoy numerous rights, including the right to examine evidence; the right to avoid particular judges; the right to appeal; the right to trial by a judicial panel; the right to confess or avoid confession; and the right to either a private attorney or a public defender. There are no preliminary hearings, and juries are not used. Judicially appointed prosecutors, working on behalf of the Ministry of Justice, bring cases against defendants and have broad discretionary powers. Prosecutors may indict, refuse to indict, or suspend indictments against defendants (Newman 2002).

Depending upon the seriousness of their offenses, prosecutors may or may not recommend bail for certain defendants. About 10 percent of all defendants have criminal trials; the remaining defendants upon conviction are subject to a wide range of community sanctions, including confinement in prison, jail, fines, forfeiture, and other penalties, such as probation. Those imprisoned may be paroled. Fines are the most frequently used punishment for minor offenses.

Probation is used most frequently as a major criminal sanction. There were 90,000 offenders in prison in 2005, and about 4 percent of all inmates are female. All prisons provide useful labor for inmates to assist in their eventual rehabilitation and reintegration.

Good institutional conduct is rewarded with parole. Inmates accumulate points for good conduct, and they may become eligible for furloughs, more progressive institutional treatment, and special privileges. Some inmates participate in work/study release programs.

Probation was officially used as early as 1982, but the probation system was not established until 1989. Special probation offices have been created in every jurisdiction, and the probation system is one of the most advanced in the world. The emphasis of probation is upon education, counseling, and guidance leading to rehabilitation and societal reintegration. In 2005 there were approximately 200,000 probationers and 70,000 parolees of different designations. Supervising those offenders were 495 probation officers in approximately thirty probation and parole offices in various cities.

Probationers are subject to various probation conditions, including community service orders and attendance center orders. Attendance centers are designed for those with various drug and alcohol addictions or dependencies. Participating in attendance center activities is compulsory (Korean Institute of Criminology 2005). Probation and parole guidelines provide for the following:

1. Legal matters of observation (allowing probation officers access to a client's premises for the purpose of monitoring the client's behavior while on probation or parole).
2. An obligation to reside in one's residence and remain employed.
3. An obligation to maintain a good family relationship.
4. An obligation to obey all probation officer directives.
5. An obligation to make advance reports if traveling for more than 1 month.

Special conditions of probation and parole may include abstinence from alcohol or drugs, avoiding certain areas, and other behavioral requirements. In 2005 more than 150,000 persons were assisted on probation or parole with low recidivism rates. Prospective parolees are subject to the orders of a Parole Examination Committee. This committee determines inmate eligibility for early release. Presentence investigation reports are examined, including an inmate's prior living conditions, family relations, friendships and acquaintances, and potential societal adaptability.

Interviews with prospective parolees are conducted, and those interviews may include participation by victims, family members, and other interested parties, including probation officers.

Time guidelines exist for different categories of offenders (see Table 3.1).

Volunteer probation officers are used extensively in probationer rehabilitation. Volunteer probation officers conduct crime prevention activities and support the activities of the probation and parole offices. Volunteers (1) assist in crime prevention activities in their communities, (2) counsel offenders, (3) assist offenders in job searches and financial aid, and (4) comply with other related concerns of the Minister of Justice. Volunteers work closely with officials to minimize school violence by monitoring and relating with juveniles more closely; providing counseling and special instruction to those under suspension of indictment; assisting probation officers in the guidance and supervision of their clients; and supporting job searches, vocational training, care, and financial aid (Chung 2006).

Sweden

Sweden is a constitutional monarchy with a parliamentary form of government. The Parliament of Sweden makes all laws, including

TABLE 3.1
Sentencing Variations and Types of Criminal Offenders in South Korea

Criminal Offenders	Length and Nature of Punishment/Parole/Probation
1. Those receiving suspended sentences or probation	Probation of one year or less
2. Those under suspended execution of sentence	Probation of one year or less
3. Parolees	Remaining period of one's original sentence
4. Juveniles on probation	Up to two years
5. Juveniles released from Juvenile Training School	Six months to two years
6. Parolees whose prison terms have provisionally expired	Three years
7. Domestic violence offenders	Six months
8. Those under suspension of indictment	Six months to one year
9. Those subject to suspended execution of sentence on probation	Community service: 500 hours or less
10. Community service orders or attendance center orders	Community service: 200 hours or less
11. Juveniles over 16 subject to community service orders	Community service: 200 hours or less
12. Community service orders for domestic violence offenders	Community service: 100 hours or less

Source: Courtesy of the author.

the criminal code. The maximum punishment in Sweden is life imprisonment, as there is no death penalty. The Swedish criminal justice system is accusatorial, consisting of a prosecutor who represents the state and a defense counsel who represents defendants. All criminal laws are embodied within the Swedish Penal Code.

The age of criminal responsibility in Sweden is fifteen. Prison sentences are not ordinarily imposed on persons under the age of twenty-one, except under extraordinary circumstances. Sweden does not distinguish between crimes and infractions. Most crime is property crime, and violent crime is rare (Wikstrom and Dolmen 2004). Defendants have the full range of constitutional rights. All defendants are entitled to a trial in which guilt must be proven beyond a reasonable doubt by prosecutors. There are no jury trials, however, and there is no plea bargaining. All defendants who are in jeopardy of receiving a prison sentence must stand trial, although only the most serious offenses actually come to trial. Prosecutors have wide discretionary powers in determining whether charges should be brought against particular suspects. Even if confessions are voluntarily given or obtained, prosecutors must make a presentation to the court to show defendant guilt beyond a reasonable doubt. A statutory maximum time for arrest and detention is 48 hours.

The court system of Sweden is three-tiered. The highest court is the Supreme Court, and the next highest court is the Court of Appeal. Those two courts taken together are considered the highest of three tiers. The other two tiers consist of district courts, which are courts of general jurisdiction, and general courts, which are similar to U.S. municipal courts. These courts hear cases involving public order offenses, traffic violations, and other offenses.

When a defendant is found guilty, a sentence is always imposed by a judge. Sentencing hearings are sometimes conducted, and during those hearings evidence of aggravating and mitigating circumstances may be presented.

A broad range of available penalties includes probation and imprisonment. Probation is a conditional sentence involving rehabilitative programming. Sentences may also be suspended and replaced with orders for counseling, community service, restitution, fines, and other sanctions. For prison sentences, the minimum time to be served is 14 days. Life imprisonment may be imposed, although fourteen to sixteen years is defined as a life sentence. Judges are advised to use prison as a last resort if it is possible to impose alternative punishments because of the individual case circumstances. Sentences are individualized and are proportional to the crime committed.

Probation sentences are made at the recommendation of the prosecutor. Probation sentences are associated with crimes for which the punishment is more severe than a mere fine. Probation programs may include electronic monitoring, home confinement, counseling, attending vocational/educational programs, mental health outpatient treatment, drug abuse counseling, and other requirements. Probation with conditions can last up to three years. Fines may also be assessed. Home confinement with electronic surveillance is used, and community service orders may be imposed.

Defendants under age twenty-one are placed with a social service agency for supervision and aftercare. These sentences are for one year, followed by two years of provisional freedom without supervision. If the offender commits a new offense while on the probationary term, however, either a new supervision period commences or the offender is incarcerated.

There are eighty prisons in Sweden, divided into national and local prisons. National prisons house offenders serving sentences of more than one year who require additional security. Local prisons are for offenders who are serving sentences of less than a year. Vocational, educational, and mental health programs and counseling are made available in all prison facilities (Probation and Parole Service 2006a). The Probation and Parole Service is under the jurisdiction of the Prison and Probation Service (Kriminalardsstyrelsen), which is directly answerable to the Ministry of Justice. The Probation and Parole Service has three major functions:

1. To provide supervision and support for offenders sentenced to probation, for offenders released from prison on early-release programs, and for offenders sentenced to community service orders, treatment orders, or home detention. In the event that some offenders fail to fulfill the demands of their programs or court orders (such as for treatment or for contact with the probation and parole office), the matter is referred to a special board, the Probation and Parole Board, for consideration.
2. To assist the courts in determining appropriate sentences through an assessment of the accused's current and past

social situation, the accused's need of and motivation for different forms of psychosocial treatment, the accused's suitability for placement in community-based programs, and the treatments likely to affect recidivism.

3. To coordinate the provision of treatment and support programs organized and administered by local government bodies and voluntary organizations and, when no appropriate programs are available in local communities, to organize and implement programs that specifically target criminal behavior (such as programs for violent offenders or alcohol- and drug-related traffic offenses) (ibid. 2006b).

Preceding any sentencing of convicted defendants, a social inquiry report is generated, including a detailed assessment of the person's needs and motivation for treatment or other forms of noncustodial care (such as community work orders or probation). Parole is an option for incarcerated offenders once they have served at least two-thirds of their prison sentence. The Probation and Parole Board hears matters of discipline regarding inmates, clients on probation, or others released from prison on parole. This board rules in all matters relating to early-release requests, sanctions for misbehavior or failure to follow program rules, and rehabilitative requirements to be met by persons sentenced to probation, parole, community work orders, community treatment orders, or home detention. The period of parole is usually one year immediately following release from prison. During that period the parolee is expected to have continuous contact with a parole officer. Parolees must keep their supervising officers informed as to their whereabouts, residence, employment, and means of financial support. Any misconduct occurring during the period may be grounds for revoking the parole program. After the period of parole has been served, the remainder of the prison sentence, whatever it may have originally been, is suspended or remitted (Department of Corrections 2006b).

The board may also rule in matters of extending the period of supervision if warranted by the facts or revoking the program for the remaining period of the incarceration. Sometimes parole is only partially revoked, for periods such as 1 month. If parole is to be revoked in its entirety, the matter is referred to district courts for further action. The board also rules in matters of treatment outside of the prison system for inmates currently serving prison sentences, and the board hears offenders' appeals of decisions made by the Prison and Probation Service. The rate of recidivism for both probationers and parolees is quite low, being under 50 percent.

Thailand

Thailand has a president and a Constitutional Court. It is considered a constitutional monarchy with seventy-six provinces, and courts of justice have jurisdiction over all criminal and civil cases. The highest court is the Supreme Court of Justice. Lesser courts include courts of appeals and courts of the first instance, basic trial courts. The National Assembly makes laws, while provincial officials and the police enforce the laws (ibid. 2006a).

In 2005 there were approximately 650,000 crimes reported, with nearly 300,000 defendants. Thailand distinguishes between violent crime (for example, murder, robbery, and kidnapping), crimes against the person (such as murder, assault, and rape), property crimes (for example, theft, blackmail, possession of stolen goods, and vandalism), interesting crimes (for example, motorcycle theft, car theft, cattle theft, taxi robbery, cheating, and fraud), and victimless crimes (such as gambling, pornography, prostitution, and narcotics offenses).

Defendants are entitled to know the charges being filed against them, and a presumption of innocence exists. Defendants have a right to a lawyer, and most defendants are entitled to bail. Prosecutors bring cases against defendants (Bureau of East Asian and Public Affairs 2005). Defendants may also be held in pretrial detention for up to 60 days: about 25 percent of those in Thai prisons and jails are pretrial detainees. There is no trial by jury. Judges decide cases based on the evidence presented. Two or more judges may sit and decide more complex or serious cases. There is no time limit governing how long trials last, and some trials may go on for years. Indigent defendants are entitled to publicly appointed counsel (Bureau of Democracy, Human Rights, and Labor 2006b). Maximum penalties include death by lethal injection, as the result of a 2001 law. However, persons under the age of eighteen cannot receive the death penalty. All sentences are indeterminate. Furthermore, all death sentences are appealable. The number of executed offenders is not large. Between 1997 and 2004, there were forty-eight executions, with only four executions in 2004 (Bureau of Rehabilitation, Department of Corrections 2005). There were 162,000 prisoners in Thailand in 2005.

Thailand has also established various community corrections programs aimed at offender rehabilitation and reintegration. The aims of these programs are to provide public protection by keeping offenders in custody or under close supervision, and to aid in the prevention of recidivism. The responsibilities and mission of community corrections are to:

1. Provide a level of supervision and custody that will offer maximum protection to the community.
2. Rehabilitate convicted offenders in order to achieve a successful adjustment upon their return to the society.
3. Provide various alternative programs for convicted offenders.
4. Provide an institutional environment that is consistent with UN standards, with minimum rules for the treatment of prisoners and related recommendations to the extent that existing circumstances allow.
5. Reduce overcrowding by encouraging the use of various alternative nonimprisonment programs for offenders who are not suited for institutional confinement.
6. Promote the knowledge of correctional techniques through systematic evaluation and research.

A definitive community corrections system has not been fully established. Much of the rehabilitation and reintegration that occurs takes place within prison systems. A five-year plan to revise and upgrade the Department of Corrections, with the overall goal to become an outstanding agency among Asian countries, was adopted in 2004. The mission of the Department of Corrections is to take offenders into custody and equip them with professional skills, rehabilitating them through meaningful and effective activities. Other objectives include helping inmates acquire professional skills, overcome their drug addictions, create better citizens among inmates, and focus activities in prisons more on learning than on punishment; using better governance or leadership in prison administration and operation; and using innovative treatment philosophies in inmate management and improvement. A later 2006 strategic plan involved the following:

1. Improving management and leadership skills of prison directors.
2. Improving human resource management for the Department of Corrections.
3. Improving the welfare system for officers.
4. Establishing consistent standards for all prisons and correctional institutions.
5. Providing secure custody for high-profile offenders.
6. Renovating prison infrastructure and improving security systems.
7. Seeking greater partnerships in corrections and community justice.

A Probation Department exists, funded by the Ministry of Justice, and about 97 percent of all offenders receive suspended sentences. Many of these offenders are placed on probation. That sentence is an acceptable alternative to prison, as it reduces the amount of prison overcrowding. Two agencies coordinate probationer supervision. One is the Adult Probation Service, which oversees adult probationers. The other is responsible for supervising youthful offenders and is called the Observation and Protection Center.

To be eligible for probation offenders must be facing prison for three years or less, and the present conviction offense must not have been committed while the offender was already on probation. Probationers will be supervised by probation officers as well as volunteer probation officers. Volunteer probation officers are recruited from among community residents and assist offenders in becoming rehabilitated and reintegrated into their communities. Halfway houses were created in 1995 for those released on probation or parole.

No precise figures about the numbers of inmates on parole are available. Inmates have usually served flat time or whatever prison sentences they receive, although some prisoners are released short of their full terms either through royal pardons or sentence commutations. All prisons have a prerelease center. These centers offer services for those offenders about to be released into their communities. They are referred to as temporary prisons and have minimum security. Most prisoners receive agricultural training and other special services to assist them in becoming more law-abiding.

References

Aronowitz, Alexis A. 2005. "The Netherlands." In *The World Factbook of Criminal Justice Systems.* Washington, DC: U.S. Department of Justice.

Associated Foreign Press. 2005. "Radical Gets Life Term for Killing Van Gogh." July 27.

Australian Institute of Criminology. 2000. *Probation and Parole 2000.* Canberra: Australian Institute of Criminology.

Australian Institute of Criminology. 2005a. "ACT Corrective Services." Canberra: Australian Institute of Criminology, December 30.

Australian Institute of Criminology. 2005b. "Community Based Corrections." Canberra: Australian Institute of Criminology, December 30.

Australian Institute of Criminology. 2006a. *Australian Crime: Facts and Figures, 2005.* Canberra: Australian Institute of Criminology.

Australian Institute of Criminology. 2006b. "Offender Development Teams and Substance Abuse." Canberra: Australian Institute of Criminology, January.

Bertrand, Francois. 2006. *Criminal Justice System of France.* Paris: Bureau of Criminal Affairs.

Biles, David. 2005. "Australia." In *The World Factbook of Criminal Justice Systems.* Washington, DC: U.S. Department of Justice.

Borricand, Jacques. 2006. "France." In *The World Factbook of Criminal Justice Systems.* Washington, DC: U.S. Department of Justice.

British Home Office. 2006. *National Community Safety Plan 2006–2009.* London: British Home Office.

Bureau of Democracy, Human Rights, and Labor. 2001. "Country Reports on Human Rights Practices." Washington, DC: Bureau of Democracy, Human Rights, and Labor, February 23.

Bureau of Democracy, Human Rights, and Labor. 2002. "Costa Rica: Country Reports on Human Rights Practices, 2001." Washington, DC: Bureau of Democracy, Human Rights, and Labor, March 4.

Bureau of Democracy, Human Rights, and Labor. 2006a. "Country Reports on Human Rights Practices." Washington, DC: Bureau of Democracy, Human Rights, and Labor.

Bureau of Democracy, Human Rights, and Labor. 2006b. "Thailand." Nonthaburi, Thailand, February 22. Bureau of Democracy, Human Rights, and Labor.

Bureau of East Asian and Public Affairs. 2005. "Background Note: Thailand." Bangkok, Thailand: October. Bureau of East Asian and Public Affairs.

Bureau of European and Eurasian Affairs. 2005. "Background Note: The Netherlands." Washington, DC: U.S. Department of State, Bureau of European and Eurasian Affairs, May.

Bureau of Rehabilitation, Department of Corrections. 2005. "Death Penalty in Thailand." Nonthaburi, Thailand: Bureau of Rehabilitation, Department of Corrections, November.

Bygrave, Lee. 1997. "Norway." In *The World Factbook of Criminal Justice Systems.* Washington, DC: U.S. Department of Justice.

Canada Correctional Services. 2005. "Adult Correctional Services, 2003/2004." *The Daily,* December 16.

Central Administration of the Correctional Service. 2006. *The Norwegian Correctional Service.* Oslo, Norway: Central Administration of the Correctional Service.

Chung, Woo Sik. 2006. "The Volunteer Probation Officer System in Korea." In *Probation and Parole System.* Seoul, Korea: Korean Probation and Parole Office.

Clavier, Sophie M. 1997. "Perspectives on French Criminal Law." Paris: Bureau of Criminal Affairs.

Cohen, Debra, and Sandra Longtin. 2004. "Canada." In *The World Factbook of Criminal Justice Systems.* Washington, DC: U.S. Department of Justice.

Commonwealth of Australia. 2006. "Probation Officer/Parole Officer." Canberra: Department of Corrective Services, March.

Conant, Gerald. 2004. "Japan." In *The World Factbook of Criminal Justice Systems.* Washington, DC: U.S. Department of Justice.

Costa Rica National Assembly. 2005. "Statistics and Trends." *2004 Penal Procedural Code.* National Assembly, December.

Department of Correctional Services. 2005. *Correctional Statistics.* South Africa: Department of Correctional Services.

Department of Corrections. 2006a. *Statistics.* Nonthaburi, Thailand: Department of Corrections.

Department of Corrections. 2006b. "Thailand Department of Corrections." Nonthaburi, Thailand: Department of Corrections.

Department of Corrective Services. 2005. *Annual Report 2004/2005.* Sydney, Australia: Department of Corrective Services.

Department of Corrective Services. 2006. "Prison Population Up." *Weekend Australian,* March 25.

Drug Policy Alliance. 2005. *Sweden: Drug Policy around the World.* Washington, DC: Drug Policy Alliance, December.

Ebbe, Obi N. I. 2005. "Ghana." In *The World Factbook of Criminal Justice Systems.* Washington, DC: U.S. Department of Justice.

Foreign Broadcast Information Service. 2004. "Russia." Washington, DC: Foreign Broadcast Information Service.

Giralt, Henry Q. 2004. "Costa Rica." In *The World Factbook of Criminal Justice Systems.* Washington, DC: U.S. Department of Justice.

Graphic Communications Limited. 2005. "A-G Wants Death Penalty Abolished." *Graphic Ghana,* October 26.

Hashimoto, Noboru. 2004. "Parole in Japan." Tokyo: Tokyo Probation Office, November.

Japan Rehabilitation Bureau, Ministry of Justice. 2006a. "Correctional Statistics." Tokyo: Japan Rehabilitation Bureau.

Japan Rehabilitation Bureau, Ministry of Justice. 2006b. "Volunteer Probation Officer Program." Unpublished paper, Onishi Yamagata, December.

Korean Institute of Criminology. 2005. *Probation and Parole in South Korea.* Seoul: Korean Institute of Criminology.

Ministry of Internal Affairs. 2006a. *The Netherlands: Criminal Justice System and Statistics.* The Hague: Ministry of Internal Affairs, March.

Ministry of Internal Affairs. 2006b. *Offenders and Punishments.* Moscow, January.

Ministry of Justice. 2005. "La delinquance des jeunes." Paris: Ministry of Justice.

Ministry of Justice. 2006a. "The Constitution of Ghana." Ghana: Ministry of Justice.

Ministry of Justice. 2006b. "Ghana: Criminal Justice, the Courts, and the Judiciary." Navrongo, Ghana: Ministry of Justice.

Miquel, Isabelle. 2002. "French Criminal Justice System." London Conference.

Moatshe, M. S. 2004. "Budget Vote: Correctional Services." Republic of South Africa, June. Johannesburg, South Africa: Ministry of Justice.

National Center for Policy Analysis. 2001. "Parole and Probation Work in Japan." Washington, DC: National Center for Policy Analysis.

Newman, Graeme R. 2002. "South Korea." In *The World Factbook of Criminal Justice Systems.* Washington, DC: U.S. Department of Justice.

New South Wales Department of Corrective Services. 2006. "Government Departments and Agencies." Sydney, Australia: Department of Corrective Services.

Nielson, Gunnar. 2005. "Crime Reduction in the UK." London: British Home Office, November.

Nikiforov, Ilya V. 2002. "Russia." In *The World Factbook of Criminal Justice Systems*. Washington, DC: U.S. Department of Justice.

Ntuli, Ronald Mpuru, and Sonwabo Victor Dlula. 2004. "Enhancement of Community-based Alternatives to Incarceration at All Stages of the Criminal Justice Process in South Africa." Johannesburg, South Africa: Department of Correctional Services.

Office to Monitor and Combat Trafficking in Persons. 2006. "Ghana: The Prison System." Navrongo, Ghana: Ministry of Justice.

Office to Monitor Trafficking in Persons. 2004. *Trafficking in Persons Report*. Office to Monitor and Combat Trafficking in Persons. Washington, DC: U.S. Department of Justice, June 14.

Penal Reform Internationale. 2005. "Introduction to Alternatives to Imprisonment." Paris: Ministry of Justice, January.

Phillips, Corretta, Gemma Cox, and Ken Pease. 2004. "Great Britain." In *The World Factbook of Criminal Justice Systems*. Washington, DC: U.S. Department of Justice.

Prison and Probation Department. 2005. *Execution of Sentence: Care and Confinement of Convicts in Norway*. Oslo, Norway: Prison and Probation Department.

Prison and Probation Department. 2006. *Norwegian Statistics on Prison and Probation, 2005*. Oslo, Norway: Prison and Probation Department.

Probation and Parole Service. 2006a. *Probation and Parole Service Nacka-Haninge: A Division of the Prison and Parole Service in Sweden*. Nacka-Haninge, Sweden: Minister of Justice and Law.

Probation and Parole Service. 2006b. *Probation and Parole Statistics for Sweden*. Nacka-Haninge, Sweden: Probation and Parole Service, January.

Public and Cultural Affairs Press. 2005. "Drug Policy and Crime Statistics." Washington, DC: United Nations, December 24.

Richards, Gene. 2006. *World Book of Criminal Justice Facts*. Washington, DC: Central Intelligence Agency.

Saskatchewan Corrections and Public Safety. 2005. "Volunteers in Probation." Saskatoon, Saskatchewan: Correctional Service of Canada, November.

Sentencing Guidelines Council. 2006. *National Allocation Guidelines 2006*. London: Sentencing Guidelines Council.

Shaw, Mark. *Reforming South Africa's Criminal Justice System*. 1996. Washington, DC: Crime and Policing Policy Project.

United Nations. 2000. "Committee against Torture, Convention against Torture and Other Cruel, Inhuman or Degrading Treatment or

Punishment." New York, November 13. Washington, DC: UN Integrated Regional Information Networks.

United Nations. 2005. "Penal Reform Planned for Prisons." Washington, DC: UN Integrated Regional Information Networks.

U.S. Department of State. 2006. *The Netherlands*. Washington, DC: U.S. Department of State, Bureau of Consular Affairs, March 24.

Van der Linden, Bart. 2000. "The Return of Early Conditional Release in The Netherlands." *Peninsula*, November. The Hague, Netherlands: Minister of Justice.

Wikstrom, Per-Olof H., and Lars Dolmen. 2004. "Sweden." In *The World Factbook of Criminal Justice Systems*. Washington, DC: U.S. Department of Justice.

Wilkinson, Reginald A. 1998. "Republic of South Africa: Department of Correctional Services." *Association of State Correctional Administrators Newsletter*, June. Johannesburg, South Africa: Ministry of Justice.

Williams, Caroline C. 2003. "Costa Rica." In *The World Factbook of Criminal Justice Systems*. Directorate of Citizen Security. Washington, DC: U.S. Department of Justice.

Winslow, Robert. 2005. *Crime and Society: A Comparative Criminology Tour of the World*. San Diego, CA: San Diego State University.

Wyvekens, Anne. 2005. "The French Juvenile Justice System: Working Group on Juvenile Justice." Paris: Ministry of Justice.

4

Chronology

A general chronology of significant events in the history of sentencing and a general timeline are presented below. This chronology lists leading U.S. Supreme Court cases that can be found in Chapter 6, where they are discussed in greater detail.

1868– The Code of Lipit-Ishtar (earliest known codifier of law
1857 BC in Sumer) is created, the earliest known codification of laws pertaining to criminal acts.

1792– The Code of Hammurabi (Babylonian code of laws,
1750 BC both criminal and civil, involving punishments for both civil and criminal offenses) is established.

100 BC– Roman centurions are established to enforce criminal
AD 200 laws and regulate citizen conduct.

AD 900 King Alfred adopts mandatory punishments in England. The *Frumentarii* are created, investigative, detective-like individuals appointed to investigate crimes and conduct criminal interrogations in the Roman Empire.

1066 The Norman Conquest results in the frankpledge system and early vestiges of crime control. Constables are appointed. Early versions of private police emerge to control citizens and to conduct crime prevention tasks.

1200– 1600	Reeves (chief law enforcement officers) are appointed for shires (counties) by the king of England for law enforcement purposes.
1557	Bridewell Workhouse is established. Workhouses house common criminals and were known for exploiting their labor for varying fees by leasing them to mercantile interests in the community.
1630– 1790	Watchmen are appointed for crime prevention purposes; shouts and rattles (noisemakers) are used to alert rural citizens to theft and other crimes.
Early 1700s	Philadelphia and other cities appoint volunteers for crime prevention patrols.
1748	Henry Fielding establishes thief-takers in London, fleet-of-foot runners who could chase down thieves, capture them, and bring them to justice.
1754	Sir John Fielding creates the Bow Street Runners, paid officers similar to thief-takers, to chase and capture criminals.
1773	The first state prison is created in the United States in Simsbury, Connecticut, and is called Newgate Prison. The site has been an abandoned copper mine.
1787	The Philadelphia Society for Alleviating the Miseries of the Public Prisons is established. Citizens and philanthropists seek to improve jail conditions and assist inmates in learning how to read and write. Religious instruction is imparted.
1790	Walnut Street Jail is constructed in Philadelphia. The facility separated women and children from adult men. The congregate system was established, and vocational and educational training for confined persons were stressed. Solitary confinement was introduced.
1792	The Pennsylvania System is created, consisting of numerous prison reforms. Corporal punishment is abol-

ished for most offenses, and hard labor, prisoner wages, and rehabilitative efforts are established.

Patrick Calquhoun emphasizes professionalism among English officers and stresses education and strict organizational principles for law enforcement.

1825   Auburn Penitentiary is established; the tier system is created, separating prisoners according to the seriousness of their offense; and the silent system is observed. The congregate system is copied from Walnut Street Jail in Philadelphia.

1829   Eastern State Penitentiary is established in Cherry Hill, Pennsylvania. The institution promotes strict regimentation: prisoners march in lockstep, close-order drill, and they are hooded so they cannot see each other. They are denied visitors and reading material.

The Metropolitan Police Act of 1829 is established, strongly promoted by Sir Robert Peel. The result is a paramilitary force designed to control crime in London and other cities; professionalism is stressed. The Metropolitan Police of London are established. This organization demands professionalism, physical and mental alertness, and educational qualifications.

1840–   Boston, New York, Chicago, Baltimore, Philadelphia, **1860**   New Orleans, and Newark adopt law enforcement organizational principles similar to those of the Metropolitan Police of London.

1850–   Tickets of leave are devised by Sir Walter Crofton in Ire- **1860**   land as an early version of parole. Captain Alexander Maconochie from Scotland shares his ideas about the mark system, a forerunner of good-time credit later used to reward U.S. prisoners and earn them time off their maximum sentences.

1870   The National Prison Association is formed in Cincinnati, Ohio. Rutherford B. Hayes, future U.S. president, is declared president of the organization, later to be

1870
(*cont.*) named the American Correctional Association. This organization shares ideas with those in other countries relating to prisons and the use of parole as early community supervision. Rehabilitation is stressed.

1876 Elmira Reformatory is constructed. This is an experimental facility created to rehabilitate offenders by offering vocational programming and other forms of instruction and education; it uses parole and other early-release methods as incentives to encourage prisoners to participate in rehabilitative and reintegrative programming.

1878 The first probation law is enacted in Massachusetts.

1880–1890 New York adopts a Persistent Felony Offender law whereby repeat offenders are subject to enhanced punishments at judicial discretion. Habitual offender or chronic offender statutes are passed in various states.

1891 The Three Prisons Act is passed by Congress, establishing prison construction for Atlanta, Georgia (1902), and Fort Leavenworth, Kansas (1906), McNeil Island, Washington (1909).

1909 The National Conference on Criminal Law and Criminology is convened, and positivist criminologists are encouraged to consider individualization of treatment and various alternative causes of criminality in their recommended treatments for criminals.

1911 Roscoe Pound (1870–1964), a jurist, scholar, and former dean of the Harvard Law School, emphasizes greater need for individualization of punishment and encourages states to adopt individualized programs.

1910–1920 Psychological screening devices are used for the first time to separate prisoners into different cell blocks in state and federal prisons.

1920 Inmate classification schemes are devised to separate prisoners into minimum-security, medium-security, and maximum-security designations based on conviction offense.

1920s   The first presentence investigation report is accepted in court as an advisory document to be used in sentencing offenders.

1925   President Calvin Coolidge signs into law the Probation Act, authorizing probation for federally sentenced offenders, to be supervised by federal probation officers.

1942   All states have parole systems.

1950s   Mandatory minimum sentences are imposed in various jurisdictions for narcotics offenses.

1950–   Designations of maxi-maxi, admin max, and supermax
1960   labels are applied to federal and state prisons designed to hold the most dangerous inmates.

1958   The Indeterminate Sentencing Act is passed by Congress.

1960s   The Boggs Act is passed, creating mandatory minimums for drug offenses.

         Dr. Thomas Gitchoff at San Diego State University pioneers the first use of privately prepared presentence investigation reports, known as the Criminological Case Evaluation and Sentencing Recommendation.

1965   The Prisoner Rehabilitation Act of 1965 is passed by Congress, establishing home furloughs, work release programs, and community treatment centers.

1966   The Narcotics Rehabilitation Act is passed by Congress, providing for drug treatment for addicted parolees.

1969   *North Carolina v. Pearce* is decided; portions of sentences served for a crime must be credited toward time served if judges impose harsher sentences in retrials and new convictions for the same offense; furthermore, any

1969
(*cont.*)
unexplained additional punishment for a new conviction in a retrial is a violation of due process rights and unconstitutional.

1970
All states and the federal government adopt indeterminate sentencing; parole boards determine the early release of sentenced offenders.

The Comprehensive Drug Abuse Prevention and Control Act is passed, repealing all mandatory sentencing penalties.

1971
The National Commission on Reform of Federal Criminal Laws recommends classification and grading of all offenses and authorized sentences; it calls for greater uniformity in the application of laws.

1973
New York pioneers the Rockefeller Drug Laws, requiring fifteen-year mandatory minimum sentences for drug trafficking.

1975
Yale Law School advocates the creation of a commission to issue sentencing guidelines, appellate review of sentences, and the abolition of parole.

1976
Maine abolishes parole.

The Parole Commission and Reorganization Act is passed and applies guidelines to all parole decisions.

1977
California adopts a determinate sentencing scheme, replacing its indeterminate sentencing scheme; early release of offenders is governed by good-time credit accumulation rather than by a parole board.

1978
The Minnesota Sentencing Guidelines Commission is formed and develops the state's first presumptive guidelines system. This system is widely copied by other states; also, truth-in-sentencing laws are created whereby offenders serve at least two-thirds of their sentence before becoming parole-eligible.

Simpson v. United States is decided; the compounding of sentences is unconstitutional where overlapping statutes exist and where a single transaction of a crime occurs.

1980–
1990

The Megargee Inmate Typology is constructed to segregate inmates into various degrees of risk or dangerousness.

1981

Bullington v. Missouri is decided; in capital cases, first trials resulting in sentences of life imprisonment that are subsequently reversed cannot be followed by sentences of the death penalty in subsequent trials and convictions for the same offense; a subsequent trial cannot result in a punishment greater than that imposed by the first in a capital case.

1982

The Pretrial Services Act is passed by Congress, providing for pretrial services in all federal districts.

1983

Forty out of fifty states pass mandatory minimum sentences to deter criminals from offending.

1984

The Bail Reform Act is passed by Congress, permitting federal district courts to consider one's dangerousness to the community in setting bail.

The Sentencing Reform Act of 1984, also called the Comprehensive Crime Control Act, is passed by Congress. It authorizes the creation of the U.S. Sentencing Commission, which is charged with rewriting existing federal criminal statutes and implementing them in October 1987.

Arizona v. Rumsey is decided; life sentences imposed for capital offenses cannot be changed in retrials to death penalty sentences; a subsequent trial cannot result in a punishment greater than that imposed by the first punishment in a capital offense case.

AIMS (Adult Inmate Management System) is created by Herbert C. Quay.

1985–
1990   An I-Level Classification System (Interpersonal Maturity Level Classification System) is devised, based on developmental and psychoanalytic theories; risk-assessment devices are used for I-Level classification purposes.

1985   *Ake v. Oklahoma* is decided; if the defendant's sanity is at issue and the state has made a psychiatric examination of an indigent defendant, the defense is entitled to a government-funded independent psychiatric evaluation for the effective defense of the accused.

1986   *Batson v. Kentucky* is decided; prosecutorial use of peremptory challenges to create all-white juries is considered discriminatory and unconstitutional.

McMillan v. Pennsylvania is decided; under mandatory minimum sentencing laws, it is not necessary for juries to make a factual determination of punishment; furthermore, the standard of proof may be "preponderance of the evidence" and not "beyond a reasonable doubt" to make a factual determination in imposing a mandatory minimum sentence; mandatory minimum sentencing laws are constitutional.

Congress enacts laws pertaining to firearm, drug, and sex offenses, as well as to repeat offenders.

The Anti-Drug Abuse Act is passed, requiring drug-related mandatory minimum sentences.

1987   The U.S. sentencing guidelines are implemented. Federal judges are obligated to sentence offenders according to sentencing guidelines; judicial discretion is curbed; opposition to the guidelines exists among about a third of all federal district court judges.

Sumner v. Shuman is decided; mandatory death penalties for any capital offense are unconstitutional because aggravating and mitigating factors cannot be considered in a bifurcated trial proceeding.

1988   *Maynard v. Cartwright* is decided; in capital cases when judges give juries instructions, they must be precise in articulating aggravating and mitigating circumstances that the jury may consider; judges may not use unconstitutionally vague phrases such as "especially heinous," "atrocious," or "cruel" when advising juries which factors to consider as aggravating or mitigating ones.

Mills v. Maryland is decided; jury instructions in capital cases in which judges lead jurors to believe that they must be unanimous in their agreement as to any mitigating factors, otherwise they must impose the death penalty, strongly imply mandatory death penalties under certain circumstances; thus such jury instructions are unconstitutional; jurors must consider all mitigating evidence as well as aggravating evidence in deciding whether to recommend the death penalty.

The Anti-Drug Abuse Act is amended to increase sentences for drug offenses.

The Omnibus Anti-Drug Abuse Act is passed, providing for five- to twenty-year mandatory minimum sentences for drug offenses.

1989   *Mistretta v. United States* is decided; a constitutional challenge alleging violation of the separation of powers doctrine results from some federal judges serving on the U.S. Sentencing Commission and rewriting federal criminal laws; lawmaking is a legislative job, not a judicial one; despite the fact that judges were on the sentencing commission making changes in punishments for violating federal criminal laws, that does not affect the constitutionality of the commission's decision-making integrity, according to an 8 to 1 U.S. Supreme Court vote on the issue, upholding the constitutionality of the sentencing guidelines.

Teague v. Lane is decided; prosecutorial use of peremptory challenges must be proved by a defendant to be

1989
(*cont.*)

discriminatory; also, subsequent claims about the use of peremptory challenges declared to be discriminatory may not be applied retroactively to prior cases in which such prosecutorial conduct is alleged.

1990

Blystone v. Pennsylvania is decided; weighing aggravating and mitigating circumstances in deciding whether to recommend the death penalty is not unconstitutional.

Supervised home release is approved.

1991

Braxton v. United States is decided; government prosecutors may not enhance a sentence based on implied stipulations under plea agreements to unproved more serious charges; prosecutors must prove all offense elements in court before a jury in order to use such offenses as sentence enhancements; stipulations to acts committed and where intent to willfully commit an illegal act is denied are insufficient grounds to impose harsher sentences.

Harmelin v. Michigan is decided; mandatory life sentences for convictions for possessing and distributing large quantities of drugs are not disproportional to the seriousness of the offense, and thus one's due process rights are not violated.

Lankford v. Ohio is decided; judges' personal feelings about the punishment to be imposed are not to be considered in capital cases, particularly when aggravating and mitigating factors are not considered by a jury; judges may not overrule juries who recommend life imprisonment and impose the death penalty where aggravating and mitigating factors have not been weighed or considered.

1993

Deal v. United States is decided; convicted offenders may have their sentences for instant offenses enhanced because of previous crimes committed, even though they may not have been caught and convicted of those offenses; escaping apprehension and conviction for prior crimes may factor into sentence enhancements for current convictions and sentences.

Smith v. United States is decided; separate and enhanced sentencing for firearms possession during the commission of a felony is constitutional as long as the firearm was used in the present conviction offense.

United States v. Dunnigan is decided; convicted offenders who have committed perjury during their trials may have their sentences enhanced because of perjured testimony; self-incrimination is not a defense for committing perjury.

Stinson v. United States is decided; the U.S. Sentencing Commission may change statutory language so that harsher punishments may be imposed, and such statutory language is binding on federal district court judges when sentencing offenders.

Arave v. Creech is decided; in capital cases if mitigating and aggravating factors are considered and the death penalty is imposed, it is not unconstitutional for judges to use phrases such as "utter disregard" or "cold-blooded pitiless slayer" in depicting offenders following a jury's recommendation of the death penalty.

Washington State passes a three-strikes-and-you're-out law, providing for life imprisonment after three felony convictions.

1994   The Crime Bill is passed by Congress, establishing truth-in-sentencing reforms. It is modeled on the federal system whereby sentenced inmates must serve 85 percent of their sentence to become parole-eligible. The bill is also known as the Violent Crime Control and Law Enforcement Act.

California adopts three-strikes-and-you're-out laws aimed at deterring offenders; the state revises this law in subsequent years as inmate populations grow.

1994
(*cont.*)

Caspari v. Bohlen is decided; double jeopardy does not occur, even in retrials for noncapital offenses, if previous convictions against defendants are used for sentence enhancements in retrials even though they were not mentioned or used in first trials.

Custis v. United States is decided; convictions for state offenses may be used to enhance sentences for federal crimes under the Armed Career Criminal Act.

United States v. Granderson is decided; U.S. sentencing guidelines pertain only to sentences of probation and incarcerative terms, not to probation revocation decisionmaking.

1996

Koon v. United States, Powell v. United States (same case) are decided; both statutory and nonstatutory factors may be considered in determining the level of the offense severity; also, guideline departures, either upward or downward, are permitted where judges write a rationale for their departures; this effectively made guidelines generally applicable and not fixed and immovable points from which federal district court judges could depart.

California modifies its three-strikes-and-you're-out sentencing scheme to delineate between violent and serious felonies and less serious felonies with proportionally less severe punishments; this change is to reduce incarceration rates among California prisons.

Melendez v. United States is decided; this case involves the recommendation from government prosecutors to decrease Melendez's sentence below the mandatory minimum sentence provided by law; the U.S. Supreme Court holds that no such departure is allowed unless recommended by prosecutors and approved by the sentencing federal district court judge.

1997

Kansas v. Hendricks is decided; sex offenders may be subject to extended commitment in civil institutions following serving maximum prison terms, provided that they are determined to pose a continuing risk to society.

O'Dell v. Netherland is decided; U.S. Supreme Court decisions cannot be retroactively applied to previous cases in which convictions have been obtained.

United States v. Gonzales is decided; mandatory sentences arising from federal convictions may be used to enhance state convictions and sentences; federal courts may authorize either concurrent or consecutive sentences for federal convictions to accompany state convictions and sentences.

The U.S. Parole Commission is phased out, and supervised releasees are created, who are persons released early from prison.

1998   *Muscarello v. United States* is decided; carrying a firearm in a glove compartment or trunk of one's car during the commission of a felony can be charged as a separate offense and subject to mandatory sentencing.

1998–   Growing emphasis is placed on the importance of inmate
2006   re-entry into society through preparole programming and postrelease programming; treatments involve individual and group counseling, vocational/educational instruction, group homes, job placement assistance, and community collaboration to minimize rejection of newly released inmates and facilitate their reintegration, ultimately reducing their potential for recidivism.

1999   *Jones v. United States* is decided; if defendants are subject to being charged with multiple offenses, those offenses must be charged; otherwise, subsequent convictions on one of those charges cannot be enhanced because of uncharged offenses; without a jury to hear and consider guilt in other offenses, those other offenses have no bearing on the instant conviction offense, and subsequent sentence enhancements are unconstitutional.

2000   *United States v. Johnson* is decided; supervised release periods for convicted offenders are unaffected by subsequently held invalid convictions for offenses if at least one or more convictions have been upheld; supervised release commences once one leaves prison; however, trial courts may modify or terminate supervised releases for certain offenders if it is clear that they have served an excessive amount of time in prison for invalid convictions for other crimes alleged.

2001   *Selig v. Young* is decided; a Washington State law committing sexually violent predators to civil custody beyond the completion of a criminal conviction and sentence served in a correctional facility is constitutional; mental health officials must provide such predators with proper treatment and care, however, in order to improve their suitability for subsequent release from civil commitment at some later date.

  Penry v. Johnson is decided; judges' jury instructions in death penalty cases that fail to include consideration of mitigating evidence presented earlier during the trial phase violate the accused's Eighth and Fourteenth Amendment rights.

  Buford v. United States is decided; state criminal convictions may be consolidated with federal convictions when considering whether to intensify a federal sentence under the sentencing guidelines.

2002   *United States v. Ruiz* is decided; impeachment information pursuant to a plea agreement does not have be disclosed to the defendant by the prosecution relative to third-party informants and others; such nondisclosures do not invalidate plea agreements, if any are in place when sentencing occurs.

  Kansas v. Crane is decided; challenge is made of the constitutionality of the Kansas Sexually Violent Predator Act; states must prove that offenders have total or complete lack of control over their dangerous behavior; the

constitution does not allow civil commitments under
the act without any lack of control determination.

Harris v. United States is decided; "brandishing" a
firearm during the commission of a crime may include
simple possession of a firearm, and such possession is a
sentencing factor to be considered rather than an element of a crime.

2003   PROTECT Act is passed by Congress, reducing the ability of federal judges to depart from sentencing guidelines.

Stogner v. California is decided; ex post facto laws are
unconstitutional, particularly if the statute of limitations relating to alleged child sex abuse crimes has expired and regardless of when the victim files complaint
with police many years following alleged incidents.

The ABA opposes mandatory minimum sentencing, allowing judges to consider all merits of each case and all
factors, extralegal and legal.

2004   *Blakely v. Washington* is decided; the U.S. Supreme Court
makes federal sentencing guidelines advisory only and
not literal.

Beard v. Banks is decided; procedural factors relating to
considering mitigating factors and reaching unanimous
agreement on them cannot be applied retroactively to
prior capital cases involving similar circumstances;
capital sentences cannot be overturned retroactively
following final U.S. Supreme Court appeals and denials
of certiorari and where fundamental fairness has not
been jeopardized.

Tennard v. Dretke is decided; jurors who are not permitted
to consider low IQ as a mitigating circumstance in a capital case deprive a defendant of the right to due process;
all mitigating evidence must be permitted in capital
cases in which the death penalty may be imposed.

2005   *Deck v. Missouri* is decided; trial courts may not use physical restraints on compliant prisoners in courtrooms in front of jurors; shackling compliant prisoners prejudices juries and denies due process to defendants.

Shepard v. United States is decided; where the government fails to show evidence that generic crimes have been committed under the Armed Career Criminal Act, mandatory minimum sentences involving generic crimes and convictions for them cannot be imposed; it is improper for the government to use police reports as the sole evidence for deciding whether crimes are generic or nongeneric.

United States v. Booker is decided; juries, not judges, must decide whether aggravating or mitigating factors are present to convict defendants beyond a reasonable doubt; judges cannot decide such facts on their own and modify sentences prescribed under the sentencing guidelines.

2006   *Brown v. Sanders* is decided; statutory aggravating and mitigating factors may be used by judges in determining sentences under sentencing guidelines.

Minnesota considers separate determinate sentencing grid for sex offenders that enhances such sentences.

5

Biographical Sketches

John Augustus (1785–1859)

Probation in the United States was conceived in 1841 by the successful cobbler and philanthropist John Augustus, although historical references to the practice may be found in writings as early as 437–422 BC. Although early actions by Judge Peter Oxenbridge Thatcher have been regarded by some scholars as the equivalent of probation—he sentenced convicted offenders to release on their own recognizance instead of jail—John Augustus is most often credited with pioneering probation in the United States.

Augustus was born in Woburn, Massachusetts, in 1785. He was a permanent resident of Boston and became a shoemaker in a successful boot-making business. His subsequent work as a volunteer probation officer is best understood within the context of the Temperance Movement. The Temperance Movement against alcohol provided the right climate for using probation. Augustus attempted to rehabilitate alcoholics and to assist those arrested for alcohol-related offenses. He was a member of the Washington Total Abstinence Society, which eventually led him to the Boston courts. Washingtonians themselves were convinced that abusers of alcohol could be rehabilitated through understanding, kindness, and sustained moral suasion rather than through conviction and jail sentences.

Appearing in a Boston municipal court one morning to observe offenders charged and sentenced for various crimes, Augustus intervened on behalf of a man charged with being a common drunkard. Instead of seeing the convicted offender placed in the Boston House of Corrections, Augustus volunteered to supervise the man for a 3-week period and personally guaranteed his reappearance. Knowing Augustus's reputation for philanthropy and trusting his motives, the judge agreed with his proposal. When Augustus returned 3 weeks later with the drunkard, the judge was so impressed with the man's improved behavior that he fined him only 1 cent, plus court costs of less than $4.00. The judge also suspended the 6-month jail term. Subsequently, Augustus assisted numerous persons appearing in court. Not all were alcohol abusers. Augustus performed an early form of candidate screening by carefully evaluating an offender's character and age, and the people, places, and things most likely to influence the person. It may be that those preliminary screenings were the first presentence investigations ever conducted, although they were informal documents and contained superficial information about the clients to be supervised.

Augustus attracted several other philanthropic volunteers to perform similar probation services. These volunteers worked with juvenile offenders as well as with adults. Although the precise number of those who benefited from the work of Augustus and his volunteers is unknown, Augustus probably supervised and assisted 1,946 persons to become law-abiding citizens during the period from 1841 to 1859. He maintained detailed notes on all of his probation activities and the clients he supervised. He was also the first to apply the term "probation" to his activity of supervising clients at the court's direction. The first probation statute was enacted in Massachusetts shortly after Augustus's death in 1859 and was widely attributed to his probation efforts.

Francis Lee Bailey (b. 1933)

Francis Lee Bailey was born in Waltham, Massachusetts, on June 10, 1933. Bailey studied at Harvard College and joined the Marine Corps in 1952. He received his law degree from Boston University in 1960. Bailey was one of the most successful defense lawyers of the late twentieth century. Bailey defended Dr. Sam Sheppard, who had been found guilty of murdering his wife in 1954. He successfully appealed Sheppard's case to the U.S. Supreme Court, arguing that biased press coverage denied Sheppard the right to due process. He won a new trial for Sheppard, who was subsequently acquitted in 1966.

Bailey also defended Albert DeSalvo, known as the Boston Strangler. Bailey arranged a plea bargain with the government on DeSalvo's behalf, sparing him the death penalty. Despite the use of the insanity defense, DeSalvo was found guilty and sentenced to life without the possibility of parole. Bailey also defended Dr. Carl Coppolino, who was accused of murdering his wife, Carmela, in 1965 and Lt. William Farber in 1963. It was believed that Dr. Coppolino had injected both of his victims with a curare-like substance, succinylcholine chloride, which at the time was undetectable in the human body by the scientific means then available. He was convicted of murdering his wife and sentenced to life, but he served twelve years of his sentence and was subsequently paroled. Bailey won him an acquittal on the charge of murdering Lt. Farber. On more than a few occasions, Bailey won acquittals for his clients by claiming that evidence had been fabricated against them by government forensics experts.

Bailey's other accomplishments included an acquittal for U.S. Army captain Ernest Medina in his 1971 court-martial for responsibility in the My Lai massacre during the Vietnam War. In the 1970s he unsuccessfully defended Patty Hearst, who had been kidnapped by the Symbionese Liberation Army (SLA) and later participated in several bank robberies with members of the SLA. Bailey is well known as a member of the "dream team" hired to defend O. J. Simpson in a Los Angeles double murder trial in the mid-1990s. One of Bailey's highlights was cross-examining Mark Fuhrman, a Los Angeles detective who committed perjury on the witness stand and was suspected of planting incriminating blood evidence at O. J. Simpson's residence. Bailey totally undermined Fuhrman's credibility in court, and it is believed that this fact was pivotal in leading to O. J. Simpson's ultimate acquittal from all charges against him.

In 2002, Bailey was disbarred by Florida and Massachusetts as a result of handling stock in the DuBoc marijuana case. Bailey filed for the reinstatement of his law license in 2005. Bailey's legal work defending clients accused of serious crimes has led to more than a few acquittals, and when convictions have been obtained by prosecutors, sentencing by judges has typically been lenient.

Zebulon Brockway (1827–1920)

Zebulon Brockway was a penologist and is regarded by some organizations as the father of prison reform. Brockway was born in Lyme, Connecticut, and began his career as a prison guard in Wethersfield, Connecticut. He was warden of the municipal alms house in Albany, New York, for two years. In 1854 he was head of the Monroe County Penitentiary in Rochester, New York. In 1861, Brockway became head of a prison, the House of Correction, in Detroit, Michigan, where he attempted to introduce what later became known as indeterminate sentences. His ideas were incorporated into a Michigan statute, but the courts subsequently nullified the statute.

Brockway was appointed as the first superintendent of Elmira Reformatory, a new type of facility for inmates established in 1876. He retained that post until 1900. The Elmira Reformatory was designed for adult men. While at the Elmira Reformatory, Brockway introduced programs of education and vocational training, physical regimens and activities, indeterminate sentences, inmate classification, and an incentive program much like the good-time policy used today, as a result of which inmates could be transferred either to areas of the reformatory with more privileges or be granted release. He wrote *Fifty Years of Prison Service,* which was published in 1912. While at Elmira Reformatory, Brockway introduced a form of military training for his inmates in order to instill discipline. He accompanied his vocational training programs with trade instruction, and his program of incentives for good behavior became widely adopted in other institutions in many other states. Eventually, his experimentation with sentencing at Elmira Reformatory led to the actual introduction of indeterminate sentencing. His indeterminate sentencing model became the standard used for sentencing schemes in most states until the 1970s.

Warren E. Burger (1907–1995)

Warren E. Burger was born in St. Paul, Minnesota, on September 17, 1907. He attended night school at the University of Minnesota, where he received a bachelor's degree. Later he enrolled in the St. Paul College of Law and received his J.D. degree in 1931. He also taught law at the St. Paul College of Law for twelve years. He was a close friend of Harry Blackmun, who eventually became one of his colleagues on the U.S. Supreme Court in the 1960s. Burger became involved in politics during the 1930s and 1940s. He strongly supported Minnesota governor Harold Stassen in his Republican bid for the presidency in 1948, although Stassen lost out to John Dewey, who became the Republican presidential hopeful. Burger was subsequently appointed by President Dwight D. Eisenhower in 1956 to the District of Columbia Circuit Court of Appeals, where he remained until 1969.

In 1968, Earl Warren indicated that he was going to retire as Chief Justice of the U.S. Supreme Court. Burger's views were known to President Richard M. Nixon. Earl Warren's resignation was accepted in May 1969, and Warren Burger was confirmed and sworn in as Chief Justice in June of the same year.

Burger participated in the *Furman v. Georgia* (1972) case, which held that the death penalty as it was being applied at the time was discriminatory on the basis of race. Burger dissented in this opinion. It was later held that Georgia had corrected the racial discrimination feature of how the death penalty was determined to be applied when the case of *Gregg v. Georgia* was upheld in 1976. Thus a four-year moratorium on the death penalty in the United States ended.

Burger approached criminal law and procedure in a very conservative way. He argued against excessive, disproportionate sentences designed to deter offenders by dissenting in the case of *Solem v. Helm* (1983), in which a life sentence was imposed on a person who cashed a fraudulent check in the amount of $100. He considered the sentence of life imprisonment in that case to be cruel and unusual punishment. The case involved a habitual offender, and various states were experimenting at the time with mandatory penalties for chronic or persistent offenders, regardless of the value of property involved in the crimes. The deterrent effect of a life sentence was intended to reduce crime, and the issue continues to be hotly debated. "Three-strikes-and-you're-out" laws have been enacted, as well as mandatory terms for persons who use firearms in the commission of crimes, such as Virginia Exile, a plan to impose mandatory five-year sentences on any conviced felon who uses a dangerous weapon, such as a firearm, during the commission of a crime. The U.S. Supreme Court has vigorously upheld a state's right to impose mandatory sentences where it is believed that such sentences will have deterrent value. The debate on this issue continues, although little evidence exists that mandatory penalties do anything more than increase prison and jail populations. Among Burger's accomplishments outside of his U.S. Supreme Court role, he helped to establish the National Institute for State Courts, located in Williamsburg, Virginia; the Institute for Court Management; and the National Institute of Corrections. These organizations seek to provide judges, clerks, and correctional officers with further professional training. Warren Burger died of congestive heart failure on June 25, 1995.

Johnnie L. Cochran (1937–2005)

Johnnie Cochran was born in Shreveport, Louisiana, on October 2, 1937. He attended UCLA as an undergraduate and obtained his law degree from Loyola Marymount. Most of Cochran's legal career was spent in Los Angeles. Cochran worked for a time in the prosecutor's office for both the City of Los Angeles and Los Angeles County. One of his early prosecutions was against Lenny Bruce, a comedian charged with obscenity in his performances. However, he subsequently became involved in racially charged criminal cases as a powerful and widely respected defense attorney.

Cochran is best known for his work as one of O. J. Simpson's attorneys in a double murder trial in 1995. Cochran was a member of the so-called dream team, consisting of F. Lee Bailey and Robert Shapiro. Cochran was known for his courtroom theatrics, and on one occasion during the Simpson trial, Cochran asked Simpson to attempt to put on a glove that had allegedly been worn by the killer of Simpson's former wife and a restaurant waiter. Simpson struggled with the glove, but it was clearly too small to fit Simpson's large hand. Cochran declared to the court shortly thereafter, "If it doesn't fit, you must acquit!" This triumphant outburst was widely quoted in the news media, and Cochran's name became even more legendary.

Early in Cochran's career as a criminal defense attorney, he defended persons against officers of the Los Angeles Police Department during a period when their conduct was being challenged on ethical grounds. Police brutality and racism were rampant, and the Rodney King incident in the early 1990s caused a major riot in greater Los Angeles, leading to even greater destruction and more injuries. (King was a black motorist. Several white police officers were acquitted of beating him without provocation and under color of their authority.) Cochran also defended Michael Jackson against child molestation charges. He went on to defend rapper Sean Combs and civil rights legend Rosa Parks. He was also an author, writing books such as *Journey into Justice* (1996) and *A Lawyer's Life* (2002).

Throughout his life, Cochran dedicated his work to civil rights issues and righting wrongs committed against blacks and other minorities. Cochran's work did not, however, always serve blacks. In the aftermath of the Rodney King case and rioting, Cochran represented a white truck driver, Reginald Denny, who was nearly beaten to death by rioting blacks in a scene that was captured on national television. Despite overwhelming visual evidence of defendant guilt in the Denny beating and subsequent trial, his assailants were acquitted by a jury. Thus the jury verdict was a clear message of jury nullification to answer how white police officers had been acquitted of crimes against Rodney King, in which similar visual evidence in videotape format had captured their crimes for all to see. Jury nullification occurs when a jury makes a decision contrary to the evidence presented, and it is usually predicated on racial or emotionally charged factors. Many persons saw the Reginald Denny beating and trial of his assailants as payback for the state acquittal of police officers who had visibly engaged in senseless brutality against Rodney King. Some of the police officers were later tried in federal court on federal charges of violating Rodney King's civil rights under color of their authority as police officers. The convictions stood, although their punishment was extremely light. Cochran will be remembered for his promotion of civil rights causes and defense of truth and justice for all. Cochran died of a brain tumor on March 29, 2005.

Sir Edward Coke (1552–1634)

Sir Edward Coke was born on February 1, 1552. He was one of the most prominent jurists in English history. Coke was admitted to the bar in 1578 after having attended Norwich School and Trinity College at the University of Cambridge. He became a member of Parliament in 1589 and became solicitor general and speaker for the House of Commons in 1592.

Between 1600 and 1605 Coke conducted several treason trials, including prosecutions against the Earls of Essex and Southampton. He was known as a tough prosecutor. In 1606, Coke was appointed Chief Justice of the Court of Common Pleas by King James I (1603–1625). Coke assisted in writing the charter of the Virginia Company and became director of one of its branches, the London Company. During his tenure as Chief Justice, Coke identified with the common citizens and their plight against the state where common law was applied. Coke's advocacy for citizens and their property rights was ultimately crafted to undermine the authority and proclamations of the king. Alienating the king with his citizen-oriented activities undermined his political future, and Coke was removed from office in 1616. Subsequently he was elected a member of Parliament and championed the rights of citizens against the king to such an extent that ultimately he was arrested and imprisoned in the Tower of London for 9 months.

Following his release from confinement, he continued his labors and writing. He advocated for citizen rights relating to protection against arbitrary imprisonment, freedom from taxation without parliamentary representation, and due process of law. His works included numerous treatises, among which was an essay on criminal law and its application to punishments and sentences. Coke's legacy was that he indirectly assisted in crafting certain parts of the U.S. Constitution and the principle of judicial review. Coke died in 1634.

Sir Walter Crofton (1815–1897)

Sir Walter Crofton was a prison reformer and director of Ireland's prison system during the 1850s. He was impressed by Maconochie's work and copied his three-stage intermediate system whereby Irish prisoners could earn their early conditional release. Crofton, also known as a father of parole in various European countries, modified Maconochie's plan whereby prisoners would be subject to:

1. strict imprisonment for a time,
2. transfer for a short period to an intermediate prison, where they could participate in educational programs and perform useful and responsible tasks to earn good marks, and
3. tickets-of-leave, whereby they would be released from prison on license under the limited supervision of local police.

Under this third, ticket-of-leave stage, released prisoners were required to submit monthly reports of their progress to police, who assisted them in finding work. A study of 557 prisoners during that period showed that only 17 had their tickets-of-leave revoked for various infractions. Thus, Walter Crofton pioneered several major functions of parole officers: employment assistance to released prisoners, regular visits by officers to parolees, and the general supervision of their activities. Whereas Alexander Maconochie had crafted the mark system for granting early release to prisoners, Crofton added an additional component: the supervised release of those who were granted freedom early, known as monitored freedom. Thus Crofton's work was the forerunner of modern-day caseloads and supervision practices among parole officers.

Alan Dershowitz (b. 1938)

Alan Morton Dershowitz was born on September 1, 1938, in New York City. Dershowitz attended Yeshiva University High School and received a B.A. degree from Brooklyn College. Later he attended Yale Law School, where he obtained a bachelor of laws (LL.B.) degree in 1962. Following his admission to the bar, Dershowitz clerked for David L. Bazelon, the chief judge of the U.S. Circuit Court of Appeals for the District of Columbia. Dershowitz credits Bazelon as being his best and worst boss. Dershowitz said of Bazelon that he was both a slave master and father figure. Needless to say, Dershowitz held Bazelon in highest esteem and regarded him as an extremely instructive jurist.

Following his clerking for Judge Bazelon, Dershowitz worked as a clerk for U.S. Supreme Court justice Arthur Goldberg. He joined the faculty of Harvard Law School in 1964, attaining the rank of full professor by 1967, an admirable feat. In 1993, Dershowitz was appointed the Felix Frankfurter Professor of Law.

Much of Dershowitz's work has been associated with criminal defense. His clients have included Patricia Hearst, Leona Helmsley, Jim Bakker, Mike Tyson, O. J. Simpson, and Harry Reems. He also represented Claus von Bulow, and the case was eventually made into a movie, *Reversal of Fortune*, starring Ron Silver and Jeremy Irons. Dershowitz had a cameo role as a judge in the motion picture.

Dershowitz has always taken the side of citizens who have been recipients of injustice at the hands of unscrupulous prosecutors and police officers. His work in civil rights is widely recognized, and he was named a Guggenheim Fellow in 1979 and received the William O. Douglas First Amendment Award in 1983. He has been awarded honorary doctorates at Yeshiva University, the Hebrew Union College, Monmouth College, Haifa University, and Bar-Han University. He is a frequent speaker on important criminal issues and is a guest on numerous television talk shows. His guest appearances at professional events and meetings are numerous and influential.

Following 9/11 and the attack by terrorists against the World Trade Center towers and the Pentagon, Dershowitz advocated that torture warrants should be issued for the purpose of obtaining immediate information from captured terrorists and associates of terrorists. While not supporting torture to extract confessions from citizens, Dershowitz believes that if there is an absolute need to acquire information quickly from terrorists to minimize further acts of terrorism, nonlethal torture should be permitted. This and other civil rights issues have placed Dershowitz in the midst of much controversy, and he has debated his various political positions at length with many interviewers and critics. In 2006, Dershowitz continued arguing unpopular issues, such as anti-Israel news media coverage, and he has claimed that Israel should not be condemned for doing what every democracy would and should do—to take every reasonable military step to stop the killing of its civilians. In August 2006, Dershowitz compared Lebanon to Austria under the Nazis in the pre–World War II era.

Despite his political controversies and ideological beliefs, Dershowitz remains one of the top defense lawyers in the United States, and he has assisted many clients in their acquittals or reduced sentences when convicted. His defense work is remarkable in that regard. His place in the sentencing process in criminal courts is unrivaled by most other defense attorneys.

Elizabeth Gurney Fry (1780–1845)

Elizabeth Fry was born in Norwich, Norfolk, England, to a Quaker family on May 21, 1780. Fry was impressionabie, and at age eighteen she became enamored with the words of William

Savary, an American Quaker, who preached on behalf of the poor, the sick, and prisoners. Fry quickly joined a voluntary movement dedicated to providing clothing and food for the poor, both in neighborhoods and in prisons. She started a Sunday school in her home to teach children how to read. In 1812, Fry visited Newgate Prison and saw conditions among prisoners that horrified her. Prisoners were sleeping on floors and washing in small cells where they slept. They did their own cooking whenever food was available, and the conditions of their confinement were in her view deplorable. Because of family problems, she was unable to devote much attention to the plight of prisoners at Newgate and other prisons until 1816. She founded a prison school for children who were imprisoned with their parents. She assisted imprisoned women and taught them how to sew and do other household chores, and she helped them read the Bible. In 1817 she founded the Association for the Improvement of the Female Prisoners in Newgate.

In 1818 her brother-in-law, Thomas Fowell Buxton, was elected to Parliament and assisted her in promoting her new ideas about assisting Newgate prisoners. He permitted Fry to give testimony and other evidence to the House of Commons committee on the conditions prevalent in British prisons. She was the first woman to present evidence of this nature to the British Parliament. Elizabeth and her brother, Joseph John, opposed capital punishment and actively sought to abolish it. At that time, citizens of England could be executed for more than 200 different types of crime. Her early appeals to the Home Secretary were rejected outright, but eventually she convinced a new Home Secretary, Sir Robert Peel, of the nobility of her views.

Fry and her brother eventually published a book, *Prisons in Scotland and the North of England,* which described numerous prisons they had visited and the deplorable conditions under which inmates were maintained. Fry also devoted some of her time to assisting the homeless of London, providing nightly shelters for them together with bedding and food. Her actions were successful and widely copied in other communities. In 1840, Fry opened a training school for nurses. Her nursing program inspired Florence Nightingale, who took a team of nurses to assist wounded soldiers in the Crimean War. Queen Victoria recognized her work and donated money to her causes. Fry died in 1845, and her memorial service was widely attended. In 2002 the Bank of England depicted

Fry on a five-pound note. In Canada her memory is honored today by Elizabeth Fry societies that advocate for imprisoned women; a National Elizabeth Fry Week in Canada is commemorated during the month of May.

Peter Greenwood (b. 1939–)

Peter Greenwood is the president and chief executive officer of Greenwood and Associates, Inc. He graduated from the U.S. Naval Academy and holds an M.S. and Ph.D. from Stanford University in industrial engineering. He founded the Rand Corporation's Criminal Justice Program, which he directed for nearly nine years. He has published extensively in the areas of violence prevention, juvenile justice, criminal careers, sentencing, corrections, law enforcement, and cybercrime.

In 1998, Dr. Greenwood was honored by the American Society of Criminology for his work in criminology by receiving the August Vollmer Award. He is a member of the Homicide Research Working Group and the Southern California High-Tech Crime Association Advisory Group, and he is former president of the California Association of Criminal Justice Research. In 2006 he served on the faculty of the Rand Graduate School, and he has served on the faculties of the University of Southern California, Claremont Graduate School, and Cal Tech, and was on the California attorney general's Panel on Research and Statistics. Dr. Greenwood assisted, together with Peter Hoffman, in devising the Salient Factor Score Index. That index, known as SFS 81, was created for the purpose of assessing federal offender risk in granting early release to federal inmates. The SFS 81 continues to be used today by the U.S. Parole Commission for persons eligible for parole under the system that existed prior to the introduction of the U.S. sentencing guidelines in 1987. Dr. Greenwood has also extensively studied California's three-strikes-and-you're-out policies and how California corrections officials and the legislature have defined "strikes." He has given numerous presentations on the subjects of sentencing and prison overcrowding. Some of his works have become classics in the field for those interested in investigating sentencing schemes and the implications of sentencing reform.

Hammurabi (1810–1750 BC)

Hammurabi was born in Babylon in 1810 BC. He became the sixth king of Babylonia in 1792 and was considered wise beyond his years. During the first twenty-five years of his reign as king, he developed alliances with several other countries, including Larsa, Mari, Ashur, and Eshnunna. Although Hammurabi fought many battles and conquered much territory, he is better known for the establishment of his Code of Hammurabi, which was based on more ancient Sumerian law. The Code of Hammurabi contained 282 laws that were chiseled into stone. The Code of Hammurabi covered four primary areas: (1) economic provisions, (2) family, (3) crime, and (4) civil matters. The code was based on equal retaliation or retribution, or an eye for an eye. It contained explicit provisions for how legal proceedings ought to be conducted, and it provided specific punishments for specific offenses. Included in his 282 laws were those pertaining to perjury and wrongful prosecutions. Thus his work was original and seminal, dealing as it did with wrongful prosecutions, which occupy a great amount of contemporary news media attention.

Hammurabi not only developed this code but also performed numerous beneficial acts to promote the economy and social life of Babylonia. He restored temples, city walls, and public buildings, and he built canals for irrigation and other purposes. He did not create a functional bureaucracy; rather, he ruled in a totalitarian or dictatorial fashion. He died in 1750 BC. His code persists today as an influential document evident in much of the literature dealing with sentencing and punishment.

John Howard (1720–1790)

John Howard was born in 1720 and worked at many jobs as a young man. Eventually he became the high sheriff of Bedfordshire, England, where he took an interest in penal reform. Earlier he had spent 2 months in France as a political prisoner and was sorely mistreated while confined. As high sheriff of Bedfordshire, Howard became a vocal advocate for penal reforms. At the time, prisoners were expected to pay fees for their upkeep during incarceration. They could earn money for those supporting fees only through hard labor, and that labor was often exploited by prison officials and guards, who hired prisoners out to private interests on a contract basis. Most prisoner earnings were pocketed by crooked prison officials. Those who couldn't pay their fees spent years attempting to bribe prison officials for early release. Conditions of confinement were terrible, unsanitary, and inhumane. Howard wrote *The State of Prisons in England and Wales,* which was a critical essay about prison conditions. His report was based upon personal visits to various places of imprisonment. Howard advocated clean, healthful accommodations, adequate clothing and linen, proper health care for prisoners, a chaplain service, productive and useful labor for prisoners, segregation of prisoners by gender, age, and nature of the offense, and for jails to be funded by the public and not by prison labor.

In 1779, Howard introduced the Penitentiary Act, which called for prisoners to work long hours in heavy manual labor during the daytime hours and be confined in individual cells at night in order to meditate and acquire remorse for their illegal behavior. Hard work and moral penitence in a sanitary environment were believed to cause changes in a prisoner's lifestyle through exposure to good work habits and religious instruction. Over time Howard's ideas were widely adopted, and Howard even succeeded in alleviating for some prisoners the psychological torment of imprisonment so customary in penitentiaries of his period. Today a John Howard Society exists, which perpetuates his ideals and principles for prison reform. Like other prison reformers, Howard was widely criticized by those who perceived prison life to be punitive and unrelated to reform and rehabilitation. Nevertheless, the Quakers were guided by Howard's moral principles and were a significant influence on converting the Walnut Street Jail in Philadelphia, Pennsylvania, into a place of self-reflection and penitence, as well as a place where prisoners could be maintained in a relatively sanitary environment to do productive work and rehabilitate themselves for subsequent reintegration into society. That the Walnut Street Jail principles were widely imitated by subsequent jail and prison reforms in the United States attests to Howard's influence on penalogical reforms and the uses of imprisonment for long-term prisoners.

Henry C. Lee (b. 1938)

Henry Lee was born on November 22, 1938, in Rugao City, Jiangau Province, China. He fled to Taiwan at the end of the Chinese

Civil War and graduated in 1960 from the Taiwan Central Police College with a degree in police science. Lee began working for the Taipei Police Department and rose to the rank of captain when he was twenty-two. He came to the United States in 1972 and earned a B.S. degree in forensic science from John Jay College of Criminal Justice in New York. He studied science and biochemistry at New York University and earned his M.S. degree in 1974. Subsequently he earned a Ph.D. in biochemistry in 1975.

Lee presently serves as the chief emeritus for scientific services for Connecticut and is a full professor of forensic science at the University of New Haven. He has helped to establish the Henry C. Lee Forensic Institute. Earlier he served as the Connecticut commissioner of public safety and as the director of the Connecticut State Police Forensic Science Laboratory, and he was the state's chief criminologist from 1979 to 2000. Since 2000 Lee has had a television show on Court TV called *Trace Evidence: The Case Files of Dr. Henry Lee,* which features his work on famous cases.

Lee is a highly regarded expert on forensic evidence. He has testified at hundreds of trials as a forensics expert and regarding evidence collected and its pertinence to the cases with which he has been affiliated. Some of his more famous cases have included the JonBenet Ramsey case, the O. J. Simpson murder trial, the Scott Peterson murder trial, and an investigation into the death of Deputy White House Counsel Vincent Foster, who apparently killed himself in Fort Marcy Park on July 20, 1993. Lee is a regular on various television programs, including the coverage of the disappearance of Natalie Holloway in 2005 in Aruba and other sensational cases covered by talk show hosts including Nancy Grace, Geraldo Rivera, and Larry King.

Much of Lee's work produces exculpatory evidence as well as inculpatory evidence. His work has led to the exoneration of various persons, thus avoiding their wrongful conviction. At the same time, his work has solidified cases against other defendants and has led to their convictions for various crimes. He continues to be a useful authority and forensics expert who enables judges to impose appropriate sentences on those convicted of various types of offenses.

Alexander Maconochie (1787–1860)

Alexander Maconochie was born in Edinburgh, Scotland, on February 11, 1787. He joined the Royal Navy in 1803 and as a midshipman saw service in the Napoleonic Wars; he was a prisoner of war from 1810 to 1814. Later Maconochie saw service in the British-American War against the United States. He was the founder and first secretary of the Royal Geographical Society in 1830 and became a professor of geography at the University of London.

As private secretary to the lieutenant governor, Sir John Franklin, Maconochie sailed to the convict settlement at Hobart in Van Diemen's Land (now Tasmania) in 1836. He was quite critical of what he saw and wrote about his adventures. His writings condemned the state of prison discipline, the convict system, the fixation of the system upon punishment alone, release of inmates back into society later without being reformed or rehabilitated, and the lack of hope among these offenders. Lord Russell, the Home Secretary of Great Britain, received Maconochie's report with deep interest and resolved to change the practice of transportation of large numbers of convicts to remote locations such as Van Diemen's Land. A committee was formed in 1837–1838, the Molesworth Committee, which was specifically designed to assess the use of transportation by English authorities. However, Maconochie's criticisms were so severe that Lord Russell subsequently dismissed Maconochie from his post.

Maconochie was deeply religious, generous, and compassionate. He believed the two guiding principles of penology should be that (1) inasmuch as cruelty debases both the victim and society, punishment should not be vindictive but should aim at the reform of the convict to observe social constraints, and (2) a convict's imprisonment should consist of task, not time, sentences, with release depending on the performance of a measurable amount of labor. Interestingly, following the Molesworth Committee's report, transportation to New South Wales was abolished in 1840, although other colonies continued to practice it. The Secretary of State for the Colonies, Lord Normanby, was so disturbed by penal conditions at the Norfolk Island prison colony that he placed Maconochie in charge of the moral welfare of convicts there, installing him as the new superintendent. In that new position Maconochie instituted a series of reforms whereby his penalogical principles could be applied. Convicts were awarded marks to encourage their effort and thrift. Sentences were served in stages, each increasing in responsibility. Cruel punishments and degrading conditions were reduced or eliminated, and a convict's sense of dignity was respected. It has been surmised that Maconochie was able to empathize with prisoners because he had once been a prisoner of war.

Unfortunately for Maconochie, his efforts at reform were rebuffed by many persons, including guards at Norfolk Island. He was prevented from applying his principles to the 1,200 convicts there by higher-ups in correctional administration, and new convicts sent to Norfolk Island were separated physically from the older ones under Maconochie's supervision. Although then-governor Sir George Gipps visited Norfolk Island in 1843 and gave Maconochie good reviews and applauded his mark system, orders had already been issued by English officials to replace Maconochie. When Maconochie left Norfolk Island, it reverted to being a place of terror under brutal masters. Nevertheless, Maconochie's legacy for Norfolk Island was that more than 1,400 convicts left the island under his administration with almost no future recidivism. Maconochie returned to England and wrote a book about his mark system. Subsequently the mark system became the foundation for what are now known as good-time credits, used in U.S. prison systems and the penal systems of other countries. Subsequently, despite being placed in the post of governor of a prison in Birmingham, Maconochie was again unjustly dismissed and his humane actions toward prisoners criticized. Despite criticisms from his contemporaries, Maconochie has had a profound influence on the course of corrections, particularly U.S. corrections, and his mark system has been widely adopted in different forms under the general term "good-time credit" as an incentive for prison inmates to be compliant and work hard to earn early release.

William Penn (1644–1718)

William Penn was an English Quaker and founder of Pennsylvania. He was born at Tower Hill, London, on October 14, 1644. His education was obtained at Christ Church, Oxford, where he became a Quaker and ultimately opposed mandatory religious services advocated by the Church of England. Because of his religious rebelliousness, he was expelled from school. Penn spent some of his early years traveling throughout Europe. In 1664 he returned to England, where he studied law at Lincoln's Inn. After a few years of study he was sent by his father to manage familial estates in the county of Cork in Ireland. Subsequently he returned to England and became a Quaker minister. He was imprisoned frequently for brief periods because of his beliefs and vocal advocacy of the Quaker faith.

In 1676, Penn continued to engage in preaching and writing on religious subjects, and eventually he arrived in the New World, the colonies, where he and several associates purchased some land in West Jersey. This land was made into a Quaker colony. In 1681, Penn received a royal grant of territory from which the boundaries of the present state of Pennsylvania were determined. He proclaimed an area later known as Philadelphia as the capital of his new territory. Penn recognized early that he ought to establish friendly relations with nearby Indian tribes, and he did so. Whereas other colonies had Indian wars and subsequent problems, Penn's colony did not. In 1684, Pennsylvania had more than 7,000 inhabitants. Penn spent much time traveling back and forth between Pennsylvania and England, largely seeking rights for the Quakers, who were at the mercy of the Church of England and persistently persecuted. Penn was accused of treason on several occasions and tried for that offense. He was acquitted, but he did not cease his efforts to intervene on behalf of his Quaker constituents.

While Penn was in Pennsylvania, he observed that corporal punishments were used with great frequency. These acts were directed largely at Indians and blacks who inhabited the area. Penn abolished corporal punishment upon his return from England and established less physical punishments for those accused of law violations. Thus Penn was an early reformer and advocated lenient treatment for those accused and subsequently convicted of crimes. The death penalty was used for numerous offenses prior to Penn's intervention, applicable to more than 220 offenses. Under Penn's rule, the death penalty was applicable to only two offenses: treason and murder. He established the Great Act, limiting these punishments. His advocacy for rehabilitative measures was not popular with the public, however. No doubt Penn's leniency toward those accused of crimes was influenced significantly by his own treatment by the English and the Church of England while he was in England. He vowed not to treat others as he himself had been treated. Thus early reforms, including rehabilitation and reintegration, can be easily traced to the work of William Penn and his Great Law, which lasted until his death on July 30, 1718. Once Penn passed away his reforms were quickly abolished, and Pennsylvania reverted to prisoner treatment equivalent to that inflicted on the Quakers by the British— one of the major reasons the Quakers had fled England.

John Roberts (b. 1955)

John Roberts was born on January 27, 1955, and is the seventeenth Chief Justice of the U.S. Supreme Court. Roberts was schooled at Harvard University, where he graduated summa cum laude and with Phi Beta Kappa honors in 1976. He then attended Harvard Law School, where he earned his law degree. Roberts is currently a member of the American Academy of Appellate Lawyers, the American Law Institute, the Edward Coke Appellate American Inn of Court, and the National Legal Center for the Public Interest. While in private practice Roberts argued thirty-nine cases before the U.S. Supreme Court, prevailing in twenty-five of those cases. Prior to his chief justiceship, Roberts served as a Circuit Court of Appeals judge for the District of Columbia. He was in private practice for fourteen years and held positions in Republican administrations in the U.S. Department of Justice and the staff of the White House Counsel.

Roberts has been instrumental in affecting laws pertaining to sentencing. He was a member of the circuit court of appeals that heard the case of *Hedgepeth v. Washington Metropolitan Area Transit Authority* (386 F.3d 1149, 2004), which involved a twelve-year-old girl who was asked if she had any drugs in her possession, was searched for drugs, taken into custody, handcuffed, driven to police headquarters, and photographed and fingerprinted, because she had violated a publicly advertised zero tolerance "no eating" policy in a Washington, D.C., subway station by eating a single french fry. Roberts wrote for a 3–0 panel affirming a district court decision that dismissed the girl's complaint, which was predicated on the Fourth and Fifth Amendments, specifically the claim that an adult would have received only a citation for the same offense, while children must be detained until parents are notified. Roberts wrote in his opinion that age discrimination and detention in this case were constitutional, noting that the question before the Court was not whether the policy was a bad idea or trivial, but rather, whether it violated the Fourth and

Fifth Amendments to the Constitution. He declared that, regardless of the minimal infraction that had occurred, the policy itself did not violate the Constitution.

Roberts upholds the Constitution and its amendments in a literal way, and thus he is less persuaded than some of the other justices by emotional and compelling arguments to see cases otherwise. In that respect he is a staunch conservative who believes in leaving previous U.S. Supreme Court decisions undisturbed unless there are strong and compelling societal interests that might dictate otherwise. Even under those circumstances, Roberts probably would be careful before overturning prior decisions by previous courts.

Barry Scheck (b. 1949)

Barry Scheck was born in Queens, New York, on September 19, 1949. Scheck received his B.S. degree from Yale University and J.D. and M.C.P. degrees from the University of California–Berkeley in 1974. Scheck is director of clinical education for the Trial Advocacy Program and the Center for the Study of Law and Ethics. He was a former staff attorney at the Legal Aid Society of New York. In 1996, Scheck received the Robert C. Heeney Award, the highest honor awarded by the National Association of Criminal Defense Lawyers. This award is given annually to the one criminal defense attorney who best exemplifies the goals and values of the association and the legal profession generally.

Scheck attracted news media attention in the 1990s during the trial of O. J. Simpson in California. Scheck's work was significant in that it challenged much of the state's DNA analysis of evidence against Simpson. One reason that Scheck became involved in the Simpson trial on the side of the defense was his earlier work with Peter Neufeld. He and Neufeld had cofounded the Innocence Project in 1992. The Innocence Project is dedicated to the use of DNA evidence to help clear innocent individuals of crimes for which they have been wrongfully convicted. As of September 1, 2006, the Innocence Project had freed 180 inmates who had been incarcerated wrongfully for various crimes.

The Innocence Project carefully screens those who claim innocence. It is a costly enterprise to test DNA evidence, and frivolous attempts by inmates to clear their names use up valuable resources better spent on more worthy convicted offenders. The

Innocence Project accepts only cases in which newly discovered scientific evidence can potentially demonstrate that a prisoner is actually innocent. Scheck and Neufeld continue to work toward freeing wrongfully convicted offenders. Scheck was prominently featured in a nonfictional work by John Grisham in 2006 entitled *An Innocent Man,* which described the wrongful conviction of Ron Williamson in Oklahoma. Williamson was on death row for nearly twenty years before Scheck and his associates were able to convince an appellate court that Williamson could not have committed the crime of murder, because his DNA did not match any DNA used as evidence against him in a 1980s murder trial.

One implication we may draw from the Innocence Project is that more than a few prosecutors are out for convictions regardless of the factual circumstances surrounding crimes. Once a potential suspect has been identified, both police and prosecutorial resources are abundantly allocated in an attempt to secure a conviction at any cost. The blind ambition of prosecutors especially is revealed through much of Scheck's work. Even when confronted by overwhelming and convincing evidence, beyond a reasonable doubt, that a wrongfully convicted person is actually innocent, many prosecutors will continue to believe that they were right initially and that the evidence they relied upon for their conviction was sound.

Scheck has caused more than a few ripples among prosecutors and the judicial system since the Innocence Project was founded. If anything, the work of the Innocence Project has caused at least some prosecutors to tread more slowly and carefully before jumping to premature conclusions and pursuing investigations against innocent suspects. Scheck's participation in trials such as the O. J. Simpson trial of the mid-1990s is a case in point. Scheck's work strongly suggested that some of the blood evidence against Simpson had been planted by one or more persons, and that some collusion had existed between the prosecutor's office and those technicians responsible for collecting and analyzing evidence at crime scenes. It will never be known how many persons have actually benefited from Scheck's work.

William Howard Taft (1857–1930)

William Howard Taft was born on September 15, 1857; he was the twenty-seventh president of the United States. Taft attended Yale

University in New Haven, Connecticut. He received a bachelor of laws degree in 1880. After he was admitted to the Ohio bar, Taft became an assistant prosecutor for Hamilton County, Ohio. Two years later he was appointed a local collector of internal revenue. He became a judge in the Ohio Superior Court in 1887. President Harrison appointed Taft to the position of solicitor general of the United States in 1892. Subsequently he became Chief Judge of the Sixth Circuit Court of Appeals. He received an honorary LL.D. degree from Yale Law School. Between 1896 and 1900, Taft was dean and professor of law at the University of Cincinnati, in addition to his judgeship.

Although Taft aspired to the U.S. Supreme Court, and although he was offered the opportunity to serve in that capacity by President Theodore Roosevelt in 1902, he declined in order to assist Filipino groups in Manila as governor-general. Roosevelt appointed Taft to serve as secretary of war from 1904 to 1908. Taft became U.S. president in 1909 and served a four-year term. He pushed for world peace during his tenure as president. Considered a progressive, Taft lowered tariffs on farm products and factory goods.

In 1921, Taft was appointed Chief Justice of the U.S. Supreme Court, a post to which he had long aspired. Thus he became the only president in history to serve also as a Chief Justice of the U.S. Supreme Court. His hand was visible in numerous civil rights decisions, as he cast vote after vote favoring civil rights and the rights of individuals over the state. Perhaps his most critical case involved *Olmstead v. United States* (277 U.S. 438, 1928). This case held that the Fourth Amendment's proscription on unreasonable search and seizure did not apply to federal wiretaps. Thus, incriminating evidence obtained through such wiretaps would be admissible against criminal defendants in court. Taft retired as Chief Justice on February 3, 1930, because of ill health. He died on March 8, 1930, of a heart attack.

Peter Oxenbridge Thatcher (1776–1842)

One of the more innovative judges during the 1830s was Boston municipal judge Peter Oxenbridge Thatcher, who was born on December 22, 1776. Thatcher was the son of a prominent jurist family of the middle 1700s, and thus it was logical that Thatcher entered law and eventually rose to the judiciary in the late 1820s.

Thatcher's early life and schooling are sketchy, and little is known about his formative years. However, his family's prominence suggests that he was well schooled and privileged. Judge Thatcher became known for his charitable work, especially for his philanthropy among the poor. He understood the plight of those confined in prisons, although he personally could not exercise his discretionary judicial power to change those conditions. However, Thatcher demonstrated considerable leniency to many who appeared in his courtroom, especially indigents.

Judge Thatcher was somewhat unusual among his Boston judicial peers during the early 1830s in that he exercised considerable judicial leniency when sentencing offenders. For instance, he ordered that some offenders be released on their own recognizance (ROR), either before or after their criminal charges had been adjudicated. Thus he is probably the first judge in history to use ROR for defendants. Ordinarily, defendants facing a trial were confined in a jail facility prior to their trial date. There simply were no exceptions to that practice. When Thatcher subsequently ordered the release of convicted offenders on their own recognizance, that amounted to an indefinite suspension of their sentence of imprisonment. Thus, Thatcher introduced the legal practice of the suspension of the execution of a sentence (SES). These SESs were known as judicial reprieves. Thatcher believed that such sentences would encourage convicted offenders to practice good behavior in their community, support their dependents through gainful employment, and refrain from committing new crimes. Judicial reprieves were the functional equivalent of probation as it is presently known. A primary difference is that Thatcher did not require those released on judicial reprieve to perform any public service, pay fines or restitution, or engage in any type of victim restitution. They were freed to return to their communities and encouraged to be law-abiding.

Probation today involves various conditions, including fines, community service, victim restitution, and other behavioral requirements. Some historians credit Judge Thatcher as the first person to introduce probation in the United States, although John Augustus is credited as being its U.S. father, in the year 1841, inasmuch as Augustus did require those released to his custody to conform their behavior to his expectations and become reformed. Nevertheless, the fact that some probation experts acknowledge Thatcher as a precedent-setter relative to the use of judicial reprieves, together with the similarity of judicial reprieves to the informal practices of Augustus, strongly roots Thatcher in the history of probation. Thatcher died in 1842.

Earl Warren (1891–1974)

Earl Warren was born in Los Angeles, California. Warren grew up in Bakersfield, and he subsequently attended the University of California–Berkeley, where he obtained his B.A. degree in legal studies and his J.D. degree in 1914. While at UC–Berkeley, Warren joined the Sigma Phi Society, a fraternal organization. He was admitted to the California bar in 1914. Warren worked in private law firms in the San Francisco Bay area and eventually became employed by San Francisco County, where he worked in the district attorney's office. He was appointed district attorney of Alameda County in 1925. In subsequent elections, Warren was elected three times to four-year terms. He was known as a tough Republican prosecutor and did much to professionalize and streamline the district attorney's office. Warren was adamant about changes made in the district attorney's office and ruled it with an iron hand. None of the convictions from his office were ever overturned on appeal.

Eventually, Warren became affiliated with the University of California–Berkeley, where he was appointed to the board of regents. He became attorney general for California in 1939 and was elected governor in 1946. During World War II, Warren supported the controversial policy of moving large numbers of Japanese-Americans from their homes and jobs to relocation camps because of pervasive citizen fear that persons of Japanese ancestry would be more likely to subvert the U.S. war effort. Subsequently, Warren apologized to Japanese-Americans and deeply regretted supporting such removal and displacement.

Warren was elected to a third gubernatorial term in 1950. Earlier, in 1948, Warren had run for vice president of the United States with Thomas Dewey, who sought the presidency. The Dewey-Warren ticket was opposed by the Truman-Barkley Democratic campaign, with Harry Truman prevailing. When General Dwight D. Eisenhower was elected president in 1952, he strongly admired Earl Warren and was impressed with his legal credentials. In 1953, President Eisenhower appointed Earl Warren as Chief Justice of the U.S. Supreme Court. Eisenhower proclaimed that Warren had the integrity, uprightness, and courage that he believed the U.S. Supreme Court needed. Interestingly, Eisenhower later became disenchanted with Warren, who became involved in and supported several liberal U.S. Supreme Court decisions that Eisenhower firmly opposed. Eisenhower remarked later and privately to others that his appointment of Warren as Chief Justice of the U.S. Supreme Court "was the biggest damned fool mistake I've ever made in my life."

One of the initial U.S. Supreme Court decisions crafted by Warren that underscored his liberalism was *Brown v. Board of Education* (1954), which effectively desegregated the public schools in the United States. At the time, blacks attended all-black schools, while whites attended all-white schools, especially in the South, although segregation of that sort was pervasive in many states, including Northern ones. Supporting the school segregation policy was an 1896 decision, *Plessy v. Ferguson,* which set forth the "separate, but equal" doctrine. That doctrine justified racial segregation on the basis that if blacks were provided with facilities equal to those of whites, the segregation inherent in such separate but equal facilities was constitutional. The Warren Court, lasting from 1953 to 1969, declared that the "separate, but equal" doctrine was not valid as it applied to schools. Many scholars have erroneously interpreted the *Brown v. Board of Education* decision as reversing the separate but equal doctrine, but it merely provided that the doctrine did not pertain to schools. It would take other U.S. Supreme Court decisions to provide that the separate but equal doctrine did not pertain to other racially separate activities, including housing, public transportation, restrooms, water fountains, and interracial marriages.

The Warren Court set numerous precedents that appeared to tie the hands of police officers when arresting and interrogating criminal suspects. Furthermore, the search and seizure powers of law enforcement officers were severely restricted as a result of several important U.S. Supreme Court decisions. For instance, in *Mapp v. Ohio* (1961), Ohio police officers were prohibited from entering a person's premises without a valid warrant to search in particular places for specified contraband. In 1966 the Warren Court decided the case of *Miranda v. Arizona,* which led to advising suspects of their right to counsel and to refuse to speak with interrogating officers when arrested for crimes. The famed "Miranda warning" stemmed from that case. Subsequently, anyone arrested for a crime was informed of the following: the right to remain silent; the right to an attorney; if they cannot afford an attorney, one will be appointed for them; they may discontinue questioning by police whenever they decide that such questioning should be discontinued; and anything they say may be recorded and used against them later in court.

Police officers in various jurisdictions rebelled against Warren Court liberalism by committing perjury on the witness stand against criminal suspects in order to circumvent U.S. Supreme Court rulings about rights violations. For instance, many police officers engaged in "dropsy testimony," in which they justified their illegal searches of a person or vehicle by claiming under oath that they had observed drugs or controlled substances drop onto the ground as suspects exited their automobile when stopped for routine traffic violations. For at least a decade, there was pervasive clumsiness among criminals who allegedly dropped illegal contraband in plain view of investigating officers, or allowed such contraband, including weapons, to protrude conspicuously from their persons or vehicle interiors, so that officers would be able to justify more extensive searches in their quest for incriminating evidence. Also during this period, citizens carried banners declaring "Impeach Earl Warren" as a protest against his liberalism. Several of Warren's critics declared that they were unsure that the document the U.S. Supreme Court was expected to apply was the U.S. Constitution or a statute. It is clear that Warren's legacy has been long-lasting, having long-term consequences for social policy and radical liberalism.

Chief Justice Warren subsequently headed an investigative commission at the request of President Lyndon B. Johnson to examine the circumstances under which President John F. Kennedy had been assassinated in 1963. The commission was known as the Warren Commission, and it subsequently concluded that the assassination of President Kennedy was the act of a single person, Lee Harvey Oswald. A large segment of the general public was convinced otherwise: that Oswald had acted in a widespread conspiracy with others. Earl Warren regretted his decision to head the commission from the outset, and he was rightly justified because of the extensive controversy the findings generated. Warren retired from the U.S. Supreme Court in 1969. Earl Warren died in 1974, and he was posthumously awarded the Presidential Medal of Freedom. The Earl Warren Bill of Rights Project is named in his honor.

References

Furman v. Georgia, 408 U.S. 238 (1972).

Gregg v. Georgia, 428 U.S. 153 (1976).

Roe v. Wade, 410 U.S. 113 (1973).

Solem v. Helm, 463 U.S. 277 (1983).

Brown v. Board of Education, 347 U.S. 483 (1954).

Mapp v. Ohio, 367 U.S. 1081 (1961).

Miranda v. Arizona, 384 U.S. 436 (1966).

Plessy v. Ferguson, 163 U.S. 537 (1896).

6

Facts and Data

This chapter presents information about inmates in U.S. prisons and jails. It includes their characteristics, including types of crimes committed. Additional information includes sociodemographic characteristics, average sentence lengths, and state and federal sentencing types and patterns. Several sentencing trends are discussed. The chapter concludes with a list of leading U.S. Supreme Court cases that have been influential in promoting changes in U.S. sentencing laws and in the nature of punishments imposed on those convicted of a crime.

Sentenced U.S. Inmates in Jails and Prisons

Jail Inmates

Jails are short-term facilities generally designed to hold local (county and city) inmates serving sentences of less than one year. However, since the 1970s and even earlier, some larger U.S. jails have held state and federal prisoners to ease overcrowding in selected institutions. These inmates serve longer terms in jails in which they can be housed, fed, clothed, and given minimal living accommodations. State and federal prisoners who are held in these jails are called contract prisoners, since contracts exist between the jails and states or the federal government. State and federal governments pay jails a fixed amount of money per prisoner per day, usually a sum exceeding significantly the ordinary expenses of accommodating local criminals. Thus contract prisoners are often a for-profit enterprise for local jails that assists them in improving their own local physical plants, hiring additional officers, providing more comprehensive training, and incorporating amenities not ordinarily found in other jails. Actually, the expenditures of state and federal governments paid to jails are often lower than the actual state and federal costs of accommodating those same inmates in their own facilities. Thus state and federal prisons benefit because local jails are able to ease prison overcrowding at a lower cost to these governments. And local jails benefit from the additional revenue received by housing a certain number of state and federal prisoners.

The functions of jails are to (1) house drunks, vagrants, and juveniles, usually for short periods, (2) hold pretrial detainees and petty offenders, (3) hold shock probationers and prison inmate overflow (contract prisoners), (4) house work releasees and the mentally ill, and (5) hold probationers and parolees for brief periods following probation or program violations.

In 2006 approximately 90 percent of all jail inmates were male, while 43 percent were white and non-Hispanic. The number of female arrestees has climbed slowly since 1990 from 9.2 percent to 14.1 percent in 2006. Figures for different ethnicities and races have remained fairly constant during the 1990s and into the 2000s. Some observers believe that selective law enforcement and racial profiling have contributed to the disproportionately large number of black jail inmates over the years, whereby they have accounted for about 46 percent of all jail inmates. More than half of all jail inmates were not convicted of any crime. At midyear 2006, it was estimated that about 94 percent of all available jail space in the United States was occupied (U.S. Department of Justice 2006).

The jail population in the United States for 2005 was 819,434 (Harrison and Beck 2006, 7). In 2005 there were 747,529 inmates held in jail, while 71,905 inmates were supervised outside of a jail facility, including weekender programs, electronic monitoring, day reporting, and home detention. The prison population of the United States for 2005 was approximately 2.186 million (U.S. Department of Justice 2006).

The gender, racial/ethnic, and conviction statuses of inmates for the years 1995, 2000, 2003, and 2004–2005 have been compared. An increasing proportion of females are incarcerated in jails across the years surveyed than in comparable prison population proportionate distributions. The proportion of female inmates grew between 1995 and 2005 from 10.2 percent to 12.7 percent. The number of white inmates grew proportionately from 1995 to 2005 from 40.1 percent to 44.3 percent, while the black proportionate inmate population declined from 43.5 percent in 1995 to 38.9 percent in 2005. However, the Hispanic proportionate distribution of jail inmates grew slightly during the same period, from 14.7 percent in 1995 to 15.0 percent in 2005. Also, fewer convicted offenders made up the jail population between 1995 and 2005, declining from 44 percent to 38 percent. The number of unconvicted offenders increased proportionately for the same period, from 56 percent to 62 percent (Harrison and Beck 2006, 8).

Prison Inmates

Prisons are state or federally funded and operated institutions housing convicted offenders under continuous custody on a long-term basis. Compared with jails, prisons are completely self-contained and self-sufficient. In 2005, there were more than 2.4 million inmates in both federal and state penitentiaries (U.S. Department of Justice, 2006). Prisons at that time were operating at 108 percent of their operating capacity. The Federal Bureau of Prisons was operating at 132 percent of its operating capacity, while New Jersey and Wisconsin were operating at 147 percent and 142 percent of their operating capacities, respectively. Erving Goffman (1961) has described a prison as a total institution, because it is an environmental reality of absolute dominance over prisoners' lives. These self-contained facilities have recreational yards, workout rooms, auditoriums for viewing feature films, and small stores for the purchase of toiletries and other goods.

The first state prison was established in Simsbury, Connecticut, in 1773. That prison was actually an underground copper mine that was converted into a confinement facility for convicted felons. It was eventually made into a permanent prison in 1790. Prisoners were shackled about the ankles, worked long hours, and received particularly harsh sentences for minor offenses. Burglary and counterfeiting were punishable in Simsbury by imprisonment not exceeding ten years, while a second offense meant life imprisonment.

The functions of prisons are to (1) provide societal protection, (2) punish offenders, (3) rehabilitate offenders, and (4) reintegrate offenders by preparing them for re-entry into society through vocational and educational training, counseling, and other institutional measures. All prisons in the United States have classifications that differentiate between prisoners and cause them to be placed under various levels of custody or security (Sullivan, 2006).

One of the main purposes for the initial inmate classification is to identify those likely to engage in assaultive or aggressive disciplinary infractions. Prisoners are eventually channeled into one of several fixed custody levels known as (1) minimum-security, (2) medium-security, and (3) maximum-security.

Minimum-security prisons are facilities designed to house low-risk, nonviolent first offenders. These institutions are also established to accommodate those serving short-term sentences. Sometimes, minimum-security institutions function as intermediate housing for those prisoners leaving more heavily monitored facilities on their way toward parole or eventual freedom. Minimum-security housing is often of a dormitory-like quality, with grounds and physical plant resembling a university campus rather than a prison. Those assigned to minimum-security facilities are trusted to comply with whatever rules are in force.

Some 60 percent of all state and federal prisons in the United States are medium- and minimum-security institutions. A majority of state and federal prison facilities are designed to accommodate medium- and minimum-security inmates. As of 2006, of all U.S. penitentiaries, all but the one in Atlanta, Georgia, were classified as maximum-security (U.S. Department of Justice 2006). Medium-security facilities at both state and federal levels offer inmates opportunities for work release, furloughs, and other types of programs.

Approximately 40 percent of all U.S. prisons are maximum-security institutions. Ordinarily, those sentenced to serve time in maximum-security facilities are considered among the most dangerous, high-risk offenders. Maximum-security prisons are characterized by many stringent rules and restrictions, and inmates are isolated from each other for long periods in single-cell accommodations. Closed-circuit television monitors often permit correctional officers to observe prisoners in their cells or in work areas. Visitation privileges are minimal, and most often no efforts are made by officials to rehabilitate inmates.

Considerable diversity exists among prisoners in state and federal institutions. These differences include the nature and seriousness of their conviction offenses, age, and psychological or medical problems. In order to cope more effectively with meeting the needs of such diverse offenders, prisons have established a variety of confinement facilities and levels of custody, depending upon how each prisoner is classified. Overall, state and federal prisoner populations increased by nearly 183 percent between 1990 and 2005. Generally, the average increase in the federal and state prison inmate population was about 5 percent per year. This information is shown in Table 6.1.

In 2005, 7 percent of all state and federal prisoners were female. Women have been incarcerated at increasing rates since the early 1990s. For instance, between 1990 and 2005, the average annual percentage of female inmates in the prison population increased 4.7 percent, outpacing male incarcerations, which rose an average of 3.0 percent for the same period. Between 1995 and 2005 the female inmate population increased by 45 percent, while the male inmate population increased by 32 percent in the same period. The more rapid rise in female incarceration is attributable

TABLE 6.1
Change in the State and Federal Prison Populations, 1990–2005

Year	Number of inmates	Annual change (percent)	Total change since 1990 (percent)
1990	773,124	—	—
1991	824,133	6.6	6.6
1992	883,593	7.2	14.2
1993	932,074	5.5	20.6
1994	1,016,691	9.1	31.5
1995	1,585,586	5.6	105.1
1996	1,646,020	3.8	112.9
1997	1,743,643	5.6	125.5
1998	1,816,931	4.2	135.1
1999	1,890,837	4.1	144.6
2000	1,937,482	2.5	150.6
2001	1,961,247	1.2	153.7
2002	2,033,331	3.7	163.0
2003	2,082,728	2.4	169.4
2004	2,131,180	2.3	175.7
2005	2,186,230	2.6	182.8

Source: Paige M. Harrison and Allen J. Beck. 2006. *Prison and Jail Inmates at Midyear 2005.* Washington, DC: U.S. Department of Justice, Bureau of Justice Statistics.

mostly to more property-related convictions among women than among men (Harrison and Beck 2006).

Between 1990 and 2005, the number of prisoners in custody in the United States increased from 1.1 million to 2.18 million. That was an average increase of 5.9 percent per year (ibid.). Among all state inmates, women made up 6.3 percent of the population in 2005. Some 50 percent of all male offenders were incarcerated for violent offenses, compared with 31.4 percent of all state female prison inmates.

Approximately 25 percent of all female prison inmates had been convicted of property offenses, compared with 19.4 percent of all male inmates. About 32 percent of the female inmates had been convicted of drug offenses, compared with 20 percent of the male inmates. Thus, disproportionately larger numbers of women than men were serving time for property and drug offenses. White inmates represented 36 percent of all state inmates, while blacks and Hispanics accounted for 46.5 percent and 14.8 percent, respectively. Forty-eight percent of the black inmates were serving time for violent offenses, compared with 48.8 percent of the Hispanic inmates and 48.6 percent of the white inmates. Whites, blacks, and Hispanics were represented fairly equally in the violent offense category. However, disproportionately larger numbers of blacks committed robbery (17.5 percent) than either whites (8.1 percent) or Hispanics (12.7 percent). About 15 percent of all white offenders were in prison for rape or sexual assault, compared with 7.1 percent of the Hispanic and 5.8 percent of the black inmates (ibid., 13). Black inmates had a larger proportion of drug offenses (25.8 percent) than either whites (13.3 percent) or Hispanics (24.2 percent). Of all major federal crime categories, drug offenses had the greatest percentage of total inmate growth, 59.3 percent, between 1990 and 2005. The actual percentage increase in the number of sentenced federal inmates for drug offenses was 140.9 percent between 1990 and 2005. That increase is attributable in large measure to the passage of antidrug legislation in the late 1980s and early 1990s.

There was also a dramatic increase in the number of sentenced federal prisoners who had been convicted of immigration, weapons, and other public order offenses. The Immigration and Naturalization Service, as well as other agencies, has cracked down on illegal immigrants, especially during the late 1990s. In the general public-order offense category, therefore, there was an increase of 32.2 percent in total federal inmate population growth between 1990 and 2005 (Harrison and Beck 2006).

Offenders on Probation in the United States

The characteristics of persons on probation in the United States for 2005 have been described. Approximately 77 percent of all probationers were male in 2005. Between 1995 and 2005, the proportion of female probationers increased from 21 to 23 percent. The racial distribution of probationers remained unchanged for much of that same period, however. White probationers increased to 56 percent in 2005 from 53 percent in 1995, while black probationers declined slightly to 30 percent from 31 percent for the same time interval. The proportion of Hispanic probationers declined slightly from 14 percent to 12 percent between 1995 and 2005.

Proportionately greater numbers of probationers are entering probation programs without serving any jail time first. In 2005, 76 percent of the probationers entered probation without incarceration, up from 72 percent in 1995. There were proportionately slightly fewer successful completions of probation programs in 2005 (60 percent), compared with a successful completion of 62 percent in 1995. About 15 percent of all probationers were returned to incarceration in 2005, compared with 21 percent in 1995 for various program violations. About half (49 percent) of all probationers in 2005 were on probation for felony convictions. Less frequent use was made of split sentencing in 2005; 8 percent of all offenders sentenced to probation were also obligated to do some jail time, compared with 15 percent in 1995. There were slightly fewer suspended sentences (24 percent) in 2005, compared with 26 percent in 1995 (Glaze and Palla 2005, 6).

Most probationers share the following characteristics: (1) probationers tend to be first offenders or low-risk offenders, (2) more property offenders than violent offenders are considered for probation, (3) more convicted women are considered for probation than convicted men, (4) not having a history of drug or alcohol use or abuse is considered a positive factor in granting probation, and (5) if there were no physical injuries resulting from the convicted offender's actions, and if no weapons were used to commit the crime, the chances for probation are greater.

Offenders on Parole in the United States

In 2005, 7 million persons were under some form of correctional supervision in the United States. Of those, 765,355, or about 11 percent, were on parole. About 10 percent of these were federal parolees, while the remainder were from state prisons. The parole population grew in the United States by 12.6 percent between 1995 and 2005. Supervised releasees in the federal system accounted for 11.7 percent of all parolees (Glaze and Palla 2005).

Some of the characteristics of parolees in the United States for 2005 have been compared with the parolee population from 1995. One of the most significant changes between 1995 and 2005 is that female parolees have increased in number from 10 percent to 12 percent of the parolee population. Racially, white parolees increased proportionately from 34 to 40 percent, while black parolees declined from 45 percent to 41 percent. The proportion of Hispanic parolees declined from 21 percent to 18 percent during the 1995–2005 period (ibid.). Further characterizing these parolees, 85 percent were on active parole status in 2005, compared with 78 percent in 1995. The greatest proportion of parolees under parole supervision in 2005 were drug offenders (38 percent), followed by property offenders (26 percent) and violent offenders (24 percent). About 52 percent of all parolees were mandatory parolees, while 31 percent were discretionary parolees. Approximately 46 percent of parolees in 2005 successfully completed their parole programs and were released from the system. About 39 percent of all parolees had been returned to incarceration, with 12 percent jailed or imprisoned for a new conviction. Parolees awaiting a parole revocation hearing totaled 26 percent, while 10 percent of all parolees leaving parole were absconders (ibid., 9).

Average Sentence Lengths for Various Offenses

As the result of massive sentencing reforms, the percentage of prison sentences among convicted state felons has significantly changed. About 68 percent of all convicted felons received incarceration in 1994, but that figure had climbed to 83 percent by 2005 (U.S. Department of Justice 2006). However, the average prison sentence had decreased from 67 months in 1994 to 62 months in 2005. For certain types of offenses, such as distribution of drugs, however, the incarceration of drug traffickers has steadily risen.

While these various sentencing schemes have changed the average sentence lengths of prison inmates, sentencing disparities have also been minimized in more than a few jurisdictions. In Minnesota, for instance, there has been a 22 percent reduction in disparity for nonprison/prison outcomes and a 60 percent reduction in sentencing inequality for overall sentence lengths for persons of different races and ethnicities convicted of identical offenses. Reductions in disparities according to racial factors also occurred over time in Pennsylvania among convicted felons. However, disparities in types of sentences and sentence lengths attributable to extralegal factors such as race, gender, or socioeconomic status continue to be found in various jurisdictions, including federal courts (ibid.).

U.S. Supreme Court General Sentencing Cases

Sentencing Decision-Making

Simpson v. United States, 435 U.S. 6, 98 S. Ct. 909 (1978)

Simpson and his brother were charged in federal court in Kentucky with two separate bank robberies in which dangerous weapons were used. They were convicted of a bank robbery charge (including the possession of a dangerous weapon) and also of the charge of using a dangerous weapon during the commission of a felony. Thus, the district judge sentenced Simpson to two consecutive prison terms for each of the statute violations. Simpson appealed. The U.S. Supreme Court reversed Simpson's conviction, declaring that sentence enhancements may not be permitted where different offenses are alleged and have stemmed from the same crime. In this case, there was a single transaction of "bank robbery with firearms." The prosecution added a second statute governing the use of weapons during the commission of felonies. The significance of the U.S. Supreme

Court decision is that sentences may not be compounded or enhanced through the misapplication of two or more different statutes. Thus, where a prosecution grows out of a single transaction, such as bank robbery with firearms, defendants may not be sentenced according to two or more different statutes covering different dimensions of the offense.

Ake v. Oklahoma, 470 U.S. 68, 105 S. Ct. 1087 (1985)

Ake was charged with two counts of first-degree murder. He declared that he was indigent, and counsel was appointed for him. He also requested the assistance of a competent psychiatrist to determine whether he was sane. Ake's defense was that he was insane, and thus it would be the state's obligation to furnish him with a psychiatrist to examine him and make a determination. A psychiatrist did so and found Ake to be incompetent to stand trial. He was confined in a mental hospital for a period of time. After 6 weeks of treatment, he was found to be competent to stand trial. His attorney asked for another psychiatric evaluation, independent of the state-provided one, but the judge denied that request, claiming the expense to be prohibitive. Ake was convicted. No testimony was given by psychiatrists during the sentencing phase of his trial. The death penalty was imposed when the state psychiatrist indicated that Ake's future dangerousness warranted it. Ake appealed. The U.S. Supreme Court reversed his conviction, holding that when a defendant has made a preliminary showing that his sanity at the time of the offense is likely to be a significant factor, the state must provide access to a psychiatrist's assistance on the issue if the defendant cannot otherwise afford one.

McMillan v. Pennsylvania, 477 U.S. 79, 106 S. Ct. 2411 (1986)

Dynel McMillan was convicted of aggravated assault for shooting a man in the right buttock during an argument over a debt. Under Pennsylvania's Mandatory Minimum Sentencing Act of 1982, anyone convicted of certain felonies and who "visibly possesses a firearm" during the commission of a felony is subject to a mandatory minimum sentence of five years. This fact may be determined by a preponderance of the evidence. McMillan appealed the conviction and five-year mandatory minimum sentence, arguing that such an issue ought to be decided by a jury trial, that the standard of proof should not be "preponderance of the evidence" but rather, "beyond a reasonable doubt," and that the act itself was invalid. The U.S. Supreme Court rejected all of McMillan's claims. First, the Court noted, the five-year mandatory minimum sentence is a *sentencing issue,* not a *jury issue.* Thus, a jury trial is not necessary for this factual determination. Further, because it is a sentencing issue, the standard of proof may be "preponderance of the evidence." The U.S. Supreme Court upheld the constitutionality of the mandatory minimum sentencing law.

Harmelin v. Michigan, 501 U.S. 957, 111 S. Ct. 2680 (1991)

Harmelin, a convicted drug dealer, was apprehended with 672 grams of cocaine. He was convicted, and a mandatory sentence of life imprisonment was imposed. Harmelin challenged the constitutionality of this sentence and also declared that it was disproportional to the crime. The U.S. Supreme Court disagreed and let his conviction and sentence stand, believing them not to have violated any of Harmelin's constitutional rights.

Deal v. United States, 508 U.S. 129, 113 S. Ct. 1993 (1993)

Deal was convicted of six different bank robberies. He was also convicted of possessing and using a firearm in each of the six robberies. These convictions yielded sentences of twenty years and five years for each of the offenses, to run consecutively. Deal appealed, arguing that the convictions and sentences were excessive. The U.S. Supreme Court upheld the constitutionality of the 105-year sentence, saying that it is not glaringly unjust to refuse to give the offender a lesser sentence merely because he escaped apprehension and conviction until the sixth crime had been committed. Thus, convicted offenders may incur sentence enhancements for various crimes they have committed but for which they have not been caught or convicted.

Smith v. United States, 508 U.S. 223, 113 S. Ct. 2050 (1993)

Smith was convicted in federal court of using a firearm during a drug sale. Essentially, he had traded a firearm for narcotics. The firearm was treated as a part of a drug transaction for purposes of sentence enhancement (for example, if a person uses a gun, he does two years in prison). Smith appealed, alleging that he wasn't "using" the firearm but rather "trading" it. The U.S. Supreme Court heard his case and upheld his conviction with the enhancement for use of the firearm by declaring that "use" and "in relation to" are for all intents and purposes the same within the meaning of the statute.

United States v. Dunnigan, 507 U.S. 87, 113 S. Ct. 1111 (1993)

Dunnigan was accused of conspiracy to distribute cocaine. She testified on her own behalf, but it was subsequently determined that she had committed perjury during her testimony. She was convicted, and the judge enhanced her sentence because of her perjury. Dunnigan appealed, arguing that her testimony was self-incriminating and that she should not be further punished because of her perjury statements. The U.S. Supreme Court disagreed and upheld her sentence enhancement. Under the U.S. Sentencing Commission Guidelines, if the court finds that the defendant committed perjury at the trial, the sentence can be enhanced.

Wisconsin v. Mitchell, 508 U.S. 476, 113 S. Ct. 2194 (1993)

Mitchell was convicted of aggravated battery and theft, and his sentence was enhanced under a Wisconsin statute because he targeted his victim by reason of the victim's race. Mitchell appealed, arguing that he should not be punished more because he had selected a person of a particular race to attack. Thus, Mitchell declared, the Wisconsin statute was unconstitutional because it violated his free speech rights. The U.S. Supreme Court heard Mitchell's case and upheld the constitutionality of the Wisconsin statute, whereby offenders may have their sentences enhanced if it is proved that they attacked their victim because of the victim's race.

Custis v. United States, 511 U.S. 485, 114 S. Ct. 1732 (1994)

Custis was convicted in federal court for possession of firearms and cocaine. He had three previous state convictions, and under the Armed Career Criminal Act, he received an enhanced sentence. He appealed, contending that the convictions in Maryland had been the result of ineffective assistance of counsel. Thus his federal sentence should not have been enhanced. The U.S. Supreme Court upheld his conviction and sentence enhancements, noting that Custis had not raised the issue of attorney competence at either of his previous Maryland convictions. Furthermore, he had plea-bargained and knowingly and intelligently waived his rights when entering guilty pleas. Thus, the Court declared, only if Custis had been convicted and denied counsel at those times could he challenge such convictions. Defendants in federal proceedings have no right collaterally to attack the validity of previous state convictions used to enhance their sentences under the Armed Career Criminal Act. However, if Custis wished to challenge his state convictions, he could do so not in federal court but rather in state court through federal habeas corpus review.

United States v. Granderson, 511 U.S. 39, 114 S. Ct. 1259 (1994)

Granderson, a letter carrier for the U.S. Postal Service, was convicted of destruction of mail and sentenced to five years' probation, although the U.S. Sentencing Guidelines provided for a 0- to 6-month incarcerative term. Subsequently, Granderson's probation was revoked when it was discovered that he possessed a controlled substance. U.S.C. Section 3565(a) of Title 18 (U.S. Code 2007), the criminal code, provides that one-third of the original sentence should be imposed as a punishment when revoking a federal probation. Thus, relying on the five-year (60-month) probationary term, the judge sentenced Granderson to 20 months of imprisonment. Granderson appealed, contending that the U.S. Sentencing Guidelines govern incarcerative terms, not probationary sentences. A circuit court of appeals reversed his sentence and ordered Granderson released. Its logic was that the original sentence had been the U.S. Sentencing Guidelines sentence of 0 to 6 months, not the original probationary sentence. Because Granderson had already served 11 months of imprisonment at the time of the appellate decision, his immediate release was ordered. The government appealed, and the U.S. Supreme Court heard the case. The Court upheld the circuit court of appeals, concluding that indeed, the U.S. Sentencing Guidelines governed this situation, not the probationary sentence imposed by the federal judge.

Koon v. United States, 518 U.S. 81, 116 S. Ct. 2035 (1996)

Police officers Koon and Powell were convicted in federal court of violating the constitutional rights of a motorist, King, under color of law during an arrest, and sentenced to 30 months' imprisonment. The U.S. district court trial judge used U.S. Sentencing Guidelines and justified a downward departure of eight offense levels from "27" to "19," to arrive at a 30- to 37-month sentence. The government appealed, contending that a downward departure of eight offense levels from "27" was an abuse of judicial discretion and that the factors cited for the downward departure were not statutory. An original offense seriousness level of "27" would have meant imposing a sentence of 70 to 87 months. The Ninth Circuit Court of Appeals rejected all of the trial court's reasons for the downward departure, and Koon and Powell petitioned the U.S. Supreme Court. The U.S. Supreme Court upheld the circuit court of appeals in part and reversed it in part. Specifically, the Court said that the primary question to be answered on appeal is whether the trial judge abused his discretion by the downward departure in sentencing. The reasons given by the trial judge for the downward departure were that (1) the victim's misconduct provoked police use of force, (2) Koon and Powell had been subjected to successive state and federal criminal prosecutions, (3) Koon and Powell posed a low risk of recidivism, (4) Koon and Powell would probably lose their jobs and be precluded from employment in law enforcement, and (5) Koon and Powell would be unusually susceptible to abuse in prison.

The U.S. Supreme Court concluded that a five-level downward departure based on the victim's misconduct, which had provoked officer use of force, was justified, because victim misconduct is an encouraged (by the U.S. Sentencing Commission) basis for a guideline departure. The Court said that the remaining three-level departure was an abuse of judicial discretion. Federal district judges may not consider a convicted offender's career loss as a downward departure factor. Furthermore, trial judges may not consider an offender's low likelihood of recidivism, because that factor is already incorporated into the Criminal History Category in the sentencing guideline table. Considering that factor to justify a downward departure, therefore, would be tantamount to counting the factor twice. The Court upheld the trial judge's reliance on the offenders' susceptibility to prison abuse and the burdens of successive state and federal prosecutions, however. The U.S. Supreme Court remanded the case to the district court, where a new sentence could be determined. Thus, a new offense level must be chosen on the basis of the victim's own misconduct, which provoked the officers, and where offender susceptibility to prison abuse and the burden of successive state and federal prosecutions could be considered. The significance of this case for criminal justice is that specific factors are identified by the U.S. Supreme Court to guide federal judges in imposing sentences on police officers convicted of misconduct and violating citizen rights under color of law. Victim response that provokes police use of force, an officer's susceptibility to abuse in prison, and the burden of successive state and federal prosecutions are acceptable factors to be considered to justify downward departures in offense seriousness, whereas low recidivism potential and loss of employment opportunity in law enforcement are not legitimate factors justifying downward departure in offense seriousness.

Melendez v. United States, 518 U.S. 120, 116 S. Ct. 2057 (1996)

Melendez was convicted of conspiring to distribute cocaine, a crime carrying a statutory minimum sentence of ten years' imprisonment. However, in a plea agreement with the government, Melendez agreed to furnish valuable information leading to the arrest and conviction of other drug dealers. The government described the assistance rendered by Melendez to the court and recommended a lesser sentence than that provided under the sentencing guidelines. Under the sentencing guidelines, Melendez's sentence would have been from 135 to 168 months, and the government moved the court to grant a downward departure from that higher range. However, the government did not move to have the court reduce Melendez's sentence below the mandatory minimum of 120 months, or ten years. The federal district judge imposed the statutory minimum ten-year sentence, and Melendez appealed, contending that the substantial assistance he had rendered to the government and their implied promise of a downward departure should be honored. Melendez had expected that his sentence would be less than the statutory ten-year minimum. The U.S. Supreme Court heard the case and affirmed the lower-court decision, holding that the district court lacked the authority to impose less than the minimum ten-year mandatory sentence where the government did not bring a motion requesting or authorizing such a departure below the ten-year minimum sentence based on substantial assistance from Melendez. Furthermore, the Court held that a motion by the government for departure from applicable guidelines based on substantial assistance does not authorize departure from statutory minimum sentences.

O'Dell v. Netherland, 521 U.S. 151, 117 S. Ct. 1969 (1997)

O'Dell was convicted of capital murder, rape, and sodomy in the Virginia case of Helen Schartner, whose body was found in February 1985. O'Dell's conviction occurred in 1988. At O'Dell's sentencing hearing, the state argued that O'Dell's future dangerousness should be considered in whether he should be given the death penalty. O'Dell sought to have the judge instruct the jury about his parole ineligibility if he should be given a life sentence, but the judge refused to give the jury such an instruction. The jury imposed the death penalty, and the conviction and sentence were upheld by the Virginia Supreme Court. Subsequently, a U.S. Supreme Court case was decided in 1994 that entitled death penalty–eligible offenders the right to have the jury informed that the offender is not parole-eligible if a life sentence is imposed. O'Dell filed a habeas corpus appeal with the U.S. Supreme Court, contending that the judge had violated his Fourteenth Amendment due-process right by failing to inform the sentencing jury about his parole ineligibility, particularly when the state introduced evidence about his future dangerousness insofar as making a decision about the death penalty was concerned. The Court heard O'Dell's appeal and affirmed the Virginia Supreme Court, holding that as the *Simmons* case was new and had occurred after O'Dell's conviction, it could not, therefore, be used to disturb O'Dell's death sentence, which had been final for six years prior to *Simmons* being decided. Thus, *Simmons* could not be made retroactively applicable to O'Dell's conviction and death sentence.

United States v. Gonzales, 520 U.S. 1, 117 S. Ct. 1032 (1997)

Gonzales, Hernandez-Diaz, and Perez were convicted in a New Mexico state court on drug-trafficking crimes and firearms violations following a drug sting operation, and the trial court sentenced them to a prison term of thirteen to seventeen years. Subsequently, they were convicted in federal court on charges arising from the same drug-trafficking offenses, including a mandatory five-year federal prison term to be served consecutively with the state and federal sentences. The district court also directed that the drug sentences run concurrently with the state sentences being served. The Tenth Circuit Court of Appeals vacated these offenders' federal sentences for the firearms violations and drug charges, holding that the federal sentences, including the mandatory five-year firearms sentence, should have run concurrently with the state sentences. This finding was based on the assumption that mandatory sentences for violating federal laws were applicable only to federal and not state crimes. The government appealed, and the U.S. Supreme Court heard the case. The Court reversed the circuit court, holding that a mandatory five-year sentence for firearms use in violation of a federal criminal statute is not limited to federal sentences but is also applicable to state sentences. Thus, U.S. district courts may impose mandatory sentences for firearms use, and these sentences may run consecutively with state sentences. Furthermore, federal courts may order drug-trafficking convictions to run concurrently or consecutively with state-imposed sentences arising from the same crimes.

Muscarello v. United States, 524 U.S. 125, 118 S. Ct. 1911 (1998)

Muscarello was convicted of unlawfully selling marijuana, which he carried in his truck to the place of the sale. He also possessed a firearm, which was locked in his glove compartment. He was found guilty of carrying a firearm during the commission of a drug crime, and a mandatory five-year term was added to his sentence for drug possession. Muscarello sought to overturn his conviction on the weapons charge, as he alleged that he was not physically carrying the weapon when arrested. A U.S. district court judge granted Muscarello's motion to quash his conviction of carrying a firearm during and in relation to drug trafficking, but the Fifth Circuit Court of Appeals reversed and remanded. The case was appealed to the U.S. Supreme Court, which affirmed Muscarello's weapons conviction. The Court held that the phrase "carries a firearm" is not limited to carrying of firearms on one's person, but also applies to a person who knowingly possesses and conveys firearms in a vehicle that the person accompanies. Thus, carrying a firearm in the glove compartment of a truck while transporting drugs was within the "carrying a firearm" statute. Even firearms locked in one's trunk are considered "carrying a firearm" for purposes of charging a separate offense and imposing a mandatory penalty.

Jones v. United States, 526 U.S. 227, 119 S. Ct. 1215 (1999)

Jones and two others carjacked an automobile by force and intimidation. Eventually they were apprehended by police, and Jones was indicted under 18 U.S.C. 2119(1), which provided upon conviction for a sentence of not more than fifteen years. However, following Jones's trial, he was sentenced to twenty-five years and appealed, contending that other carjacking elements under 18 U.S.C. 2119 were not charged in the indictment and thus the sentence was excessive. The U.S. Supreme Court heard Jones's appeal and examined the provisions of 18 U.S.C. 2119, which provides that a person possessing a firearm who takes a motor vehicle from the person or presence of another by force and violence or by intimidation shall (1) be imprisoned not more than fifteen years, (2) if serious bodily injury results, be imprisoned not more than twenty-five years, and (3) if death results, be imprisoned for any number of years up to life. The indictment made no reference to Section 2119's numbered subsections. Furthermore, Jones was told at his arraignment that he faced a maximum fifteen-year sentence for carjacking, and that the jury instructions at his trial defined that offense only by referencing 18 U.S.C. 2119(1). The U.S. Supreme Court reversed Jones's conviction, holding that the additional subsections (2) and (3) of 18 U.S.C. 2119 constituted separate offenses, all elements of which must be proved beyond a reasonable doubt. As these offenses were not mentioned in the indictment, it was improper for the trial judge to sentence Jones to any term in excess of fifteen years. The Court stressed that under the existing carjacking statute, 18 U.S.C. 2119, three distinct offenses are outlined rather than a single offense with a choice of three maximum penalties. The Supreme Court said, "We think the better reading is of three distinct offenses, particularly in light of the rule that any interpretive uncertainty should be resolved to avoid serious questions about the statute's constitutionality."

United States v. Johnson, 529 U.S. 53, 120 S. Ct. 1114 (2000)

Johnson was convicted of multiple drug and firearms felonies in 1990. A sentence of 171 months was imposed, consisting of three concurrent 51-month terms, to be followed by two consecutive 60-month terms. In addition, a three-year mandatory term of supervised release was ordered to be served for the drug possession offenses. After Johnson had served several years in prison, two of his convictions were held to be invalid. As a result, he was ordered to be set free, as he had served two and a half years too much prison time. Nevertheless, a three-year term of supervised release was yet to be served on the remaining conviction. Johnson filed a motion to reduce his supervised release time by the amount of extra prison time he had served. The motion was denied in a federal district court, but the Sixth Circuit Court reversed and granted the motion. The government appealed and the U.S. Supreme Court heard the case. The Court reversed the Sixth Circuit, holding that the term of Johnson's supervised release commenced upon his actual release from prison, not on the date when he should have been released. The Supreme Court said that supervised release periods do not run while a prisoner remains in the custody of the Bureau of Prisons. The Court added, however, that the trial court was at liberty, "as it sees fit," to modify or terminate Johnson's supervised release obligations after one year of completed service according to 18 U.S.C. Section 3583(e)(1).

Penry v. Johnson, 532 U.S. 782, 121 S. Ct. 1910 (2001)

Penry was convicted of first-degree murder in 1989 in a Texas court and sentenced to death. However, the conviction was overturned because it violated the Eighth Amendment. Penry was retried in 1990 and again found guilty of capital murder. During the penalty phase of the proceedings, the defense put on extensive evidence of Penry's mental impairments and childhood abuse. Prosecutors introduced and read into the record over a defense objection a 1977 psychiatric evaluation of Penry prepared at his attorney's request in another court matter unrelated to the murder at issue. The report concluded in part that if Penry were released, he would be dangerous to others. Subsequently, the judge gave the jury detailed instructions including a consideration of mitigating circumstances, and Penry was again sentenced to death. However, the judge provided jurors a document with the original special issues from Penry's first trial. Again a question arose about whether the judge had adequately permitted the jury to consider and give effect to the particular mitigating evidence.

Penry appealed through a habeas corpus action, claiming in part that the introduction into evidence of his earlier psychiatric report was a violation of his Fifth Amendment right against self-incrimination. Further, Penry contended that the judge's jury instructions were inadequate because they did not permit the jury to consider and give effect to his particular mitigating evidence. The state denied Penry habeas corpus relief, and Penry appealed to the U.S. District Court, which affirmed the Texas trial court. An appeal to the circuit court of appeals resulted in a similar affirmation of the sentence, and Penry appealed to the U.S. Supreme Court seeking habeas corpus relief. The Supreme Court heard the case and held that the introduction of the earlier psychiatric examination during Penry's sentencing phase did not warrant habeas corpus relief. However, the Court also held that the judge's instructions on mitigating circumstances failed to provide the jury with a vehicle to give effect to mitigating circumstances of mental retardation and childhood abuse as required by the Eighth and Fourteenth Amendments. Thus, the U.S. Supreme Court reversed in part, and affirmed in part, the decision of the trial court.

Harris v. United States, 536 U.S. 545, 122 S. Ct. 2406 (2002)

Harris was convicted in a U.S. district court of selling narcotics. Harris ran a pawnshop and carried an unconcealed semiautomatic pistol at his side during working hours. Although he was not charged with brandishing a firearm during the act of selling narcotics, the judge considered "brandishing" a firearm in relation to a drug-trafficking offense as a sentencing factor and imposed a mandatory minimum sentence of seven years. Harris objected, contending that "brandishing" a firearm was an element of a separate statutory offense for which he was neither indicted nor convicted. The district court judge and the Fourth Circuit rejected Harris's argument and upheld his sentence. The U.S. Supreme Court heard the case and affirmed, holding that the possession of a firearm during the commission of a criminal offense was a sentencing factor rather than an element of a crime, and that allowing the judge to find that factor did not violate Harris's constitutional rights.

Blakely v. Washington, 542 U.S. 296, 124 S. Ct. 2531 (2004)

Pursuant to a plea bargain agreement in Washington, Ralph Blakely pleaded guilty to kidnapping his estranged wife and was convicted of second-degree kidnapping involving domestic violence and the use of a firearm. In his plea agreement, Blakely admitted to the kidnapping and to limited facts that supported a maximum sentence of 53 months under Washington's guidelines sentencing scheme. However, the judge rejected the prosecutor's recommended 49- to 53-month sentence and instead imposed an exceptional sentence of 90 months, 37 months longer than contemplated by the plea agreement. The judge justified his departure because of "deliberate cruelty" exhibited by Blakely, because the maximum sentence is up to ten years, and because "deliberate cruelty" is an aggravating factor under Washington's Sentencing Reform Act. Blakely appealed, contending that this sentencing procedure denied him the right to have a jury determine all facts legally essential to his sentence. The Washington Supreme Court denied Blakely's appeal, and the case was heard by the U.S. Supreme Court. The Court invalidated Blakely's 90-month sentence, holding that because the facts supporting Blakely's exceptional sentence were neither admitted in the plea agreement nor found by a jury, the sentence violated his Sixth Amendment right to a trial by jury. The Supreme Court elaborated, stating that the trial judge could not have imposed the exceptional 90-month sentence solely on the basis of the facts admitted in the guilty plea. According to U.S. Supreme Court precedent, statutory maximum sentences are maximum sentences that judges may impose solely on the basis of the facts reflected in a jury verdict or admitted by the defendant. The Court further noted that this decision does not question Washington's sentencing guidelines scheme or its constitutionality. Rather, it reflects the scope of judicial discretion in sentencing under the circumstances of this case.

Deck v. Missouri, 544 U.S. 622, 125 S. Ct. 2007 (2005)

Carman Deck was convicted of first-degree murder in a Missouri court. During the sentencing phase, Deck was shackled in leg irons, handcuffs, and a belly chain, in front of the jury, and the death penalty was imposed. Deck appealed, and the death sentence was set aside by the Missouri Supreme Court. Deck was re-sentenced, again shackled in leg irons, handcuffs, and a belly chain, in front of a new jury, and the Missouri Supreme Court affirmed the sentence. Deck appealed to the U.S. Supreme Court, and it heard the case. The Court reversed the conviction and remanded the case back to the trial court for new proceedings. The U.S. Supreme Court held that the due process clause prohibits routine use of physical restraints visible to the jury during the guilt phase of criminal proceedings. Courts may not routinely place defendants in visible restraints during the penalty phase of capital proceedings. Shackling in this case was not shown to be specifically justified by the circumstances, and thus this offended due process.

Shepard v. United States, 544 U.S. 13, 125 S. Ct. 1254 (2005)

Reginald Shepard pleaded guilty to and was convicted of being a felon in possession of a firearm. Under the U.S. Sentencing Guidelines, Shepard's sentence would be 30 to 37 months, but the government sought a fifteen-year mandatory minimum sentence under the Armed Career Criminal Act (ACCA) in view of the fact that Shepard had three prior convictions for burglary. The government claimed that Shepard's burglaries were "generic burglaries," as defined under the ACCA, which defines generic burglaries as those committed in a building or enclosed space, thus constituting violent crimes. Shepard's burglary convictions occurred in Massachusetts, and Massachusetts has a broad range of burglary categories that render them nongeneric burglaries.

The government failed to show the district court evidence that Shepard's burglaries were generic burglaries according to the ACCA, and the court refused to impose the fifteen-year mandatory minimum sentence. The government appealed, and the First Circuit Court of Appeals reversed the district court. Shepard appealed to the U.S. Supreme Court, which heard the case. The Court reversed the appellate court, holding that the government had failed to show that Shepard's burglaries were generic in the context of the ACCA, and furthermore, that it would be improper for a sentencing court to look to police reports in making a "generic burglary" decision under the ACCA as the government had earlier requested.

Brown v. Sanders, ___U.S.___, 126 S. Ct. 884 (2006)

Sanders was convicted of first-degree murder in California, as well as robbery, burglary, and attempted robbery. In a bifurcated trial, the jury deliberated and found four special circumstances, each of which would render Sanders eligible for the death penalty. The jury recommended the death penalty, and it was imposed. Later, on appeal, Sanders argued that two of the factors were invalid, and an appellate court agreed. Sanders further argued that considering invalid aggravating factors as special circumstances added an improper element of aggravation to jury deliberations concerning whether the death penalty should be imposed. The Ninth Circuit Court of Appeals reversed the death sentence, and the state appealed. The U.S. Supreme Court heard the case and reversed the Ninth Circuit, holding that the fact that two of the four eligibility factors found by the jury, any one of which would have rendered Sanders eligible for the death penalty, were determined to be invalid did not affect the constitutionality of the death sentence ultimately imposed. No improper element of aggravation occurred as a result of these factors that were later determined to be invalid.

The U.S. Sentencing Guidelines

Mistretta v. United States, 488 U.S. 361, 109 S. Ct. 647 (1989)

Mistretta was convicted of selling cocaine. The U.S. Sentencing Guidelines were officially in effect after November 1, 1987, and Mistretta's criminal acts and conviction occurred after that date; thus he was subject to guidelines-based sentencing rather than indeterminate sentencing, which the federal district courts had previously followed. Under the former sentencing scheme, Mistretta might have been granted probation. However, the new guidelines greatly restricted the use of probation as a sentence in federal courts, and thus Mistretta's sentence involved serving an amount of time in prison. Mistretta appealed his conviction, arguing that the new guidelines violated the separation-of-powers doctrine, as several federal judges were members of the U.S. Sentencing Commission and helped to formulate laws and punishments, an exclusive function of Congress. The U.S. Supreme Court upheld Mistretta's conviction and declared the new guidelines to be constitutional, not in violation of the separation-of-powers doctrine.

Stinson v. United States, 508 U.S. 36, 113 S. Ct. 1913 (1993)

Stinson pleaded guilty to a five-count indictment resulting from a bank robbery. He was sentenced according to the U.S. Sentencing Guidelines and the statutory language that the instant offense of conviction be a crime of violence. Later, the statutory language was changed to expressly exclude the felon-in-possession offense from the crime-of-violence definition. The sentencing court ignored that language change, however, and sentenced Stinson to the more serious penalty range. Stinson appealed, and the U.S. Supreme Court overturned his sentence, saying that the lower court had erred when it ignored the Sentencing Commission language change. Such commentary by the Sentencing Commission is binding on federal court judges.

Buford v. United States, 532 U.S. 59, 121 S. Ct. 1276 (2001)

Paula Buford was convicted of armed bank robbery and sentenced to 188 months after a finding by the federal district court judge that she was a career offender. Buford had five prior convictions, four relating to a series of gas station robberies. The fifth conviction was for a drug offense. The sentencing judge consolidated these prior convictions in determining whether Buford was a career offender and should receive the maximum sentence under the U.S. Sentencing Guidelines. Buford challenged the consolidation of these convictions, in which the drug offense was included in order to determine her career offender status. Buford did not contest the factual circumstances of each of the prior convictions. State criminal courts in Wisconsin had previously sentenced Buford to three prison terms for the five crimes (six years for the drug crime, twelve years for two robberies, and fifteen years for the other two robberies), and the courts had ordered that all three sentences run concurrently. However, she raised a procedural issue that would seek to clarify the consolidation-related legal principles and bring consistency to her sentence. Thus, she challenged the right of the appellate court to review her sentence deferentially rather than de novo. The U.S. Supreme Court heard the case and affirmed the right of the appellate court to review Buford's case deferentially. Buford's 188-month sentence remained unchanged.

United States v. Ruiz, 536 U.S. 622, 122 S. Ct. 2450 (2002)

Ruiz was convicted in a U.S. district court of importing marijuana. The U.S. Attorney's Office attempted to formulate a plea agreement with Ruiz wherein she would plead guilty, waive indictment and a trial, as well as an appeal, in exchange for a reduced sentence recommendation. However, the prosecutor specified that Ruiz must waive her right to any impeachment information relating to any informants or other witnesses, as well as information supporting any affirmative defense she might raise if the case were to go to trial. Ruiz refused to waive that right, although she subsequently pleaded guilty absent a plea agreement. At sentencing, she asked the judge to grant her the same reduced sentence that the government had offered if she had accepted the plea agreement. The prosecutor opposed her request, and it was denied. The Ninth Circuit vacated Ruiz's sentence, and the government appealed to the U.S. Supreme Court, which heard the case. The Court reversed the Ninth Circuit ruling and reinstated Ruiz's conviction, holding that the Constitution does not require the government to disclose impeachment information prior to entering into a plea agreement with a criminal defendant. Furthermore, a plea agreement requiring the defendant to waive her right to receive information from the government relating to any affirmative defense she would raise at trial does not violate the Constitution.

United States v. Booker, 543 U.S. 220, 125 S. Ct. 738 (2005)

Booker and another defendant in an unrelated case, Fanfan, were convicted of cocaine distribution in separate jury trials in different federal district courts. In Booker's case, a sentence of twenty-one years and 10 months was prescribed for his conviction offense by the U.S. Sentencing Guidelines. However, during the sentencing hearing, the judge found additional facts by a preponderance of the evidence to support a sentence of from 360 months to life and gave Booker a thirty-year sentence. In Fanfan's case, a judge made a similar finding and imposed a harsher sentence, sixteen years instead of the six years prescribed by the U.S. Sentencing Guidelines. Both cases were appealed, Booker's to the 7th Circuit and Fanfan's to the 1st Circuit. Both circuit courts overturned these convictions, holding that any fact(s) that increase the penalty for a crime beyond the prescribed statutory maximum must be submitted to a jury and proved beyond a reasonable doubt. The government appealed both cases, and the U.S. Supreme Court heard them. The Court affirmed the circuit court decisions and vacated the enhanced sentences for both Booker and Fanfan. The Court held that the federal sentencing guidelines are subject to Sixth Amendment jury trial requirements, and that if a judge authorizes a punishment on the finding of a fact, that fact, no matter how the judge labels it, must be found by a jury beyond a reasonable doubt.

Sex Offender Laws

Kansas v. Hendricks, 521 U.S. 346, 117 S. Ct. 2072 (1997)

Hendricks was convicted in 1984 of sexually molesting two thirteen-year-old boys. Hendricks had a lengthy history of child sexual abuse convictions. In 1994, Hendricks was scheduled to be released from prison to a halfway house, but Kansas had recently enacted the Sexually Violent Predator Act, which establishes procedures for the civil commitment of persons who, because of a mental abnormality or a personality disorder, are likely to engage in predatory acts of sexual violence. Kansas thus invoked the act against Hendricks and ordered his civil commitment to a mental hospital for an indeterminate period. Hendricks challenged the civil commitment on several grounds, including double jeopardy, the prohibited application of ex post facto laws, and a violation of his substantive due-process rights. The Kansas Supreme Court invalidated the act, finding that the precommitment condition of a mental abnormality did not satisfy what it perceived to be the substantive due-process requirement that involuntary civil commitment must be predicated on a mental illness finding. It did not address Hendricks's double jeopardy or ex post facto claims. Kansas officials appealed to the U.S. Supreme Court, which heard the case. The Court reversed the Kansas Supreme Court, holding that the act's definition of mental abnormality satisfies "substantive" due-process requirements. Furthermore, the act does not violate Hendricks's rights against double jeopardy or its ban on ex post facto lawmaking, as the act does not establish criminal proceedings, and involuntary confinement under it is not punishment in any criminal context.

Seling v. Young, 531 U.S. 250, 121 S. Ct. 727 (2001)

Andre Young was convicted of six rapes over three decades and was scheduled for release from prison in October 1990 in Washington State. One day prior to his release, the state filed a petition to commit Young as a sexually violent offender. A commitment hearing was held, and it was determined that Young posed a threat as a sexually violent offender under Washington State's Community Protection Act of 1990, which authorizes civil commitment of such offenders. Young appealed, arguing that his civil commitment constituted double jeopardy and that the law was unconstitutional. Furthermore, Young alleged that the conditions of his confinement were incompatible with rehabilitation and too restrictive. Washington State courts rejected his arguments, and he appealed to the U.S. Supreme Court, which heard the case. The Court upheld Young's civil commitment and rejected his double jeopardy argument. It further held that the Washington State law was constitutional. The Court did not address whether the mental health center in which Young was being housed and treated was operating properly. Rather, the Court left that determination to the Washington State courts. The U.S. Supreme Court noted that offenders have a cause of action at the state level if the mental health center fails to fulfill its statutory duty to care adequately and to provide individualized treatment for sex offenders.

Kansas v. Crane, 536 U.S. 407, 122 S. Ct. 867 (2002)

Michael Crane was convicted of lewd and lascivious behavior and pleaded guilty to aggravated sexual battery for two incidents occurring in 1993. He exposed himself to a tanning salon attendant and a video store clerk. In the case of the video store clerk, he demanded oral sex and threatened to rape her. Subsequently, the state court evaluated Crane and adjudicated him a sexual predator under Kansas's Sexually Violent Predator Act (SVPA). That act permits the civil detention of a person convicted of any of several enumerated sexual offenses, if it is proven beyond a reasonable doubt that the person suffers from a mental abnormality, a disorder affecting emotional or volitional capacity that predisposes the person to commit sexually violent acts or that makes the person likely to engage in repeated acts of sexual violence. Crane was committed to civil custody. Crane appealed, and the Kansas Supreme Court reversed the civil commitment of Crane, holding that the SVPA requires that the state must prove that the defendant cannot control his or her dangerous behavior, and that the trial court had made no such finding. Kansas appealed to the U.S. Supreme Court, which heard the case. The U.S. Supreme Court reversed the Kansas Supreme Court and held that (1) the SVPA does not require the state to prove the offender's total or complete lack of control over his or her dangerous behavior, and that (2) the federal constitution does not allow civil commitment under the act without any lack of control determination. The significance of the U.S. Supreme Court action is that a state must show that a defendant is likely to engage in sexually violent conduct in the future, but not in any absolute sense. There is no rule obligating the state to prove that any defendant must lack total control regarding violent sexual conduct. Rather, the phrase stressed is that the state must demonstrate that the defendant possesses an abnormality or disorder that makes it difficult, if not impossible, to control the dangerous behavior (compare *Kansas v. Hendricks* [1997]).

Stogner v. California, 539 U.S. 607, 123 S. Ct. 2446 (2003)

In 1998, a California jury indicted Marion Stogner on several counts of sex-related child abuse committed several decades earlier, from 1955 through 1973. The statute of limitations on those crimes was three years during that particular time interval. However, California enacted an ex post facto statute in 1993 governing sex-related offenses that was amended with additional provisions in 1996. The new law provided for prosecutions of sex-related crimes in which the statute of limitations had already expired, provided that authorities prosecuted defendants within one year following a victim's first complaint to police of the crime. Stogner moved to dismiss the complaint on grounds that the ex post facto nature of the new law was unconstitutional. The trial court agreed and dismissed the complaint. However, a California appeals court reversed, thus permitting Stogner's prosecution for these prior crimes. Stogner persisted in his appeal to the U.S. Supreme Court, which heard his case. The Court reversed the California court, holding that California's law subjects individuals such as Stogner to prosecution long after the state has, in effect, granted amnesty, telling them that they are at liberty to return to their country.

Reconvictions and Resentencing

North Carolina v. Pearce, 395 U.S. 711, 89 S. Ct. 2072 (1969)

Pearce was convicted of assault with intent to commit rape and was sentenced to twelve to fifteen years. Several years later he filed a habeas corpus petition, alleging that an involuntary confession had been admitted as evidence against him at his trial. He was subsequently retried, was convicted, and this time was sentenced to eight years. This sentence, when added to the time he had already spent in prison, amounted to a term longer than his original sentence. Pearce appealed, arguing that the additional time imposed was a punishment for having his original conviction set aside. The U.S. Supreme Court heard this appeal and set aside the sentence, saying that although nothing prohibits judges from imposing harsher sentences in retrials than the sentences imposed in earlier trials, constitutional guarantees obligate the government to give full credit of previous time served against the new sentence. The U.S. Supreme Court also said that any unexplained additional punishment is a violation of due process.

Bullington v. Missouri, 451 U.S. 430, 101 S. Ct. 1852 (1981)

Bullington was charged with capital murder. His case was heard by a jury, which found him guilty. In the sentencing phase, the jury had to decide between the death penalty and life imprisonment as a punishment, and they recommended the latter. Subsequently, Bullington's conviction was reversed and a new trial resulted. Bullington was again convicted. This time, the jury decided in favor of the death penalty. Bullington appealed, and the U.S. Supreme Court heard his case. It set his death penalty sentence aside, saying that the first jury's refusal to impose the death penalty was an acquittal for that form of punishment. A subsequent trial cannot result in a punishment greater than that imposed by the first in a capital case (compare *Arizona v. Rumsey* [1984] *and Caspari v. Bohlen* [1984]).

Arizona v. Rumsey, 467 U.S. 203, 104 S. Ct. 2305 (1984)

Rumsey, convicted of murder, was sentenced to life imprisonment by the judge. His case was overturned and set for retrial. A new trial also resulted in a conviction for murder. This time the death penalty was imposed by the judge, who cited aggravating factors that outweighed mitigating ones. Rumsey appealed on the grounds that the second penalty was more severe than the first. The U.S. Supreme Court overturned the death penalty sentence, saying that in capital cases in resentencing proceedings, the punishment cannot be greater than that imposed in the first sentencing. Thus, states cannot impose the death penalty on convicted murderers following prior trials in which life imprisonment was imposed. The U.S. Supreme Court declared that the first judge's refusal to impose the death penalty operated as an acquittal of that punishment, not the offense itself. Thus, judges who impose life sentences in lieu of the death penalty cannot later impose the death penalty as a greater punishment (compare *Bullington v. Missouri* [1981] for a case involving a jury decision involving the same issue).

Caspari v. Bohlen, 510 U.S. 383, 114 S. Ct. 948 (1994)

Bohlen and others were convicted of robbing a jewelry store in Missouri in 1981. The judge determined that Bohlen was also a persistent offender and was thus in violation of Missouri's persistent-offender statute. The jury convicted him of first-degree robbery, and the judge sentenced him to three consecutive terms of fifteen years in prison. Bohlen appealed, and the Missouri Supreme Court overturned his conviction because no proof of his being a persistent offender had been presented at his trial. The case was retried, this time to allow the prosecution the opportunity of showing proof of Bohlen's four prior felony convictions and his status as a persistent offender for a commensurate sentence. Again the trial judge sentenced Bohlen to three consecutive terms of fifteen years in prison, and again Bohlen appealed on the grounds that the second trial had violated his Fifth Amendment right against double jeopardy. Bohlen's conviction and consecutive sentences were upheld by the U.S. Supreme Court, which said that it is well established that there is no double-jeopardy bar to the use of prior convictions in sentencing persistent offenders (at 954). The significance of this case is that the double-jeopardy issue does not apply in resentencing proceedings in noncapital cases (compare such cases as *Bullington v. Missouri* [1981] *and Arizona v. Rumsey* [1984]).

Acceptance of Responsibility

Braxton v. United States, 500 U.S. 344, 111 S. Ct. 1854 (1991)

Braxton entered guilty pleas to charges of assaulting federal officers but pleaded not guilty to the more serious charge of intent to kill a U.S. marshal. The government accepted these pleas, but when applying the U.S. Sentencing Guidelines it applied an enhancement more applicable to the charge to which Braxton had pleaded not guilty. Thus Braxton was sentenced as though he had actually committed the crime of "intentionally attempting to kill a United States marshal." The government argued that Braxton had "stipulated" to the essence of the charge, that he had deliberately fired a shotgun through his front door when U.S. marshals came to arrest him. Braxton appealed the more severe sentence. The U.S. Supreme Court heard the appeal and vacated the sentence, holding that there was nothing in Braxton's stipulation that he ever intended to kill a U.S. marshal. Because that was a necessary element of an "intent to kill a United States marshal" charge, the sentence had to be vacated and the case remanded for resentencing.

Aggravating and Mitigating Circumstances

Batson v. Kentucky, 476 U.S. 79, 106 S. Ct. 1712 (1986)

In Kentucky, a black man, Batson, was convicted by an all-white jury of second-degree burglary. The prosecutor had used all of his peremptory challenges to exclude the few black prospective jurors from the jury pool. Ordinarily, peremptory challenges may be used to strike particular jurors without the prosecutor's having to provide a reason for doing so. In this case the use of peremptory challenges was rather transparent, and Batson appealed. In a landmark case, the U.S. Supreme Court decided that peremptory challenges may not be used for a racially discriminatory purpose. Thus, creating an all-white jury by deliberately eliminating all prospective black candidates was discriminatory. The Court ruled in favor of Batson.

Sumner v. Shuman, 483 U.S. 66, 107 S. Ct. 2716 (1987)

In Nevada, Shuman was convicted of first-degree murder and sentenced to life without parole. While in prison, he murdered another inmate and was convicted of this second murder. This time he was sentenced to the death penalty. He appealed. Nevada had a statute imposing a mandatory death penalty on prisoners who commit murder while imprisoned and already serving life terms. The U.S. Supreme Court overturned Shuman's death sentence, indicating that mandatory death penalties are unconstitutional because they do not consider aggravating and mitigating circumstances.

Maynard v. Cartwright, 486 U.S. 356, 108 S. Ct. 1853 (1988)

Cartwright shot and killed a man and slit his wife's throat. These victims had formerly employed him. An Oklahoma jury found Cartwright guilty of first-degree murder. When the judge gave the jury instructions during the penalty phase of the trial, he used the phrase "especially heinous, atrocious, or cruel" in describing various aggravating circumstances they were to consider. Cartwright challenged his death sentence on the grounds that such a statement was unconstitutionally vague. The U.S. Supreme Court agreed with Cartwright, and his death sentence was vacated, as the instruction, determined to be unconstitutionally vague, had not offered sufficient guidance to the jury in deciding whether to impose the death penalty.

Mills v. Maryland, 486 U.S. 367, 108 S. Ct. 1860 (1988)

Mills was an inmate of the Maryland Correctional Institution in Hagerstown. He stabbed his cellmate to death with a homemade knife and was charged with murder. A trial was held and the jury found Mills guilty. Instructions from the judge at the beginning of the sentencing phase led jurors to believe that they must agree unanimously on mitigating circumstances before they could consider them in Mills's case. If they could not agree, then they had to render a death penalty decision. Because they were not unanimous regarding any mitigating circumstances, they decided on the death penalty as required by the judge's instructions. Thus, a mandatory element was introduced into the penalty phase, which is unconstitutional in relation to death penalty decisions. Mills appealed, arguing that very point to the U.S. Supreme Court. The Court overturned Mills's conviction, concluding that there was a substantial probability that reasonable jurors, upon receiving the judge's instructions, might well have thought that they were precluded from considering any mitigating evidence unless all twelve jurors agreed on the existence of such a circumstance. The Court said that the jurors must consider all the mitigating evidence. The possibility that a single juror could block such consideration, and consequently require the jury to impose the death penalty, was not to be risked. Therefore, the death penalty sentence was vacated.

Teague v. Lane, 489 U.S. 288, 109 S. Ct. 1060 (1989)

Teague, a black man, was accused of attempted murder. During jury selection, the prosecutor used all of his ten peremptory challenges to exclude blacks from the jury. Teague was eventually convicted by an all-white jury. In the meantime, *Batson v. Kentucky* (1986) had recently been decided, which established that blacks could not be excluded from jury duty by use of peremptory challenges. Teague sought to make that rule retroactive in his case, thus causing his conviction to be overturned and a new trial conducted. The U.S. Supreme Court rejected the retroactive principle relating to *Batson,* holding that convicted offenders are barred from making retroactive claims involving racial discrimination in jury selection. Furthermore, Teague had failed to make a convincing case that the peremptory challenges had been used in a discriminatory fashion.

Blystone v. Pennsylvania, 494 U.S. 299, 110 S. Ct. 1078 (1990)

Blystone was convicted of first-degree murder, robbery, and criminal conspiracy to commit homicide. The sentencing jury was instructed to consider aggravating and mitigating circumstances and to impose the death penalty if aggravating circumstances outweighed the mitigating ones. The death penalty was imposed on Blystone, and he appealed, contending that the weighing procedure of aggravating and mitigating circumstances made the death penalty a mandatory penalty and thus unconstitutional. The U.S. Supreme Court rejected Blystone's argument, saying that the Pennsylvania statute of weighing the aggravating and mitigating circumstances was not unconstitutional.

Lankford v. Idaho, 500 U.S. 110, 111 S. Ct. 1723 (1991)

In this rather complicated case, Lankford and his brother were charged with first-degree murder but entered a guilty plea in exchange for a minimum ten-year term. The judge refused to approve the plea agreement and the case went to trial. The defense and prosecuting attorneys proceeded as though the ten-year minimum term was being sought as a punishment and the death penalty was not contemplated. When the brothers were convicted of the murder, the judge asked whether either party wished to cite aggravating or mitigating circumstances to determine the type of sentence imposed. Neither side indicated that, and in the sentencing phase the two brothers were recommended for long prison terms. The judge, however, decided that the punishment was too lenient and imposed the death penalty on both brothers, citing several aggravating circumstances in justification. The brothers appealed. The U.S. Supreme Court overturned the death penalty because neither side had been permitted to argue the merits of aggravating or mitigating circumstances. The judge's personal feelings in the matter had come too late in the proceeding for either side to address the aggravating and mitigating circumstances. Thus, the Court ruled that the sentences of death were unconstitutional because the judge had failed to provide adequate notice that they would be imposed.

Arave v. Creech, 507 U.S. 463, 113 S. Ct. 1534 (1993)
Creech, confined in the Idaho Penitentiary, was convicted of the murder of another inmate. At his trial the judge sentenced him to death, basing his decision, in part, on aggravating circumstances. He used the phrases "utter disregard" and "the cold-blooded pitiless slayer." Creech appealed the sentence, contending that the phrase "utter disregard" was invalid. The U.S. Supreme Court upheld Creech's conviction, holding that the phrase "utter disregard" did not violate any constitutional provisions.

Beard v. Banks, 542 U.S. 406, 124 S. Ct. 2504 (2004)
George Banks was convicted of twelve counts of murder in Pennsylvania in the early 1980s, and Banks's convictions became final in 1987. Subsequently, the U.S. Supreme Court decided *Mills v. Maryland* (1988) and *Teague v. Lane* (1989). *Mills* made it unconstitutional for juries to be prevented from considering mitigating factors in capital cases in which those factors were not agreed upon by the jury unanimously. The *Teague* case barred retroactive application of later U.S. Supreme Court decisions to earlier cases with some limited exceptions. Banks sought habeas relief in federal court subsequent to 1987, claiming among other things that the jury in his case had disregarded mitigating factors that were not found unanimously. His habeas petition was denied on the merits in U.S. district court, and he appealed to the Third Circuit Court, which reversed and remanded the case, concluding that the *Teague* analysis was unnecessary. Pennsylvania appealed, and the U.S. Supreme Court heard the case. The Court reversed the Third Circuit and held that (1) convictions become final for purposes of determining the applicability of the *Teague* rule on the date the U.S. Supreme Court denied certiorari after Banks's convictions were affirmed on appeal, (2) the *Mills* rule announced a

new rule of constitutional law for *Teague* purposes, and (3) *Mills* was not a watershed rule of criminal procedure implicating fundamental fairness, for purposes of meeting *Teague*'s nonretroactivity exception. The *Mills* rule does not fall within either of *Teague*'s exceptions, and therefore it cannot be applied retroactively to Banks.

Tennard v. Dretke, 542 U.S. 274, 124 S. Ct. 2562 (2004)

Robert Tennard was convicted of capital murder in Texas in 1986. Evidence presented at his trial indicated that Tennard and two accomplices killed two of Tennard's neighbors and robbed their house. Tennard stabbed one of the victims to death. Tennard was charged with capital murder and subsequently convicted. During the trial, Tennard's defense counsel introduced evidence which showed that Tennard had an IQ of 67, as well as testimony from a rape victim of Tennard's which suggested that Tennard's limited mental faculties and gullible nature mitigated his culpability in his conviction offense of first-degree murder. It was also established that Tennard had suffered some childhood abuse. During the penalty phase, the jury was instructed to consider Tennard's appropriate punishment by answering two "special issues" questions used at the time in Texas to establish whether life imprisonment or death would be imposed. These issues were (1) was the conduct of Tennard that led to the death of the deceased committed deliberately with the reasonable expectation that the death of the deceased or another would result? and (2) is there a probability that Tennard would commit criminal acts of violence that would constitute a continuing threat to society? Neither of those issues was sufficient to address whether Tennard's mental retardation or history of childhood abuse could be considered as mitigating circumstances.

The jury recommended the death penalty, and the judge sentenced Tennard to death. Tennard appealed his conviction and sentence, alleging that his death sentence violated his Eighth Amendment rights and that the jury was not permitted to consider evidence of his mental retardation as a mitigating factor. Tennard's appeals were rejected by the Texas Supreme Court, which held that evidence of low IQ alone was insufficient to demonstrate mental retardation, and that Tennard had failed to show that the crime he committed was attributable to his low IQ. Tennard then asked the Fifth Circuit Court of Appeals to issue a certificate of appealability (COA), which was denied. Agreeing with the Texas Supreme Court, the Fifth Circuit declared that Tennard had failed to present any constitutionally relevant evidence of a "uniquely severe permanent handicap with which the defendant was burdened through no fault of his own," or any evidence that "the criminal act was attributable to this severe permanent condition." Subsequently Tennard appealed to the U.S. Supreme Court, which heard the case. The Court reversed Tennard's conviction and remanded the case to the Texas courts. The U.S. Supreme Court held that Tennard had made a substantial showing of a denial of a constitutional right because jurors were not permitted to consider his low IQ as evidence of mental retardation. Furthermore, the "constitutional relevance" test used by the Fifth Circuit was improper and has no foundation in U.S. Supreme Court decisions, since Tennard's low IQ evidence was relevant mitigating evidence. Impaired intellectual functioning has a mitigating dimension beyond the impact it has on the ability to act deliberately. The prosecutor in Tennard's case expressed the most problematic interpretation of special issues by suggesting that Tennard's low IQ was irrelevant in mitigation but relevant to future dangerousness.

References

Glaze, Lauren E., and Seri Palla. 2005. *Probation and Parole in the United States, 2005.* Washington, DC: Bureau of Justice Statistics.

Goffman, Erving. 1961. *Asylums.* Garden City, NY: Anchor Press.

Harrison, Paige M., and Allen J. Beck. 2006. *Prisoners and Jail Inmates at Midyear 2005.* Washington, DC: Bureau of Justice Statistics.

Sullivan, Christopher. 2006. "Classification and Specialization: Assessing the Relevance of Conviction Offense as a Means of Defining Offending Patterns." Unpublished paper presented at the annual meeting of the Academy of Criminal Justice Sciences. Baltimore, MD, March.

U.S. Code. 2007. *United States Code.* Washington, DC: U.S. Government Printing Office.

U.S. Department of Justice. 2006. *State and Federal Corrections Statistics.* Washington, DC: U.S. Department of Justice.

7

Directory of Organizations

Many organizations are associated with sentencing, either directly or indirectly. Some of these organizations are international, while most listed and described in this chapter are U.S.-based organizations and agencies. Virtually every organization listed here assists defendants in various ways. In some instances persons have been convicted wrongfully, and there are several organizations that take on unpopular cases in order to clear the names of those who have been falsely convicted. Some organizations make use of technological resources more than do others. In some instances, certain organizations have used DNA as a biological mechanism to secure a prisoner's release where DNA evidence has been preserved from a crime scene. This list is not comprehensive. In most instances, there are Internet links with affiliate organizations and sites that may be of interest.

American Bar Association
321 N. Clark Street
Chicago, IL 60610
Telephone: (800) 285-2221
Internet: http://www.abanet.org

The American Bar Association (ABA) was founded on August 21, 1878, in Saratoga Springs, New York, by a hundred lawyers from twenty-one states. The legal profession as we know it today barely existed at that time. Lawyers were generally sole practitioners who trained under a system of apprenticeship. There was no national code of ethics and no national organization to serve as a forum for discussion of the increasingly intricate issues involved in legal practice.

The first ABA constitution, which is still substantially the charter of the association, defined the purpose of the ABA as being the advancement of the science of jurisprudence and the promotion of the administration of justice and a uniformity of legislation throughout the country. Today ABA membership is in excess of 400,000. The ABA provides law school accreditation, continuing legal education for those desiring it, information about the law, programs to assist judges and lawyers in their work, and initiatives to improve the legal system for the public. The overall mission of the ABA is to be the national representative of the legal profession, serving the public and the profession by promoting justice, professional excellence, and respect for the law. The ABA recruits persons from a variety of backgrounds who seek opportunities for challenging and substantive work.

Certain ABA goals pertain to increasing the racial and ethnic diversity of attorneys admitted to the bar through focusing upon pipeline issues. These goals encompass the following: (1) take steps to increase the awareness of the ABA leadership about the need for and benefits of greater racial and ethnic diversity in the profession, (2) make pilot projects available for ABA and affiliated entities to conduct racial and ethnic diversity pipeline programs, (3) act as a national clearinghouse and information source on increasing racial and ethnic diversity in the pipeline to share information and develop strategies, (4) provide a mechanism for people and entities with an interest in expanding racial and ethnic diversity in the pipeline to share information and develop strategies, (5) provide services for any organization to carry out programs and increase racial and ethnic diversity in the pipeline, and (6) partner with other ABA and non-ABA entities on programs and projects concerning racial and ethnic diversity issues in the pipeline.

The most important role of the ABA is its creation and maintenance of a code of ethical standards for lawyers. The Model Code of Professional Responsibility (1969) and newer model rules of professional conduct promulgated in 1983 have been adopted in forty-nine state jurisdictions and the District of Columbia. The ABA publishes the *ABA Journal*. The ABA has a house of delegates that acts as the organization's primary body for adopting new policies and recommendations as a part of the association's official position. Accrediting law schools is an important function as well, since the organization assists in the training of lawyers who defend clients accused of crimes. Defense lawyers must meet with prosecutors and work out plea agreements in many cases so their clients can benefit from greater leniency at the time of sentencing. The ABA prepares lawyers for this practice, among its other activities and initiatives.

American Civil Liberties Union (ACLU)
125 Broad Street
New York, NY 10004-2400
Telephone: (212) 549-2500
Internet: http://www.aclu.org

The American Civil Liberties Union (ACLU) was founded in 1920 by Roger Baldwin, Crystal Eastman, Albert DeSilver, and others. It is a nonprofit, nonpartisan organization and presently has a membership of more than 500,000. The U.S. system of government is founded on two counterbalancing principles: that the majority of the people governs through democratically elected representatives, and that the power even of a democratic majority must be limited to ensure individual rights. Majority power is limited by the Constitution's Bill of Rights, which consists of the original ten amendments ratified in 1791, including three post–Civil War amendments (13th, 14th, and 15th) and the 19th amendment (adopted in 1920).

The mission of the ACLU is to preserve all of these protections and guarantees: (1) First Amendment rights—freedom of speech, association, and assembly, freedom of the press, and freedom of religion supported by the strict separation of church and state, (2) right to equal protection under the law—equal treatment regardless of race, sex, religion, or national origin, (3) right to due process—fair treatment by the government whenever the loss of your liberty or property is at stake, and (4) right to privacy—freedom from unwarranted government intrusion into your personal and private affairs.

The ACLU works to extend these rights to segments of the population that have traditionally been denied these fundamental rights, including Native Americans and other people of color, lesbians, gay men, bisexuals and transgendered persons, women, mental health patients, prisoners, people with disabilities, and the poor.

The ACLU has maintained the position that civil liberties must be respected, even in times of national emergency. The ACLU is supported by annual dues and contributions from its membership, including grants from private foundations and individuals. No government funding is accepted.

Amnesty International
5 Penn Plaza, 14th Floor
New York, NY 10001
Telephone: (212) 807-8400
Fax: (212) 463-9193
Internet: http://www.web.amnesty.org

Amnesty International (AI) was founded in 1961 by Peter Benenson, a British lawyer. It was originally his intention to launch an appeal in Britain with the aim of obtaining amnesty for prisoners of conscience all over the world. The committee working for this cause soon acquired extensive documentation about this category of prisoner; it was so extensive that the committee discovered that it would have to carry out the work more systematically and comprehensively and on a more permanent basis. AI is a world-embracing movement that works for the protection of human rights. It is independent of all governments and is neutral in relation to its political goals, ideologies, and religious divisions. AI works for the release of women and men who have been arrested for their convictions, the color of their skin, or their ethnicity, race, or other factors, provided that they have not themselves used force or exhorted others to resort to violence. AI proclaimed 1977 as Prisoners of Conscience Year and collected signatures for an appeal addressed to the General Assembly of the United Nations.

In 1963 a general secretariat was established, and Sean MacBride, a subsequent Nobel Prize winner, became chairman of AI. In 1971, AI had more than 1,000 voluntary groups in twenty-eight countries, and its membership figures were constantly growing. AI has continuously worked for the forgotten prisoners, those who are prisoners of conscience. Furthermore, AI opposes the death penalty and seeks its abolition wherever it is used. It is also against torture and the ill-treatment of prisoners. These are the three most important tasks AI has set for itself. In 2006 there were 1.8 million members of AI in more than 150 countries. Major policy decisions for AI are made by an international council of representatives from all national selections. AI's national selections and local volunteer organizations are primarily responsible for funding the movement, since no funds are sought or accepted from any government. AI is independent of any government, political ideology, economic interest, or religion. It does not support or oppose any government or political system, nor does it support or oppose the views of the victims whose rights it seeks to protect. It is concerned solely with the impartial protection of human rights.

Center for Wrongful Convictions
Northwestern University School of Law
357 East Chicago Avenue
Chicago, IL 60611
Telephone: (312) 503-3100
Internet: http://www.law.northwestern.edu/depts/clinic/
    wrongful/mission.htm

The Center for Wrongful Convictions (CWC) is dedicated to identifying and rectifying wrongful convictions and other serious miscarriages of justice. CWC was cofounded in 1999 by Steven Drizin and Lawrence C. Marshall and has three major components: (1) representation, (2) research, and (3) community services. CWC faculty, staff, cooperating outside attorneys, and Bluhm Legal Clinic students investigate possible wrongful convictions and represent imprisoned clients with claims of actual innocence. The research component focuses upon identifying systemic problems in the criminal justice system and, together with the community services component, on developing initiatives designed to raise public awareness of the prevalence, causes, and social costs of wrongful convictions and to promote reform of the criminal justice system. Additionally, the community services component assists exonerated former prisoners to cope with the difficult process of reintegration into society.

The work of Steven Drizin and others who have helped shape the goals of CWC has focused on unfair police interrogations and tactics and false confessions. Collaborations with other attorneys have led to legal reforms and initiatives dedicated to freeing wrongfully convicted persons. The CWC's efforts also include seeking to abolish the death penalty for juveniles in all U.S. jurisdictions. CWC works closely with the American Bar Association, the Juvenile Law Center, and Amnesty International.

Human Rights Watch
350 Fifth Avenue, 34th Floor
New York, NY 10118-3299

Telephone: (212) 290-4700
Fax: (212) 612-4333
e-mail: hrwnyc@hrw.org
Internet: http://www.hrw.org

Human Rights Watch (HRW) was begun in 1978 as Helsinki Watch, to monitor compliance with Soviet bloc countries with the human rights provisions of the landmark Helsinki Accords. In the 1980s, American Watch was established to counter the notion that human rights abuses by one side in the war in Central America were somehow more tolerable than abuses by the other. The organization grew to cover other world regions, until all of the "Watch" committees were united in 1988 to form Human Rights Watch.

HRW is dedicated to protecting the human rights of persons around the world. HRW stands with victims and activists to prevent discrimination, to uphold political freedom, to protect people from inhumane conduct in wartime, and to bring offenders to justice. HRW investigates human rights violations and holds abusers accountable. HRW challenges governments and those who hold power to end abusive practices and respect international rights law.

HRW is the largest human rights organization based in the United States. It consists of more than 150 dedicated professionals—lawyers, journalists, academics, and country experts of many nationalities and diverse backgrounds—who work around the world. Often HRW joins with groups in both the United States and other countries to further their common goals. A growing contingent of volunteers supplements the work of trained professionals who work to further HRW's interests.

HRW's staff and researchers conduct fact-finding investigations into allegations of human rights abuses in all regions of the world. HRW publishes these findings and distributes its publications worldwide. This publicity is intended to embarrass abusive governments in world eyes and in the court of world opinion, in order to bring about changes that will vest citizens of different countries with human rights. In extreme circumstances, HRW will call for the withdrawal of economic and military support of those countries where human abuses occur. Then HRW representatives meet with the world leaders involved and attempt to resolve their differences with the citizens they represent. HRW believes that international standards of human rights apply to all people equally, and that sharp vigilance and timely protest are necessary to prevent tragedies from occurring in which human lives may be lost because of overt or covert rights violations. HRW remains objectively neutral, accepting no money from any government or government-funded agency. Its survival and perpetuation are dependent upon contributions from private foundations and citizens throughout the world.

Innocence Project
100 Fifth Avenue, 3rd Floor
New York, NY 10011
Telephone: (212) 364-5340
Internet: http://www.innocenceproject.org

The Innocence Project (IP) of the Benjamin N. Cardozo School of Law was created by Barry C. Scheck and Peter J. Neufeld in 1992. It was established and remains a nonprofit clinic. The IP handles only cases in which postconviction DNA testing of evidence can yield conclusive proof of one's innocence. As it is a clinic, students handle most of the case work while supervised by a team of attorneys and staff.

Most clients of IP are poor and forgotten and have exhausted all of their legal avenues of relief. The only hope they have is that biological evidence from their case still exists and can be subjected to DNA testing. All IP clients go through an extensive screening process to determine whether DNA evidence could prove their claims of innocence. Thousands of convicted offenders currently await an evaluation of their cases by IP.

The IP is the forerunner in the field of wrongful convictions. The IP has grown to become much more than the court of last resort for inmates who have exhausted their appeals and their financial resources. IP is now organizing the Innocence Network, a group of law schools, journalism schools, and public defender offices across the country that assists inmates who are trying to prove their innocence whether or not the cases involve biological evidence that can be subjected to DNA testing. The IP consults with legislators and law enforcement officials at the state, local, and federal levels, conducts research and training, produces scholarship, and proposes a wide range of remedies to prevent wrongful convictions from occurring while continuing to work to free innocent inmates through the use of postconviction DNA testing.

One important objective of IP is to heighten citizen awareness and concern about the failings of the criminal justice system.

It is a facet of this society that eventually touches all of its citizens in several important ways. The prospect of innocent persons languishing in jail, or worse, being put to death for crimes they did not commit, should be intolerable for every American regardless of race, politics, gender, origin, or creed.

Institute for Court Management
300 Newport Avenue
Williamsburg, VA 23815-4147
Telephone: (800) 616-6160
Fax: (757) 564-2108
Internet: http://www.ncsconline.org

The Institute for Court Management (ICM) has a mission to educate, inform, and support the management and leadership of state courts. It is a division of the National Center for State Courts. ICM is dedicated to providing the highest level of service and leadership to the state courts. It is the premier judicial-branch educational organization, universally recognized for quality curriculum and customer service. ICM is committed to (1) customer satisfaction, (2) excellence in education, training, and professional development, (3) continuous learning: faculty and staff are encouraged to evaluate their level of technical, interpersonal, and conceptual skills, (4) diversity and valuing the differences in people, cultures, and ideas, (5) breaking down organizational and departmental boundaries and supporting the free exchange of ideas, knowledge, and information among faculty and staff, and (6) prudent use and accountability of public resources.

ICM has an Advisory Council that provides advice and support regarding the development of new programs and faculty, offers suggestions for improving existing courses and methods of instruction, and assists in the long- and short-term planning of curriculum and court administration effectiveness. The members of the Advisory Council are appointed by the executive director of ICM after consultation with the president of the National Center for State Courts. Members serve three-year terms.

International Court of Justice
Peace Palace
2517 KJ The Hague
The Netherlands
Telephone: (31) (0) 70 302 23 23

Telefax: (31) (0) 70 364 99 28
Internet: http://www.icj-cij.org/icjwww/igeneralinformation
  .htm

The International Court of Justice is headquartered in the Peace Palace at The Hague in The Netherlands. It is the official judicial body for the United Nations, functions as a world court, and hears and decides disputes between nations over international crimes, the use of natural resources, and other matters of an international nature. It also functions in an advisory capacity to give individual member-states advice and counsel regarding international matters that may arise and what possible alternative actions may be taken. The International Court of Justice originated by charter on April 18, 1946, stemming from UN committee action in 1945 to create an international tribunal that could function in an impartial manner to settle disputes and other matters between member nations, also referred to as states.

The International Court of Justice was preceded by the Permanent Court of International Justice, which existed from 1922 to 1946, although the idea for this court was set forth in discussions and actions at The Hague Peace Conference of 1899. This body eventually became the International Court of Justice. The Permanent Court of International Justice was the creation of the League of Nations. The League of Nations was formed following World War I in 1919 with goals that included disarmament, preventing war through negotiation and diplomacy, and improving global welfare. The founding of the League of Nations was strongly influenced by U.S. president Woodrow Wilson.

The International Court of Justice is composed of fifteen permanent judges who are elected by the UN General Assembly and the UN Security Council. Judges serve nine-year terms and may be re-elected. Elections occur every three years, so that there is constant turnover among judges representing different member countries. Judges may sit as an entire bench, or they may sit in three-judge or five-judge panels to hear less important cases or disputes between nations. Sometimes smaller three-judge or five-judge panels are assigned to hear cases of a specialized nature, in which the testimony of experts is critical and must be closely evaluated and considered. In 2006 the president of the International Court of Justice was Dame Rosalyn Higgins from the United Kingdom, while the vice president was Awn Shawkat Al-Khasawneh from Jordan.

UN members are automatically parties to the Court's statutes. In all cases in which disputing parties agree to submit to the rulings of the Court, these rulings are binding on the participating nations. The jurisdiction of the Court in any case is on the basis of mutual consent between parties. Four methods are used by the Court to establish jurisdiction:

1. Parties may refer cases to the Court. Although this method does not involve compulsory jurisdiction, explicit consent is given where both parties desire a matter to be resolved.
2. The Court has jurisdiction in all matters in which modern treaties are in force. Most treaties have provisions concerning compromise, providing for dispute resolution and binding arbitration by the Court.
3. Optional clause declarations may be made by member states. These declarations often contain reservations and particular exclusions; thus they are not compulsory, and the countries are not bound to abide by the terms of a concluded arbitration. By 2005, sixty-five nations had declarations in force.
4. Jurisdiction may occur through prior declarations and treaties made under the Permanent Court of International Justice. Thus, jurisdiction is transferred from older treaties to influence contemporary decision-making.

The Security Council of the United Nations has a duty to comply with all International Court of Justice decisions involving member-states. If the disputing parties are Security Council members and do not comply with the recommendations of the arbitration board, enforcement action may be recommended to the Security Council. Of course the Security Council has the right to veto any enforcement action against any of its members, and thus there is no way to force compliance. The International Court of Justice decides all cases in accordance with international law. Judicial decision-making is largely influenced by international conventions, international customs, and general principles of law recognized by civilized nations.

National Alliance of Sentencing Advocates and Mitigation Specialists (NASA)
National Legal Aid and Defender Organization

1140 Connecticut Avenue, NW, Suite 900
Washington, DC 20036
Telephone: (202) 452-0620
Fax: (202) 872-1031
Internet: http://www.nlada.org

The National Alliance of Sentencing Advocates and Mitigation Specialists (NASA) is a section of the National Legal Aid and Defender Association and is dedicated to the promotion of fair, humane, and equitable sentencing and confinement decisions for all American people. NASA is designed to advance the field of sentencing advocacy by fostering the professional development of its members and upholding the ethical standards of practice of the organization.

National Bar Association
1225 11th Street, NW
Washington, DC 20001
Telephone: (202) 842-3900
Fax: (202) 289-6170
Internet: http://www.nationalbar.org

The National Bar Association (NBA) was established in 1925. It represents the interests of African-American attorneys throughout the United States. The association has several affiliate chapters located throughout the country, including the Barristers' Association of Philadelphia and the Garden State Bar Association. At the time of its formation, the NBA had fewer than 1,000 black lawyers to represent, and fewer than 250 of them joined the NBA at the time it was organized. Today the organization boasts a substantial membership and exists in most states. The objectives of the NBA are to advance the science of jurisprudence; to improve the administration of justice; to preserve the independence of the judiciary and uphold the honor and integrity of the legal profession; to promote professional and social intercourse among the members of the American and the international bars; to promote legislation that will improve the economic condition of all American citizens, regardless of race, sex, or creed, in their efforts to secure free and untrammeled use of the franchise guaranteed by the Constitution of the United States; and to protect the civil and political rights of all citizens and residents of the United States.

The NBA has operated a lawyer referral center for those accused of crimes, especially minorities; fostered longtime alliances with various legal organizations, including the American Bar

Association; and offered classes to elementary and secondary school students in different jurisdictions about the nature of the U.S. criminal justice system. It continues to protect the civil rights of citizens and residents of the United States through its efforts. It is a nonprofit organization and relies on grants and donated monies and member dues for its perpetuation. It hosts frequent seminars and actively combats egregious acts perpetrated against minority citizens by the criminal justice system, through the means of providing legal services at little or no cost to defendants. It also advises other nations in their legal matters. The NBA strives to achieve equality in how the law is applied in sentencing decisions at all levels, local, state, and federal.

National Center for State Courts
300 Newport Avenue
Williamsburg, VA 23185-4147
Telephone: (888) 450-0391
Fax: (757) 564-2034
Internet: http://www.ncsconline.org

The mission of the National Center for State Courts (NCSC) is to improve the administration of justice through leadership and service to state courts and courts throughout the world. Through original research, consulting services, publications, and national educational programs, NCSC offers solutions to enhance court operations with the latest technology; collects and interprets the latest court data about court operations nationwide; and provides information about the proven "best practices" for improving court operations. NCSC is an independent nonprofit organization. It seeks to disseminate information to state court leaders about key national policy issues, including sentencing, and helps to advocate policies to Congress and other influential bodies. NCSC supports several important organizations and their work, including the ABA. Services available to the courts include a resource guide for trial judges, court administrators, and court community constituents who want to know more about courts and criminal procedure. The Internet site for NCSC offers high-level overviews of NCSC's mission, services, and activities as well as providing a comprehensive database of information requested by state courts. A major aim is to improve the quality of state judiciary throughout the United States at all levels.

National Institute of Corrections
320 First Street, NW
Washington, DC 20534
Telephone: (800) 995-6453
Telephone: (202) 307-3106
Fax: (303) 682-0558
Internet: http://nicic.org

The National Institute of Corrections (NIC) is an agency within the U.S. Department of Justice, Federal Bureau of Prisons. The NIC was created in 1974. It received its first funding as a line-item in the federal budget in 1977. The NIC is headed by a director appointed by the U.S. attorney general. A sixteen-member advisory board is also appointed by the U.S. attorney general to provide policy direction for the institute. NIC provides training, technical assistance, information services, and policy/program development assistance to federal, state, and local corrections agencies. Through cooperative agreements, NIC awards funds to support its program initiatives. NIC also provides leadership to influence correctional policies, practices, and operations nationwide in areas of emerging interest and concern to correctional executives and practitioners as well as public policy-makers.

NIC's mission is to provide a center for correctional learning and experience. It advances and shapes effective correctional practices and public policies that respond to the needs of corrections through collaboration and leadership, and it provides assistance, information, education, and training. The outcomes of NIC's activities include: (1) effectively managed prisons, jails, and community corrections programs and facilities, (2) enhanced organizational and professional performance in corrections, (3) community, staff, and offender safety, (4) improved correctional practices through the exploration of trends and public policy issues, and (5) enhanced NIC services through improved organizational staff effectiveness. Offices include Community Corrections/Prisons, Office of International Assistance, Office of Correctional Job Training and Placement, and Administrative Offices.

National Legal Aid and Defender Association
1140 Connecticut Avenue, NW, Suite 900
Washington, DC 20036
Telephone: (202) 452-0620

Fax: (202) 872-1031
Internet: http://www.nlada.org

The National Legal Aid and Defender Association (NLADA) is the nation's leading advocate for frontline attorneys and other equal justice professionals—those who make a difference in the lives of low-income clients and their families and communities. NLADA was founded in 1911 as the result of combining fifteen legal aid societies together to form a National Alliance of Legal Aid Societies. Arthur von Briesen of the Legal Aid Society of New York was the first president of the organization. The name of the organization was changed several times but was eventually changed to its present name in 1958. Representing legal aid and defender programs, as well as individual advocates, NLADA is the oldest and largest national, nonprofit, membership association devoting 100 percent of its resources to serving the broad equal justice community. NLADA serves the equal justice community in two ways: (1) providing first-rate products and services, and (2) as a leading national voice in public policy and legislative debates on the many issues affecting the equal justice community. It also serves as a resource for those seeking more information on equal justice in the United States. NLADA files amicus briefs on behalf of many persons charged with crimes. It seeks due process, including provisions for counsel for indigents.

The Police Foundation (PF)
1201 Connecticut Avenue, NW
Washington, DC 20036
Telephone: (202) 833-1460
Fax: (202) 659-9149
e-mail: pfinfo@policefoundation.org
Internet: http://www.policefoundation.org

Founded in 1970 through a Ford Foundation grant, the Police Foundation (PF) has as its purpose helping police be more effective in doing their job, whether it be deterring robberies, intervening in potentially injurious family disputes, or working to improve relationships between the police and the communities they serve. To accomplish its mission, the PF works closely with police officers and police agencies across the country, and it is in their hard work and contributions that PF's accomplishments are rooted. The PF works as a catalyst for change and an advocate for new ideas in restating and reminding the public about the fundamental purposes of policing and in ensuring that an important link remains intact between the police and the public they serve. The PF is a member of the Community Policing Consortium.

Portland Copwatch/People Overseeing Police Study Group (PCPOPSG)
P.O. Box 42456
Portland, OR 97242
Telephone: (503) 236-3065
e-mail: copwatch@teleport.com
Internet: http://www.teleport.com/~copwatch/

The Portland Copwatch/People Overseeing Police Study Group (PCPOPSG) is a grassroots group promoting police accountability through citizen action. It was formed as a project of Peace and Justice Works (PJW) in 1992. PCPOPSG also participates in community forums on police accountability, and it regularly attends meetings of Portland, Oregon's, review board, also known as the Police Chief's Forum. The PCPOPSG publishes a newsletter, *People's Police Report,* which includes information about local and national police accountability efforts. Police behavior is observed in different parts of Portland, and contacts are made and information is spread throughout the community. The goals of PCPOPSG are: (1) to empower victims of police misconduct to pursue their grievances, with the goal of resolving individual cases and preventing future occurrences; (2) to educate the general public and in particular target groups of police abuse on their rights and responsibilities; and (3) to promote and monitor an effective system for civilian oversight of police. One of the first lines of defense for fair court treatment and subsequent sentencing equitability is fair treatment by police. Accountability mechanisms are in place to ensure that citizen-police encounters are smooth and that one's rights are observed at all stages following an arrest.

The RAND Corporation
1776 Main Street
Santa Monica, CA 90407-2138
Telephone: (310) 393-0411
Fax: (310) 393-4818
Internet: http://www/rand.org

The RAND Corporation (RC) was created on May 14, 1948, following World War II. RAND is a contraction of Research and

Development, and the organization quickly became an independent, nonprofit group dedicated to furthering and promoting scientific, educational, and charitable purposes for the public welfare and the security of the United States. For nearly sixty years RC decision-makers in both the public and private sectors have objectively sought to analyze and devise solutions for various challenges facing the world. These challenges include economic issues, social issues, and related problems of education, poverty, crime, and the environment, as well as national security concerns.

During the 1970s and 1980s, RC undertook various projects related to sentencing offenders. RC examined the impact of the three-strikes-and-you're-out law enacted by the California legislature. It was apparent that Californians and others were being impacted by a fear of crime, sympathy for crime victims and their families, and anger at violent criminals. RC sought to provide hard evidence for voters to consider concerning the various implications of the three-strikes law. How much crime reduction could be expected as a result of the law? What about the alternatives? And where will the money come from? RC sought to answer these questions with research from those on its staff with corrections interests. Peter Greenwood and Joan Petersilia are two of the many persons who undertook an analysis of those and related issues with positive and influential results. Analytical models were constructed that predicted how populations of offenders on the street and in prison would change under the differing sentencing provisions of the new law and under various alternatives. Using data on those populations, researchers were able to estimate crime rates and costs. Also investigated has been intensive supervised probation and parole for various types of offenders, including drug offenders. The results of RC research have helped to shape and modify public opinion and legislative actions in recent years. RC research continues in those and other important sentencing and offender supervision areas.

The Sentencing Project
5143 Tenth Street, NW, Suite 1000
Washington, DC 20004
Telephone: (202) 628-0871
Fax: (202) 628-1091
Internet: http://www.sentencingproject.org

The Sentencing Project (SP) is a national organization working for a fair and effective criminal justice system by promoting reforms in sentencing law and practice, and alternatives to incarceration. The SP was founded in 1986 to provide defense lawyers with sentencing advocacy training and to reduce the reliance on incarceration. Since that time, the SP has become a leader in the effort to bring national attention to disturbing trends and inequities in the criminal justice system, with a successful formula that includes the publication of groundbreaking research, aggressive media campaigns, and strategic advocacy for policy reform.

As a result of the SP's research, publications, and advocacy, many people know that this country is the world's leader in incarceration, that one in three young black men is under the control of the criminal justice system, that 5 million Americans can't vote because of felony convictions, and that thousands of women and children have lost welfare, education, and housing benefits as a result of convictions for minor drug offenses. The SP is dedicated to changing the way Americans think about crime and punishment.

United States Sentencing Commission
Office of Publishing and Public Affairs
One Columbus Circle, NE, Suite 2-500
Washington, DC 20002-8002
Telephone: (202) 502-4590
Fax: (202) 502-4699
e-mail: pubaffairs@ussc.gov
Internet: http://www.ussc.gov

The United States Sentencing Commission (USSC) was created by the Sentencing Reform Act of 1984 as a part of the Comprehensive Crime Control Act of 1984. The sentencing guidelines established by the commission are designed to (1) incorporate the purposes of sentencing (for example, just punishment, deterrence, incapacitation, and rehabilitation), (2) provide certainty and fairness in meeting the purposes of sentencing by avoiding unwarranted disparity among offenders with similar characteristics convicted of similar criminal conduct, while permitting sufficient judicial flexibility to take into account relevant aggravating and mitigating factors, and (3) reflect to the extent practicable, advancement in the knowledge of human behavior as it relates to the criminal justice process.

The USSC is charged with the ongoing responsibility of evaluating the effects of sentencing guidelines on the criminal justice system, recommending to Congress appropriate modifications of substantive criminal law and sentencing procedures, and establishing a research and development program on sentencing issues. Additionally, the Sentencing Reform Act abolished parole for offenders sentenced under the guidelines so that the sentence received would basically be the sentence served. Under the federal law, federal inmates may earn up to 54 days of credit a year for good behavior, otherwise known as good time. That figure is approximately 15 percent of a year, and it complies with a truth-in-sentencing federal provision subsequently approved by the USSC in that federal offenders must serve at least 85 percent of their sentences before becoming eligible for early release from prison.

The USSC was created primarily to codify existing criminal laws and make them more uniform. Furthermore, considerable judicial abuse of discretion was prevalent throughout the federal judiciary and among circuits. Critics of pre-USSC judicial officiating and decision-making cited the following as factors justifying the creation of the USSC: (1) the previously unfettered sentencing discretion of federal trial judges needed to be more structured, (2) the administration of punishment needed to be more certain, and (3) specific offenders (for example, white collar, violent, and repeat offenders) needed to be targeted for more serious penalties. Subsequently, Congress authorized a permanent commission charged with formulating national sentencing guidelines, known as presumptive guidelines, to define the parameters for federal trial judges to follow in their sentencing decisions.

The new sentencing guidelines went into effect on November 1, 1987. There were several challenges to those guidelines, most notably *Mistretta v. United States* (1989). The *Mistretta* case argued that the federal sentencing guidelines were unconstitutional because they violated the separation of powers doctrine. That was because some members of the USSC were also federal district court judges. Thus judges were both creating law and implementing it, apparently violating the separation of powers doctrine. Justice Scalia agreed with that position, although the other members of the U.S. Supreme Court rejected the argument and upheld the constitutionality of the guidelines. Subsequent U.S.

Supreme Court decisions (*United States v. Booker*, 2005; *Blakely v. Washington*, 2004) decided that the Sixth Amendment right to a jury trial applies to the federal sentencing guidelines. A remedial opinion by the U.S. Supreme Court, however, excised two provisions from the guidelines that removed their mandatory application. Today federal district court judges are obliged to consult these guidelines and take them into account when sentencing federal offenders, although the guidelines are not binding on these judges. Circuit courts of appeal may review any appeals alleging unreasonableness on the part of district court trial judges if it is believed that their decisions in the application of the guidelines are unreasonable.

In theory, the sentencing guidelines promulgated by the USSC provide federal district court judges with fair and consistent guideline ranges to consult at the time of sentencing. The guidelines take into account both the seriousness of criminal conduct as well as the defendant's criminal record. Each offender is assigned to a criminal history category and one of forty-three offense levels. Where those values intersect in the body of a guidelines table defines a range of months that judges may choose for sentencing purposes. Judges must choose a sentence from within the guideline range unless one or more factors result in contemplating a different sentence. Since the USSC cannot create every conceivable contingency for sentencing, there is room for subjective interpretation among federal district court judges. Usually, whenever departures from guidelines are contemplated by federal judges, they must write a rationale articulating the reason(s) for their departure. Those reasons are usually acceptable to appellate courts, should defendants decide to challenge them or their constitutionality.

Sources

Blakely v. Washington, 124 S.Ct. 2531 (2004).
Mistretta v. United States, 488 U.S. 361 (1989).
United States v. Booker, 125 U.S. 738 (2005).

The Vera Institute
233 Broadway, 12th Floor
New York, NY 10279
Telephone: (212) 334-1300
Fax: (212) 941-9407
e-mail: contactvera@vera.dot.org
Internet: http://www.vera.org

The Vera Institute began in 1961 with an experiment conducted by Louis Schweitzer, an active philanthropist, and Herb Sturz, a young magazine editor. They recognized the injustice of the U.S. bail system that granted liberty based upon income. Together they created the Vera Foundation (VF), which later became the Vera Institute of Justice (VIJ). With a small group of researchers working in tandem with some of New York City's criminal courts, they explored the bail problem and devised a solution. The experiment in bail reform led to widespread release on one's own recognizance, or ROR, where it was proved that New Yorkers too poor to afford bail but with strong community ties could be safely released before trial and would subsequently reappear for their hearings. Supplemental funding was obtained in 1966 from the Ford Foundation to further VIJ's interests.

The mission of the VIJ is to work closely with governmental leaders and civil society to improve services that people rely upon for safety and justice. The VIJ develops innovative, affordable programs that often grow into self-sustaining organizations; studies social problems and current responses; and provides practical advice and assistance to governmental officials in New York and around the world. VIJ's staff are leading more than two dozen separate projects, each aiming to reveal more about the meaning of justice even as they make a difference in the lives of individuals. These projects include efforts to serve troubled and delinquent children at home instead of in juvenile institutions; to reduce violence against women; to help state leaders develop affordable and humane sentencing policies; and to strengthen police-community relations. Today VIJ is a leader in developing unexpected yet practical and affordable solutions to some of the toughest problems in the administration of justice, and thereby making justice systems more humane, fair, and efficient for everyone.

One division of the VIJ is the Center on Sentencing and Corrections (CSC), which provides support to governmental officials charged with addressing their jurisdiction's sentencing and corrections policies. CSC's staff and researchers study and analyze state sentencing and correctional programs. They have developed a national database and archive to assist states in better understanding how their systems work and how they compare with the sentencing systems of other jurisdictions. Both jails and prisons are targets of CSC intervention and study. Evaluations are made of various types of sentencing plans and how regional jails and prisons will be impacted or affected by those changes.

Because so many entering inmates of prisons and jails have drug-related dependencies, the CSC studies treatment options for non-violent drug offenders and has worked aggressively with policy-makers in various states, including New York, to improve contemporary parole practices to better meet the needs of drug-dependent offenders.

Victim-Offender Reconciliation Project (VORP)
20 Battern Park Avenue, Suite 708
Asheville, NC 28801
Telephone: (828) 253-3355
Fax: (828) 255-3315
e-mail: martyprice@vorp.com
Internet: http://www.vorp.com

An alternative dispute resolution is victim-offender reconciliation. Victim-offender reconciliation is a specific form of conflict resolution between the victim and the offender. Face-to-face encounter is the essence of this process. Elkhart County, Indiana, has been the site of the Victim-Offender Reconciliation Project (VORP) since 1987. The primary aims of VORP are (1) to make offenders accountable for their wrongs against victims, (2) to reduce recidivism among participating offenders, and (3) to heighten responsibility of offenders through victim compensation and repayment for damages inflicted. A subsequent mission statement was released in 2004. The mission of VORP has been revised to bring restorative justice reform to our criminal and juvenile justice systems, to empower victims, offenders, and communities to heal the effects of crime, to curb recidivism, and to offer society a more effective and humane alternative to the growing outcry for more prisons and more punishment.

VORP was established in Kitchener, Ontario, Canada, in 1974 and was subsequently replicated as PACT, or Prisoner and Community Together, in northern Indiana near Elkhart. Subsequent replications in various jurisdictions have created different varieties of Alternative Dispute Resolution (ADR), each variety spawning embellishments, additions, or program deletions deemed more or less important by that particular jurisdiction. The Genessee County (Batavia), New York, Sheriff's Department established a VORP in 1983, followed by programs in Valparaiso, Indiana; Quincy, Massachusetts; and Minneapolis, Minnesota, in 1985. In Massachusetts, the program was named EARN-IT and was operated through the Probation Department. More than twenty-five different states have one or another version of VORP. One of these sites involved a study of offender recidivism and ADR. Investigations of ADR and its effectiveness have tended to reduce recidivism among affected offenders. Associates of VORP include mediators and trainers with backgrounds in psychotherapy, education, public administration, and law. VORP serves nonprofit organizations, government agencies, and individuals.

8

Resources

Annotated Print Resources

Books and Journal Articles

Allender, David M. 2004. **"Offender Reentry: A Returning or Reformed Criminal?"** *FBI Law Enforcement Bulletin* 73: 1–10.

Offender re-entry into the community is an increasingly important topic in community corrections and corrections generally. The question is whether prisons and jails adequately prepare inmates for their subsequent transition into communities in which their lives are less regimented. Not only are living conditions severely different, but adaptations of newly released offenders are expected. These adaptations to normal community living assume that inmates have received the necessary vocational and educational training, counseling, and other services while confined, so that they may successfully adapt to community living and lead law-abiding lives. The reality is that most prisons fail to prepare inmates for subsequent community living, and the various causes of that failure are examined. One cause is the lack of money with which to hire sufficient personnel to perform training services. Money earmarked for corrections is often diverted by state legislatures to local noncorrections-related projects. Accountability mechanisms are nonexistent in many jurisdictions. Thus, it is unclear how the money is allocated to projects and activities unrelated to the correctional services originally intended for such funds. The problems of accountability for correctional expenditures are examined and contrasted with the failure of many inmates to adjust adequately to community living.

Belenko, S. 2006. **"Assessing Released Inmates for Substance-Abuse-Related Service Needs."** *Crime and Delinquency* 52: 94–113.

Many inmates released from prison unconditionally or on parole suffer from continuing substance-abuse problems. These problems need to be addressed effectively by appropriate and mandated community programming. Despite the recognition of the necessity for such programming, many communities lack the funds or resources to provide such services to growing numbers of offenders in need of treatment. The implications of offender needs and existing community services are explored.

Bergeron, Christine E., and Stuart J. McKelvie. 2004. **"Effects of Defendant Age on Severity of Punishment for Different Crimes."** *Journal of Social Psychology* 144: 75–90.

Research examines the effects of defendant age on the severity of punishment for various crimes. After reading a murder or theft vignette in which the perpetrator was a twenty-, forty-, or sixty-year-old man, ninety-five undergraduates gave sentence and parole recommendations for the offender's act. Punishment was harsher for the murder than for the theft. For murder, participants treated the twenty- and sixty-year-old men less harshly than the forty-year-old men, which confirms previous archival findings. However, this inverted U-shaped function occurred for murder only. Results are discussed in the context of the just-desert and utilitarian rationales that guide sentencing. Suggestions for future research are discussed.

Dembo, R., et al. 2005. **"Evaluation of the Impact of a Policy Change on Diversion Program Recidivism and Justice System Costs."** *Journal of Offender Rehabilitation* 41: 93–122.

Diversion programs are examined as they impact formal court processing of criminal cases. Are diversion programs accomplishing their goals of heightening offender accountability, ensuring public safety, and individualizing offender treatment? Findings suggest that diversion is a useful and productive alternative to formal offender processing. Court delays are reduced by diverting less serious property cases to alternative dispute resolution and victim-offender reconciliation projects. The implications of diversion for offender attitudes and future recidivism are examined.

Denov, Myriam S., and Kathryn M. Campbell. 2005. **"Understanding the Causes, Effects and Responses to Wrongful Conviction."** *Journal of Contemporary Criminal Justice* 21: 224–249.

One egregious consequence of a vigorous prosecution is the conviction of innocent persons. Overwhelming circumstantial evidence may be presented resulting in the wrongful conviction of persons who have committed no crime. The systemic features of the appellate process are examined in this context. It is quite difficult for higher courts to overturn wrongful convictions, since the system is weighed heavily in favor of prosecutors and the state. It is assumed by higher courts that trial courts were correct in convicting persons initially, and it takes overwhelming evidence to convince higher courts otherwise. Since many of those who are wrongly convicted are coincidentally indigent and cannot mount the same quality of defense as more affluent offenders, this raises questions of fairness in terms of minority and socioeconomic factors. The causes, effects, and responses to wrongful conviction are explored and several solutions proposed.

Doob, Anthony N., and Cheryl Marie Webster. 2003. **"Sentence Severity and Crime: Accepting the Null Hypothesis."** In *Crime and Justice: A Review of Research, Volume 30.* Michael Tonry, ed. Chicago: University of Chicago Press, 143–195.

This review probes an aspect of general deterrence: the effects of sentence severity on crime. It concentrates primarily on studies conducted over the past decade, with special consideration of those that examine the dramatic changes in sentencing policy that occurred during the 1990s. The literature in this area has been studied many times in the past twenty-five years. Most reviews conclude that there is little or no consistent evidence that harsher sanctions reduce crime rates in Western populations. Nevertheless, scholars have been reluctant to conclude that variation in the severity of sentence does not have differential deterrent impacts. A reasonable assessment of the research to date justifies the notion that sentence severity has no effect on the level of crime in society. The time has come to accept the null hypothesis.

Draine, M., T. L. Sia, and D. F. Dansereau. 2006. **"Improving Early Engagement and Treatment Readiness of Probationers: Gender Differences."** *Prison Journal* 86: 1552–1572.

A comparison of male and female offenders placed on probation shows that women have greater success rates on probation than men. The reasons for these differences are examined. Women are more likely than men to be responsive to community programs designed to assist them in making the transition to community living and remaining law-abiding. Male-female differences are assessed. Various factors are considered as explanations for why women are more successful on probation, and why men have more difficulty in making successful probation adjustments.

Farrell, Jill. 2003. **"Mandatory Minimum Firearm Penalties: A Source of Sentencing Disparity?"** *Justice Research and Policy* 5: 95–115.

This study examines how mandatory minimum firearm penalties are applied in Maryland. Data are obtained from Maryland circuit courts for all multiple- and single-count violent offenses that occurred between July 1, 1987, and July 1, 1995 (19,995). Only 37 percent of eligible offenders are ultimately convicted under the mandatory minimum statute, and they receive approximately three years more on their sentence as a result of the mandatory minimum. The penalty is not applied randomly, but prosecutors do exhibit an organized effort to target the more serious offenders who commit more serious crimes. Race and gender, however, also exert a significant effect on the outcome, controlling for prior record, offense severity, offense type, other demographic characteristics, and case processing variables. Specifically, black offenders are more likely to receive the mandatory penalty than whites, and women are less likely to receive the penalty than men. Whereas it is possible that race and gender are only proxies for other, unobserved characteristics, this finding serves as an upper boundary on the size of the gender and race effect in prosecutorial discretion, and it demonstrates the potential for disparity in the charge bargaining stage of the sentencing process. Future research should pay close attention to multiple stages in the sentencing process and multiple-count data to estimate unwarranted disparity whenever possible.

Fleury, Steiner Benjamin, and Victor Argothy. 2004. **"Lethal Borders: Elucidating Jurors' Racialized Discipline to Punish in Latino Defendant Death Cases."** *Punishment and Society* 6: 67–84.

Contemporary anti-immigration and tough-on-crime images of the threatening alien have direct implications for understanding how modern death sentencing decisions are racialized. This research focuses on the historic racialization of Latin Americans in popular culture, in key state legislative initiatives, and in capital punishment decisions. Data, drawn from the Capital Jury Project, are based on the narratives of thirty-five jurors who served in some fourteen cases in Texas and California in which a Latino defendant was sentenced to death. Erecting a racial binary, capital jurors as penal activists impose the death sentence on Latino defendants as part of a broader assimilationist-infused strategy for doing punishment. It is argued that, in a historically racist society such as the United States, the decision to impose the death sentence itself is mobilized as a broader, historically situated form of racialized discipline.

Harris, Victoria, and Christos Dagadakis. 2004. **"Length of Incarceration: Was Their Parity for Mentally Ill Offenders?"** *International Journal of Law and Psychiatry* 27: 387–393.

Two groups of detainees in U.S. county jails—mentally ill offenders (MIOs) and nonmentally ill offenders (NMIOs)—are examined to answer two questions: (1) if previous criminal history was controlled for and the sample size of a comparative study was greatly increased, would the results suggesting that MIOs were incarcerated for a significantly longer period of time hold? and (2) how large an effect does the presence of a mental illness have on the length of incarceration for MIOs? Data were obtained through official records for 127 detainees who were housed in the psychiatric unit at the King County Correctional Facility in Seattle, Washington, during 1990, and 127 detainees who were incarcerated during 1990 but not on the psychiatric unit. Whereas MIOs had a lower rate of previous misdemeanor arrests, there was no statistical difference found in the length of incarceration for the index misdemeanor crime. This suggests that factors other than age, gender, current crime severity, mental illness, and previous criminal history were involved in the determination of the length of incarceration. NMIOs statistically also had significantly more severe histories of prior felony arrests, yet no difference in the mean incarceration length was found. A larger percentage of MIOs served their entire sentence. Based on relative homelessness, however, a lower rate of MIOs were released on bail or personal recognizance. Overall, when age, gender, and crime severity are considered, mental illness does not statistically influence length of incarceration. The presence of a mental illness may easily result in a longer incarceration for an individual. There was a disparity in the length of sentence for both serious and minor crimes, although the difference was not statistically significant.

Hartwell, Stephanie. 2004. **"Triple Stigma: Persons with Mental Illness and Substance Abuse Problems in the Criminal Justice System."** *Criminal Justice Policy Review* 15: 84–99.

This study focuses on individuals with a dual diagnosis and examines policies creating the trajectories for mentally ill people with substance-use problems and their community re-entry after involvement with the criminal justice system. Subjects were divided into three groups: a preadjudication group (n = 171), a postadjudication group serving a prison or misdemeanor sentence averaging 4 months (n = 212), and a postadjudication group serving a prison or felony sentence averaging four years (n = 118). Tracking data were gathered from the Forensic Transition Team program administered by the Massachusetts Department of Mental Health. In comparison with offenders with mental illness, the dually diagnosed were more likely to be serving sentences related to their substance use, to be homeless and to violate probation after release, and to recidivate to correctional custody. An examination of substance abuse histories, short-term community outcomes, and service trends 3 months postrelease suggests various public policy and social service directions.

Henham, Ralph. 2004. **"Conceptualizing Access to Justice and Victims' Rights in International Sentencing."** *Social and Legal Studies* 13: 27–55.

This essay and review addresses some of the theoretical and conceptual difficulties of understanding the meaning and relevance of notions of access to justice and rights for victims in the context of international sentencing. In particular, it suggests the need for such conceptualizations to engage with the nature of the international sentencing process as a transformative mechanism in which fact and value are negotiated to correspond with the moral ideologies of the powerful. For international penalty to progress beyond partisan ideology, rhetorical symbolism and the dynamics of retribution and vindictiveness require us to recognize and comprehend how moral values and action are linked through process, and the significance of that for the legitimacy of punishment. For victims and victim communities in international conflict, this means conceiving of participation and rights as processual reality, and recognizing that any constructive engagement with notions of truth and justice must be grounded in context.

Holleran, David, and Cassia Spohn. 2004. **"On the Use of the Total Incarceration Variable in Sentencing Research."** *Criminology* 42: 211–240.

This research questions the use of the total incarceration response variable that has been incorporated into sentencing studies over the past thirty years. Specifically, using 1998 data from the Pennsylvania Commission on Sentencing, it demonstrates that prison and jail represent two distinct institutions, and that the judge's decision on disposition should take that factor into account. Based on these findings, researchers should reconsider the use of the total incarceration variable, which combines prison and jail into a single response category.

Ireland, Connie Stivers, and JoAnn Prause. 2005. **"Discretionary Parole Release: Length of Imprisonment, Percent of Sentence Served, and Recidivism."** *Journal of Crime and Justice* 28: 27–49.

Length of imprisonment of a sample of inmates, the actual percentage of time served, and the amount of recidivism are observed over a three-year period following discretionary release through parole board action. Although recidivism rates were lower for those who had served greater portions of their sentences before being paroled, the differences between these parolees and those paroled after serving shorter sentences were not significant statistically. Questions pertaining to how much time should be served before parole consideration are examined. Length of imprisonment does not appear to be a deterrent to future recidivism among those paroled after serving shorter or longer portions of their sentences.

Jeffries, Samantha, Garth Fletcher, and Greg Newbold. 2003. **"Pathways to Sex-based Differentiation in Criminal Court Sentencing."** *Criminology* 41: 329–353.

This research examines the process of sex-based differentiation in sentencing outcomes for 194 men and 194 women sentenced between 1990 and 1997 in Christchurch, New Zealand. Subjects were selected from two court registers: the High Court's "Return of Prisoners Tried and Sentenced" and the District Court's "Return of Persons Committed for Trial and Sentence." Only cases involving drug, violent, and property offenses for adult offenders (aged seventeen and over) were analyzed. Consistent with past research, results showed that judicial processing treated women more leniently than men. Path analyses revealed that judges were less likely to sentence women than men to imprisonment because of gendered information and decisions made earlier in the judicial process, such as criminal history, length of custodial remands, and presentence recommendations by probation officers. In contrast, judges exercised considerably more leniency toward women than men in setting the length of prison terms, even after statistically controlling for all sex-differentiated factors such as criminal history.

Johnson, B. D. 2005. **"Contextual Disparities in Guidelines Departures: Courtroom Social Contexts, Guidelines Compliance, and Extralegal Disparities in Criminal Sentencing."** *Criminology* 43: 761–796.

Whenever judges depart from sentencing guidelines, it is expected and mandated that they will provide a rationale in writing for doing so. The factors justifying the guideline departure must be clearly articulated. It is often difficult to separate legal from extralegal factors when making sentencing guideline departure decisions. An examination of the extralegal factors responsible for guideline departures is made, and suggestions for correcting departures based on racial, gender, ethnic, and socioeconomic factors are provided.

Kovandzic, Tomislav V. 2001. **"The Impact of Florida's Habitual Offender Law on Crime."** *Criminology* 39: 179–203.

This study examines the impact of Florida's habitual offender law on crime. It attempts to mitigate the problems found in similar studies, such as a failure to consider the incapacitation effects that may be responsible for most of the law's impact but that may not appear until years after the law is passed; failure to address simultaneity issues; and omitting needed control variables to avoid spurious or suppressed results. A multiple time-series design of pooled annual data for fifty-eight counties in Florida from 1980 to 1998 was analyzed. Crime rates were measured using Uniform Crime Report data; habitual offender law data were obtained from inmate files provided by the Florida Department of Corrections.

Procedures that criminologists can use to overcome methodological problems plaguing habitual offender law research are outlined. Procedures include conducting a sentencing outcome analysis to estimate the extra amount of prison time imposed on offenders, using the Granger causality test to help resolve simultaneity issues between habitual offender laws and crime, and using a multiple time-series design that provides for a large sample size and allows one to enter proxy variables for unknown factors that affect crime.

Florida's habitual offender law may have slightly reduced rape, robbery, assault, burglary, larceny, and auto theft, but there is little evidence that changes in crime immediately follow passage or application of the law. Four possible explanations are discussed. Florida's habitual offender law has not been very effective at reducing crime; the legislature should consider repealing it and sentencing repeat offenders under the state's sentencing guidelines.

Kovandzic, Tomislav V., John J. Sloan, and Lynne M. Vieraitis. 2004. **"'Striking Out' as Crime Reduction Policy: The Impact of 'Three Strikes' Laws on Crime Rates in U.S. Cities."** *Justice Quarterly* 21: 207–239.

This study estimates the overall and state-specific effects of three strikes laws on UCR index crimes using a multiple time-series design. City-level, time-series, cross-sectional data were obtained for the years 1980 to 2000 for all 188 U.S. cities with a population of 100,000 or more in 1990, and for which relevant UCR data were available. Of the 188 cities, 110 were in states that had passed three strikes laws between 1993 and 1996. No credible statistical evidence was found that the passage of three strikes laws reduces crime by deterring potential criminals or incapacitating repeat offenders. Furthermore, no evidence of an immediate or gradual decrease in crime rates and homicide rates was positively associated with the passage of three strikes laws. The findings for the state-specific analysis were mixed, with some states showing increases in some crimes, and other showing decreases. As such, policymakers should reconsider the costs and benefits associated with three strikes laws. Although the laws have failed to produce what is arguably one of the most important benefits, a reduction in crime, researchers have identified numerous costs associated with three strikes and other habitual offender laws, including racial disparity in their application and the financial costs of increased trials and of providing medical care to aging prisoners. Researchers should also continue to explore this topic, especially in light of the continual advances in research methodology.

Kunselman, Julie C., Kathrine A. Johnson, and Michael C. Rayboun. 2003. **"Profiling Sentence Enhancement Offenders: A Case Study of Florida's 10–20–Lifers."** *Criminal Justice Policy Review* 14: 229–248.

This study creates a profile of criminals incarcerated under Florida's 10–20–Life statute—the initial stage of a postimpact analysis of the statute. Passed in July 1999, Florida's 10–20–Life legislation requires that an offender who possesses a firearm during the commission of a crime must serve a minimum term of imprisonment of ten years. An offender who discharges a weapon during a crime must serve a minimum term of twenty years. Finally, an offender who discharges a firearm and inflicts death or great bodily harm must serve a minimum term of not less than twenty-five years and not more than life. Individual and criminal offense data on all incarcerated 10–20–Life offenders (1,065 as of November 1, 2001) are collected from the Florida Department of Corrections. Subjects are overwhelmingly male (96 percent), and one-half are ages twenty-three to forty-one. Some 80 percent of offenses are for felonies committed while in possession of a firearm or concealed weapon, and robbery with a firearm or deadly weapon. Slightly more than half of the offenders are sentenced to a term of three years; the remaining receive ten or more years. The average sentence is eight years. The average sentence length is significantly higher for blacks than for others sentenced under 10–20–Life. Moreover, blacks received all nine of the life sentences.

Kurlychek, Megan C., and Brian D. Johnson. 2004. **"The Juvenile Penalty: A Comparison of Juvenile and Young Adult Sentencing Outcomes in Criminal Court."** *Criminology* 42: 485–517.

This is an investigation of the sentencing of juvenile offenders processed in adult criminal court by comparing their sentencing outcomes to those of young adult offenders in similar situations. The expanded juvenile exclusion and transfer policies of the 1990s have led to an increase in the number of juveniles convicted in adult courts; thus, it is critical to better understand the judicial decision-making process involved. Data were obtained from the Pennsylvania Commission on Sentencing for the sentencing outcomes of 1,042 juveniles and 33,962 young adults (ages eighteen to twenty-four) processed in the state's adult criminal justice system over a three-year period (1997–1999). Overall, juvenile offenders in adult court are sentenced more severely than their young adult counterparts. Moreover, juvenile status interacts with and conditions the effects of other important sentencing factors, including offense type, offense severity, and prior criminal record. These findings suggest that judges may attribute less importance to traditional legal variables when sentencing juveniles in court, and that the impact of both offense severity and prior record is significantly less for juvenile offenders than for young adult offenders. Although this finding may suggest that juvenile status overshadows other traditional sentencing considerations typically found to impact sentencing in adult court, future research is needed to substantiate that claim. Nevertheless, this decreased reliance on legal criteria may be related to the overt salience of juvenile status in adult court. That is, while all other legal and extralegal factors included in this analysis are typical considerations before the adult court judge, juvenile status is a unique identifier for this category of offender that is not present in the majority of sentencing decisions. As such, courtroom actors may afford it more weight relative to other sentencing considerations.

Lowencamp, Christopher T., and Edward J. Latessa. 2005. **"Developing Successful Reentry Programs: Lessons Learned from the 'What Works' Research."** *Corrections Today* 67: 72–76.

Attention is focused on successful parolees who adjust to community living after serving various prison terms. Whether inmates are released through discretionary parole or mandatory parole seems to make little difference in their subsequent community adjustment. Focus is given to preparole programs provided to these inmates while confined. Vocational and educational training seem to factor prominently into their subsequent successful (or unsuccessful) community adjustment, and whether their law-abiding behavior is affected significantly. Counseling, individual or group, is considered quite important in determining whether offenders can make satisfactory psychological and social adjustments to community living. Sentencing solutions should include court-ordered counseling and other services, regardless of whether institutions can provide them. The failure of institutions to provide such services should obligate those institutions to demand funding to furnish the necessary personnel and other ancillary materials and resources necessary to effectively provide for the needs of offenders in preparole stages. Various solutions are considered.

Mann, Ruth E., et al. 2004. **"Approach versus Avoidance Goals in Relapse Prevention with Sexual Offenders."** *Sexual Abuse: A Journal of Research and Treatment* 16: 65–75.

This work is an investigation into the clinical effects of a deliberately positively focused relapse prevention (RP) approach for sex offenders focusing on the creation of a "good life." It hypothesizes that clients completing this approach would develop more commitment to preventing relapse and engage the RP intervention more effectively than those completing the more traditional avoidance-oriented RP intervention. A total of forty-seven inmates convicted of sex offenses were randomly assigned to the two groups, which were matched on age, risk, and sentence length. All participants completed an 8-month group treatment program. Data were gathered from the RP Interview, the Self-Esteem Questionnaire, risk diaries, and therapist ratings and interviews. Results indicated that subjects who completed the approach-focused intervention had a greater engagement in treatment as measured by homework compliance and willingness to disclose lapses. Furthermore, these offenders were rated by therapists as being more genuinely motivated to live without offending by the end of treatment. However, marked differences failed to emerge between the groups with regard to changes in self-esteem following treatment. Implications of the findings for treatment delivery are noted.

Mauer, M., and Meda Chesney-Lind. 2002. *Invisible Punishment: The Collateral Consequences of Mass Imprisonment.* New York: New Press.

This book examines the implications for a large sample of prisoners for subsequent reentry into society, adaptation to societal standards, and coping with freedom after being imprisoned for various sentence lengths. The social and psychological effects of imprisonment are questioned, together with an analysis of the absence of effective vocational and educational programming, and psychological group or individual counseling available or unavailable to those incarcerated. Conditions of imprisonment are examined as they relate to offender integration.

Mauer, Marc, Ryan S. King, and Malcolm S. Young. 2004. *The Meaning of "Life": Long Prison Sentences in Context.* Washington, DC: Sentencing Project.

Drawing on official statistics, this report assesses the dramatic increase in the imposition of life sentences in the context of incapacitation and public safety, fiscal costs, and the sentencing goal of punishment. Currently, 9.4 percent of offenders in state/federal prison are serving a life sentence. Of those, 26.3 percent are serving a sentence of life without parole. The number of lifers rose by 83 percent between 1992 and 2003. In six states—Illinois, Iowa, Louisiana, Maine, Pennsylvania, and South Dakota—all life sentences are imposed without the possibility of parole. The increase in prison time for lifers results from changes in state policy rather than continuous increases in violent crime. A total of 79.4 percent of lifers released in 1994 had no arrests for a new crime in the three years following release. That compares to an arrest-free rate of 32.5 percent for all inmate releases. Finally, imposing a life sentence carries a potential cost to taxpayers of $1 million.

McBride, Elizabeth C., Christy Visher, and Nancy LaVigne. 2005. **"Informing Policy and Practice: Prisoner Reentry Research at the Urban Institute."** *Corrections Today* 67: 90–93.

Prisoner re-entry research has disclosed numerous defects in preparole programming at numerous correctional institutions throughout the United States. A lack of funding, qualified personnel, and programming is at the root of many offenders' problems when attempting to readjust to normal community living. Success rates of parolees are highly dependent upon the nature and extent of training they receive while confined in prison environments, including vocational and educational counseling, group and individual therapy, anger management courses, and other practical experiences designed to assist in their eventual rehabilitation and reintegration. Present policies are examined and suggestions for improving policies are considered.

Merritt, Nancy, Terry Fain, and Susan Turner. 2006. **"Oregon's Get Tough Sentencing Reform: A Lesson in Justice System Adaptation."** *Criminology and Public Policy* 5: 5–36.

One result of a get tough policy relating to sentencing is growing inmate populations in prisons and jails, as more offenders are given longer sentences with the expectation that they will serve greater portions of those sentences under truth-in-sentencing accompanying statutes. The implications of such a get-tough policy are explored, both from a practical standpoint of funding the creation of new institutions for confining these growing numbers of offenders and the need for public safety.

Ray, Katherine E. Brown, and Leanne Fiftal Alarid. 2004. **"Examining Racial Disparity of Male Property Offenders in the Missouri Juvenile Justice System."** *Youth Violence and Juvenile Justice* 2: 107–128.

On the basis of 1994 juvenile court data on 4,284 male juvenile property offenders, this study investigates the extent of racial disparity and discrimination in six Missouri counties. Logistic regression analyses were used to test the probability of juveniles being processed in the system at four decision-making points: referral, detention, adjudication, and disposition, controlling for available legal factors and county type. Evidence emerged of contextual racial discrimination in some jurisdictions at the petition, detention, and adjudication stages. In all counties combined, blacks were more likely to be formally referred and detained before adjudication, whereas whites were more likely to be adjudicated. The earlier intake decision produced the most collective racial disparity, a finding reported in other studies. The importance of jurisdictional differences among counties is demonstrated.

Roberts, Julian V. 2003. **"Public Opinion and Mandatory Sentencing: A Review of International Findings."** *Criminal Justice and Behavior* 30: 483–508.

This article examines the findings from public opinion surveys related to mandatory sentencing. Evidence from several countries indicates that public support for mandatory sentencing is quite limited. Support is strongest when a general question is posed that permits respondents to supply their own image of the kinds of offenders likely to be affected by mandatory sentencing laws and when there is no reference to the impact of mandatory sentencing laws on the principles of sentencing (such as a loss of proportionality in sentencing). When confronted with specific cases, however, the public rejects mandatory sentences, especially strongly in the case of nonviolent offenders. Moreover, the limited research evidence suggests that few members of the public are aware of mandatory penalties, and providing information about such sentences has no effect on either their perceptions of crime seriousness or their confidence in the sentencing process. This suggests that whatever their merits, mandatory sentences of imprisonment do not necessarily advance the goals of deterrence. Furthermore, there is only limited public support for the sentencing goals of denunciation and deterrence that underlie mandatory sentencing. The public appears to be more concerned with desert-based sentencing, which emphasizes proportional punishments to which mandatory minima are anathema. By limiting a court's ability to impose a proportional sentence, mandatory minima can violate the principle of proportionality, and that is likely to undermine, rather than enhance, public confidence in the courts. Nonetheless, whatever happens with respect to these punitive laws, it is important to have a comprehensive and accurate view of where the public stands. To achieve a fair and valid assessment of public attitudes, therefore, respondents must be made aware of the effects of mandatory sentences on proportional, desert-based sentencing. They should also be provided with specific examples of the range of cases affected by mandatory sentencing legislation.

Roberts, Julian V., and Edna Erez. 2004. **"Communication in Sentencing: Exploring the Expressive Function of Victim Impact Statements."** *International Review of Victimology* 10: 223–244.

The role of the victim in the sentencing process continues to generate controversy among scholars and practitioners. This essay and review addresses some of the persistent objections to allowing victim input into sentencing. By placing the debate on victim input within its historical context, it suggests that the movement to provide victims with a voice has been derailed, as the communicative model of victim input—originally envisioned by the reform movement as its justification—was replaced by a model stressing the influence of victim impact statements on sentencing. Much of the lingering opposition to victim input rights has been animated by this "impact" model, which is theoretically misconceived, empirically unsupported, and at odds with major sentencing aims. The communicative model, which reflects the original intent and purpose of the victim reform concerning input, is reintroduced, and its benefits for both victims and offenders are elaborated. Two examples from the field are provided, and a call is made to reassess current theory and practice regarding victim integration in sentencing. Policy recommendations are outlined.

Rodriguez, Nancy. 2003. **"The Impact of Three-Strikes-and-You're-Out Sentencing Decisions: Punishment for Only Some Habitual Offenders."** *Criminal Justice Policy Review* 14: 106–127.

This research focuses on how implementation of habitual offender laws has affected the sentencing of repeat, violent offenders. Using both additive and interactive models, the research uses criminal history records and prior three-strike offenses to measure sentence length of convicted felony offenders in Washington State. Data on 19,403 convictions from July 1993 through June 1997 are collected from the State of Washington Sentencing Guidelines Commission. Hispanics and blacks receive shorter sentences than whites, whereas male and younger offenders receive longer sentences than females and older offenders. The influence of criminal history records and prior strikes on sentencing decisions is indirectly associated with offense type (that is, person, property, sex, and drug cases). Findings clearly demonstrate the importance of capturing how legal variables effect the sentencing process of those sentenced under persistent offender laws. Directions for future research are suggested.

Ruback, R. Barry, Jennifer N. Shaffer, and Melissa A. Logue. 2004. **"The Imposition and Effects of Restitution in Four Pennsylva-**

nia Counties: Effects of Size of County and Specialized Collection Units." *Crime and Delinquency* 50: 168–188.

The effects of restitution are examined in several Pennsylvania counties. Court, probation, and collection office records in four Pennsylvania counties were chosen because they varied along two dimensions: population size and the use of specialized units for the collection of monetary sanctions. From each county, restitution-eligible cases were sampled from both 1994 and 1996 to test the effects of a 1995 statutory change mandating restitution. Multivariate models indicated that restitution was significantly more likely to be ordered for property crimes, offenses that were more easily quantified, offenses against businesses, and offenses committed after the statutory change. Moreover, restitution was more likely to be imposed and a higher percentage was likely to be paid in counties with smaller populations and in those in which probation officers handled the collection of economic sanctions than in counties in which they were handled by specialized collection units.

Schlesinger, T. 2005. **"Racial and Ethnic Disparity in Pretrial Criminal Processing."** *Justice Quarterly* 22: 170–192.

The criminal justice system has long been accused of operating on the basis of extralegal factors, particularly factors related to race and ethnicity. Numerous studies have examined those and other extralegal factors as they relate to criminal processing. Inconclusive evidence has been disclosed, although there have been instances in which clear and convincing evidence of racial and ethnic discrimination in offender processing has occurred. Correcting such disparities rests both with judges and parole boards. Various accountability mechanisms are suggested for avoiding the appearance of disparities in processing attributable to extralegal factors. Suggestions are made for holding judges and paroles more accountable in their decision-making relating to sentencing under a racially and ethnically neutral scenario.

Simourd, David J. 2004. **"Use of Dynamic Risk/Need Assessment Instruments among Long-term Incarcerated Offenders."** *Criminal Justice and Behavior* 31: 306–323.

Research examines the Level of Service Inventory-Revised (LSI-R) by exploring the predictive validity of the instrument among long-term incarcerated offenders. Dynamic risk/need assessment instruments are useful tools in the effective treatment and management of offenders. The LSI-R is a dynamic risk/need assessment instrument that has been used extensively among a variety of offender samples. Although considerable research has shown that the instrument is valid and reliable, there is a lack of information on the predictive validity of the instrument among longer-term offenders. In the current study, the LSI-R was completed by a sample of 129 Canadian federally incarcerated offenders serving a mean sentence length of five years. Scores on the LSI-R were compared with various recidivism criteria during a 15-month follow-up period. Overall, the instrument had acceptable reliability and predictive validity and distinguished recidivists from nonrecidivists. As such, the LSI-R can effectively be applied to long-term offenders as well as showing promise as an important risk/need assessment instrument among a variety of offender samples. Given the technical quality of the LSI-R and other similar dynamic risk/need assessment instruments, perhaps the time has come to shift focus away from the production-line pace of developing new risk assessment tools. Instead, research energy might be better channeled toward issues that have been largely ignored during the risk assessment technology boom. Specifically, attention is lacking in quality assurance strategies, links between assessment and rehabilitation, and the unique factors among individuals that make them more or less susceptible to clinical intervention.

Solomon, Amy L. 2006. **"Does Parole Supervision Work? Research Findings and Policy Opportunities."** *APPA Perspectives* 30: 26–37.

Parole supervision is examined insofar as it assists parolees to make successful adjustments into their communities. Problems of parolee re-entry are explored, and a focus is directed toward prisons in which these inmates are supposed to receive training, vocational and educational, as well as other services, including individual and group counseling. Such preparole programming is considered essential to making successful adjustments to community living on the outside. Inmates without such preparole experiences present supervision problems for their parole officers, who are frustrated in that they lack the means to assist offenders in becoming successfully reintegrated. The issues and problems of preparole institutional programming are examined and compared with the services provided by paroling authorities and the qualifications of officers expected to supervise large numbers of untrained and unprepared clients.

Steen, Sara, and Mark A. Cohen. 2004. **"Assessing the Public's Demand for Hate Crime Penalties."** *Justice Quarterly* 21: 91–124.

This work is an analysis of public attitudes toward punishment for hate crimes, using telephone interview data from a nationally representative sample of adults (N = 1,300). The most general finding to emerge was that there is minimal public support for harsher penalties for offenders who commit hate crimes than for offenders who commit identical crimes with no specific motivation. The second important finding was that respondents' concerns about hate crimes depend on which minority groups are targeted. Specifically, there appeared to be some support for harsher penalties for hate crimes against Jewish victims. Finally, while most respondents' demographic characteristics did not have an impact on sentencing decisions for either nonhate or hate crimes, attitudes toward punishment, treatment, and minority rights had a significant effect on those decisions.

Tonry, Michael. 2004. *Thinking about Crime: Sense and Sensibility in American Penal Culture.* Oxford, UK: Oxford University Press.

This essay discusses America's preoccupation with crime problems and policies such as the war on drugs, zero tolerance policing, and three-strikes-and-you're-out policies. The U.S. criminal justice system has lost its way, and political cynicism and fear have replaced good intentions. The crime control policies that we currently implement are fueled by short-term thinking and knee-jerk reactions so as not to appear "soft on crime." Attitudes toward crime in the United States are cyclical and change with problems and media presentations. Specific solutions are proposed that can serve as a platform for criminal justice reform.

Ullmer, Jeffery T., and Brian Johnson. 2004. **"Sentencing in Context: A Multilevel Analysis."** *Criminology* 42: 137–177.

Hierarchical modeling is used to test hypotheses about contextual-level influences and cross-level interaction effects on local court decisions. Criminal sentencing data for 1997 to 1999 were drawn from the Pennsylvania Commission on Sentencing. Contextual data were taken from the census, the U.S. Uniform Crime Reports, and the 1999 County and City Extra. Cases were limited to the most serious offense per judicial transaction and to those sentenced under the 1997 guidelines. Most of the explanatory "action" was at the individual case level in criminal sentencing. In addition, evidence emerged of local contextual features—court organizational culture, court caseload pressure, and racial and ethnic composition—affecting sentencing outcomes, either directly or in interaction with individual factors. Theoretical implications are discussed, as are the dilemmas among civil rights, local autonomy, and organizational realities of criminal courts.

Vogel, Brenda L. 2003. **"Support for Life in Prison without the Possibility of Parole among Death Penalty Proponents."** *American Journal of Criminal Justice* 27: 263–274.

This study compares death penalty supporters who favor the alternative of life in prison without the possibility of parole (LWOP) to death penalty supporters who oppose that option. Telephone interviews are conducted with 556 adult residents of Orange County, California. More than 45 percent of respondents in the two groups viewed LWOP as a viable alternative to the imposition of capital punishment. Although findings reveal few statistically significant differences between the groups, those in the higher-income brackets are more likely to oppose the LWOP alternative. Developing a clearer picture of death penalty supporters willing to support the LWOP option will not only contribute to death penalty opinion literature but may also better inform opponents committed to the demise of capital punishment and allow them to champion that cause more effectively.

Weidner, Robert, Richard Frase, and Iain Pardoe. 2004. **"Explaining Sentence Severity in Large Urban Counties: A Multilevel Analysis of Contextual and Case-level Factors."** *Prison Journal* 84: 184–207.

A hierarchical logistic model is used to examine the impact of legal, extralegal, and contextual variables on the decision to sentence felons to prison in a sample of large urban counties in 1996. Individual-level data were obtained from the State Court Processing Statistics Program of the Bureau of Justice Statistics. None of the four contextual (county-level) variables (the level of crime, unemployment rate, racial composition, and region) increased the likelihood of a prison sentence, but ten case-level factors, both legal and extralegal, and several macro-micro interaction terms were influential. Overall, these results demonstrate the importance of considering smaller geographic units (that is, counties instead of states) and controlling for case-level factors in research on interjurisdictional differences in prison use. Further research in this area will, therefore, ultimately help pinpoint the (combination of) contextual characteristics possessed by jurisdictions with relatively moderate punishment practices. An overarching goal of future inquiry is to identify the key organizational contextual determinants that keep punishment in check.

Williams, Jackson. 2003. **"Criminal Justice Policy Innovation in the States."** *Criminal Justice Policy Review* 14: 401–422.

This study examines factors influencing states' adoptions of four criminal justice policy innovations: Truth-in-Sentencing laws (TIS); three-strikes-and-you're-out laws; boot camps for convicted offenders; and juvenile court transfer provisions. The data contain forty-eight cases for forty-eight states (excluding Hawaii and Alaska) and consist of cross-sectional observations of whether a state had adopted TIS by 1997, instituted a three-strikes law by 1997, instituted a boot camp program by 1995, and enacted or toughened a juvenile transfer program provision between 1992 and 1995. States' crime rates are positively correlated with adoption of the measures, but other objective state factors, such as sentence length, are not. Strained state resources do not deter legislatures from enacting these policies, and voter ideology and political culture have less than expected impact. It appears that criminal justice policy innovations, at least those of the crime control variety, are most highly responsive to the problem environment only at the general level of public consciousness and not responsive to more specific formulations of policy problems. Specifically, political entrepreneurs, rather than state characteristics, are responsible for the adoption.

Annotated Nonprint Resources

Journals, Magazines, Bulletins, and Newsletters

American Jails
American Jail Association
1135 Professional Court
Hagerstown, MD 21740-5853
Telephone: (301) 790-3930
Fax: (301) 790-2941
Internet: http://www.aja.org

Bimonthly refereed magazine publishing articles pertaining to jail operations, management, construction, inmate mental health and welfare, and all other aspects of jail life. Includes articles on probation, parole, and community corrections, for both juveniles and adults. Examines sentencing schemes in existence in all jurisdictions and their implications for jail functions and operations.

Corrections Compendium
American Correctional Association
206 North Washington Street
Suite 200
Alexandria, VA 22314
Telephone: (800) 222-5646
Fax: (703) 224-0040
Internet: http://www.aca.org

Bimonthly refereed publication by the American Correctional Association. Features essays and surveys on selected topics covering the full range of corrections, including community and institutional corrections. Investigates sentencing variations among states and the federal government, including how good time is calculated and distinguished. Examines contemporary issues of relevance to practitioners and theorists. Provides book reviews and commentaries on the current state of law relating to all types of corrections.

Corrections Today
American Correctional Association
206 North Washington Street

Suite 200
Alexandria, VA 22314
Telephone: (800) 222-5646
Fax: (703) 224-0040
Internet: http://www.aca.org

Monthly publication by the American Correctional Association focusing on all aspects of corrections, including community and institutional corrections. Articles focus largely on prison issues, such as overcrowding, mental health of inmates, inmate management, sentencing issues, legal actions, and summaries of current research by prominent practitioners and theorists. Thematic issues address different prison and community corrections issues in timely ways.

Federal Probation
Administrative Office of the U.S. Courts
Washington, DC 20544
Telephone: (202) 502-1600
Fax: (202) 502-1677
Internet: http://www.uscourts.gov/library/pfcontents.html

A refereed journal published three times a year by the Administrative Office of the U.S. Courts. Focuses upon probation, parole, sentencing policies and practices, and all forms of corrections. Dedicated to current thought, research, and practice in corrections and criminal justice for both juvenile and adult correctional systems.

Perspectives
American Probation and Parole Association
P.O. Box 11910
2760 Research Park Drive
Lexington, KY 40511-8482
Telephone: (859) 244-8203
Fax: (859) 244-8001
Internet: http://www.appa-net.org/contact.htm

Referred magazine published bimonthly by the American Probation and Parole Association. Includes articles by practitioners and theorists pertaining to all aspects of probation and parole, including community corrections. Focuses on both offenders and agency officials who work with offenders. Supervisory techniques and technological advances relating to offender supervision are highlighted.

Government Documents and Agency Publications

Bonczar, Thomas P., and Tracy L. Snell. 2005. *Capital Punishment, 2004.* Washington, DC: U.S. Department of Justice, Bureau of Justice Statistics. NCJ 206322.

This work examines all states with capital punishment and capital punishment trends. Cross-tabulations are made according to race, ethnicity, gender, and age of those executed. It reports on the number of persons on death row at year's end, 2004, and reports the methods of execution used by state. The document also reports numbers of persons released from death row administratively because of exculpatory evidence and wrongful convictions.

Brien, Peter. 2005. *Reporting by Prosecutors' Offices to Repositories of Criminal History Records.* Washington, DC: U.S. Department of Justice, Bureau of Justice Statistics. NCJ 205334.

This work examines the reporting of case dispositions by state court prosecutors to state criminal history repositories. The report examines the final disposition information reported, the methods used to transmit, and the length of time required to provide a final disposition. It describes the impediments that many prosecutors encounter that inhibit providing case declinations and other final disposition information to the repository.

DeFrances, Carol J. 2003. *State Court Prosecutors in Small Districts, 2001.* Washington, DC: U.S. Department of Justice, Bureau of Justice Statistics. NCJ 196020.

Results are presented from the 2001 National Survey of Prosecutors (NSP), which collected data on all chief prosecutors that handled felony cases in state courts of general jurisdiction. The report covers prosecutors' offices that served a district with a population under 250,000. It summarizes the budgets for prosecutors' offices and profiles their staffs of attorneys, investigators, victim advocates, and support personnel. The report also presents data on threats against staff and prosecution of computer-related crime. The other survey areas include the number of felony cases closed, the use of DNA evidence, and the number of juvenile cases proceeded against in criminal court.

Durose, Matthew R., and Patrick A. Langan. 2004. *Felony Sentences in State Courts, 2002.* Washington, DC: U.S. Department of Justice, Bureau of Justice Statistics. NCJ 206916.

Felony Sentences in State Courts presents statistics for adults who were convicted of a felony and sentenced in a state court. The data were collected through a nationally representative survey of 300 counties in 2002. Within the twelve offense categories reported are the number and characteristics (for example, age, sex, race) of offenders who were sentenced to prison, jail, or probation. Trends from 1994 to 2002 highlight the number and characteristics of adults convicted of felonies and the types and lengths of sentences imposed. This periodic report is published every two years.

Durose, Matthew R., and Patrick A. Langan. 2005. *State Court Sentencing of Convicted Felons, 2002.* Washington, DC: U.S. Department of Justice, Bureau of Justice Statistics.

This publication examines state court convictions of a national sample of felons for both violent and nonviolent offenses. Sentence lengths are cross-tabulated with gender, race, ethnicity, and other factors. Trends in sentencing are discussed. Numerous statistical tables are presented to illustrate these trends.

Durose, Matthew R., and Christopher J. Mumola. 2004. *Profile of Nonviolent Offenders Exiting State Prisons.* Washington, DC: U.S. Department of Justice, Bureau of Justice Statistics. NCJ 207081.

This is a description of the general characteristics of prison populations serving time for nonviolent crimes as they exit state prisons. Nonviolent crimes are defined as property, drug, and public order offenses that do not involve a threat of harm or an actual attack upon a victim. To conduct this analysis, data were collected under two statistical programs. One program collected data on those discharged from prisons in fifteen states in 1994; the other was a survey of inmates in state correctional facilities in 1997. This report examines the responses of inmates who indicated to interviewers that they expected to be released within 6 months.

Glaze, Lauren E., and Seri Palla. 2005. *Probation and Parole in the United States, 2004.* Washington, DC: U.S. Department of Justice, Bureau of Justice Statistics. NCJ 210676.

The number of persons on probation and parole by state at year's end 2004 is reported here in comparison with totals for year's end 1995 and 2000. The states with the largest and smallest parole and probation populations and the largest and smallest rates of community supervision are identified, along with the states with the largest increases in probation and parole. The race and gender of those populations are also described, together with the percentages of parolees and probationers completing community supervision successfully, or failing because of a rule violation or a new offense.

Greenfeld, Lawrence A. 1995. *Prison Sentences and Time Served for Violence.* Washington, DC: U.S. Department of Justice, Bureau of Justice Statistics. NCJ 153858.

Violent offenders released from state prisons in 1992 served 48 percent of their sentences, an average of 43 months in confinement, both jail and prison, on an average sentence of 89 months. Prison release practices for violent offenders in thirty-one states reveal wide disparity and greater consensus on the duration of time spent in confinement. The report also estimates the hypothetical impact on time served of changing the percentage of sentence served and discusses how the states differ in percentage of sentence served.

Harrison, Paige M., and Allen J. Beck. 2006. *Prison and Jail Inmates at Midyear, 2005.* Washington, DC: U.S. Department of Justice, Bureau of Justice Statistics. NCJ 213133.

This document presents data on jail and prison inmates collected from the National Prisoner Statistics counts and the Census of Jail Inmates 2005. The annual report provides the number of inmates and the overall incarceration rate per 100,000 residents for each state and the federal system. It offers trends since 1995 and the percentage change in prison populations since midyear and year's end 2004. The midyear report presents the number of prison inmates held in private facilities and the number of prisoners under eighteen years of age held by state correctional authorities. It includes total numbers for prison and jail inmates by gender, race, and Hispanic origin, as well as counts of jail inmates by conviction status and confinement status. The report also provides findings on rated capacity of local jails, percentage of capacity occupied, and capacity added.

Hughes, Timothy A. 2001. *Trends in State Parole, 1990–2000.* Washington, DC: U.S. Department of Justice, Bureau of Justice Statistics. NCJ 184735.

Trends in State Parole examines the changing nature of offenders entering and leaving parole and the effects on the trends and composition of the prison population. The report compares discretionary and mandatory releases to parole with the type of discharge from parole supervision. Data are presented on the success and failure rates of offenders on parole by criminal history, sentence length, time served in prison, and offense distribution. The report also profiles specific characteristics and needs of offenders re-entering the community, including drug and alcohol use history, homelessness, and mental health status.

James, Doris J., and Lauren E. Glaze. 2006. *Mental Health Problems of Prison and Jail Inmates.* Washington, DC: U.S. Department of Justice, Bureau of Justice Statistics. NCJ 213600.

This work presents estimates of the prevalence of mental health problems among prison and jail inmates using self-report data on recent history and symptoms of mental disorders. The report compares the characteristics of offenders with a mental health problem to those without, including current offense, criminal record, sentence length, time expected to be served, co-occurring substance dependence or abuse, family background, and facility conduct since current admission. It presents measures of mental health problems by gender, race, Hispanic origin, and age. The report also describes mental health problems and mental health treatment among inmates since admission to jail or prison. Findings are based on the Survey of Inmates in State and Federal Correctional Facilities, 2004, and the Survey of Local Jails, 2002.

Motivans, Mark. 2006. *Federal Criminal Justice Trends, 2003.* Washington, DC: U.S. Department of Justice, Bureau of Justice Statistics. NCJ 205331.

This report presents data on federal criminal justice trends from 1994 to 2003. It summarizes the activities of agencies at each stage of the federal criminal justice case process. It includes ten-year statistics on the number arrested (with detail on drug offenses); number and disposition of suspects investigated by U.S. attorneys; number of persons detained prior to trial; number of defendants in cases filed, convicted, and sentenced; and the number of offenders under federal correctional supervision (for example, incarceration, supervised release, probation, and parole).

Perry, Steven W. 2006. *Prosecutors in State Courts, 2005.* Washington, DC: U.S. Department of Justice, Bureau of Justice Statistics. NCJ 213799.

Prosecutors in State Courts presents findings from the 2005 National Survey of Prosecutors, the latest in a series of data collections about the nation's 2,300 state court prosecutors' offices that tried felony cases in state courts of general jurisdiction. This study provides information on the number of staff, annual budget, and felony cases closed for each office. Information is also available on the use of DNA evidence, computer-related crimes, and terrorism cases prosecuted. Other survey data include special categories of felony offenses prosecuted, types of nonfelony cases handled, number of felony convictions, number of juvenile cases proceeded against in criminal court, and work-related threats or assaults against office staff.

Rottman, David B., and Shauna M. Strickland. 2006. *State Court Organization, 2004.* Washington, DC: U.S. Department of Justice, Bureau of Justice Statistics. NCJ 212351.

Detailed comparative data is presented by state trial and appellate courts in the United States. Topics covered include the number of courts and judges; process for judicial selection; governance of court systems, including judicial funding, administration, staffing, and procedures; jury qualifications and verdict rules; and processing and sentencing procedures for criminal cases. Diagrams of court structure summarize the key features of each state's court organization.

Urban Institute. 2006. *Prisoner Reentry and Community Policing: Strategies for Enhancing Public Safety.* Washington, DC: Urban Institute.

The use of police officers in communities as supplements to probation and parole officer supervision of parolees is examined. A growing number of communities are utilizing police officers in capacities unrelated to traditional law enforcement duties. Should police officers be responsible for assisting parole officers in supervising their clients? That question and others are examined, and the moral and ethical issues of police involvement in parole officer functions are examined.

Videotapes and DVDs

Absence of Malice
Type: DVD
Length: 117 minutes
Date: 1981
Cost: $16.99
Source: Movies Unlimited
3015 Darnell Road
Philadelphia, PA 19154-4344
Telephone: (800) 668-4344
Internet: http://www.moviesunlimited.com

Paul Newman stars as the son of a former crime boss who is now engaged in a legitimate liquor wholesaling business. He becomes involved in an investigation of another crime figure inadvertently, and the U.S. Attorney's Office and various assistant U.S. attorneys attempt to cajole him into giving them incriminating information about those targeted for investigation. Sally Field plays a reporter who secures Newman's confidence and learns things that she reports in her newspaper. The information causes one of Newman's close friends to commit suicide. The film is an excellent depiction of prosecutorial misconduct and how the legal system can be easily manipulated to bring about desired ends, often to the detriment of innocent persons and their friends. The title of this film refers to printing unsubstantiated rumors about what may or may not be true, and such information is disseminated in the press without malice.

American Law: How It Works
Type: DVD
Length: 30 minutes
Date: 2004
Cost: $229
Source: Insight Media
2162 Broadway
New York, NY 10024-0621
e-mail: cs@insight-media.com
Internet: http://www.insight-media.com

This documentary examines the legal system in the United States from its origins in English common law to current legislative and judicial processes. It covers such terms as *habeas corpus, voir dire,* and *stare decisis,* and explores several important landmark U.S. Supreme Court decisions affecting civil liberties.

Another Man's Crime
Type: VHS
Length: 50 minutes
Date: 2003
Cost: $89
Source: Insight Media
2162 Broadway
New York, NY 10024-0621
e-mail: cs@insight-media.com
Internet: http://www.insight-media.com

This documentary explores the incidence of wrongful convictions for crimes. It presents and discusses the story of a police officer who was sent to prison for murder despite his innocence. The program shows how his release from custody and exoneration did not rely on new DNA evidence or an appeal to the courts, but on the conscience of a man he never met who eventually confessed to the crime.

Burden of Innocence
Type: VHS
Length: 60 minutes
Date: 2003
Cost: $119
Source: Insight Media
2162 Broadway

New York, NY 10024-0621
e-mail: cs@insight-media.com
Internet: http://www.insight-media.com

This is a documentary of what happens to people who are considered innocent by DNA testing and then released from prison without financial assistance or support. This PBS program examines the social, psychological, and economic challenges of five exonerated prisoners as they struggle to repair the damage inflicted by wrongful convictions.

Capital Punishment: An Evolving Standard
Type: DVD
Length: 30 minutes
Date: 2005
Cost: $129
Source: Insight Media
2162 Broadway
New York, NY 10024-0621
e-mail: cs@insight-media.com
Internet: http://www.insight-media.com

This documentary examines issues surrounding capital punishment in the United States. It discusses the U.S. Supreme Court's decision that ended capital punishment for juvenile offenders (*Roper v. Simmons,* 2005), executions of minors and adults since 1976, and the application of international standards to U.S. law. The program examines the Eighth Amendment and the consideration that capital punishment is cruel and unusual punishment.

Clarence Darrow
Type: DVD
Length: 120 minutes
Date: 1974
Cost: $23.99
Source: Movies Unlimited
3015 Darnell Road
Philadelphia, PA 19154-4344
Telephone: (800) 668-4344
Internet: http://www.moviesunlimited.com

This movie describes the life of Clarence Darrow, one of the most prominent defense attorneys of his time. He defended Leopold and Loeb in the 1920s in their thrill killing of a youth simply to prove that they could commit the perfect crime. Darrow is best known for his role in the "Monkey Trial," which occurred in Dayton, Tennessee, in the 1920s and involved a schoolteacher, John Scopes, who taught evolution in his history class against school policy. The film is an absorbing portrayal of Darrow and his motives prompting him to pursue defense work on behalf of those unable to afford adequate legal services.

Crime of Insanity
Type: VHS
Length: 60 minutes
Date: 2002
Cost: $119
Source: Insight Media
2162 Broadway
New York, NY 10024-0621
e-mail: cs@insight-media.com
Internet: http://www.insight-media.com

This PBS video explores the insanity plea through the trial of Ralph Tortorici, a disturbed university student who took a class hostage and seriously wounded one of his classmates. The defense of insanity was raised at his trial. The documentary explores the implications for defendants where the insanity plea is raised as an affirmative defense.

The Dark Side of Parole
Type: VHS
Length: 50 minutes
Date: 2000
Cost: $89
Source: Insight Media
2162 Broadway
New York, NY 10024-0621
e-mail: cs@insight-media.com
Internet: http://www.insight-media.com

This documentary examines the growing debate over whether parole boards are too quick to release dangerous inmates, and it considers the cases of a parolee who raped and killed a college student and a former inmate who was released because of prison overcrowding and then committed murder. It raises several issues, including those challenging the ability of parole boards to make decisions relating to the future dangerousness of inmates.

The Death Penalty
Type: DVD
Length: 50 minutes
Date: 2004
Cost: $24.95
Source: Films for the Humanities and Sciences
P.O. Box 2053
Princeton, NJ 08543-2053
Telephone: (800) 257-5216
Internet: http://www.films.com

This documentary explores the arguments for and against the death penalty. It examines the difficult legal, political, and religious issues involved through extensive and intensive interviews with experts on both sides of the debate. A unique insight into capital punishment is provided by an interview with one of the first jailhouse lawyers in the United States, Caryl Chessman, a rapist and kidnapper who appealed his death sentence successfully for twelve years. A reasoned examination of capital punishment is presented.

The History of Punishment
Type: VHS
Length: 53 minutes
Date: 1998
Cost: $159
Source: Insight Media
2162 Broadway
New York, NY 10024-0621
e-mail: cs@insight-media.com
Internet: http://www.insight-media.com

Definitions of crime and punishment in an individual society reveal much about the society's values and history. This program explores the history of punishment, beginning with early compensatory forms of justice, the Code of Hammurabi, and the Law of Moses. It examines Socrates' execution, Roman and medieval forms of justice and punishment, and contemporary forms of societal retribution.

Interviews with Judges and Prosecutors
Type: VHS
Length: 60 minutes
Date: 2005
Cost: $35
Source: The Enlightenment Sentencing Project
1000 N. 4th St.
Fairfield, IA 52557
Telephone: (314) 521-4390
Internet: http://www.enlightenedsentencing.org/orders/htm

This program features several interviews with judges, probation and parole officers, and prosecutors. It details their experiences and the sorts of defendants and clients they interact with daily. Judges relate how they sentence offenders, and they provide some of the reasons for sentencing inequities.

Punishment
Type: VHS
Length: 100 minutes
Date: 2002
Cost: $89
Source: Insight Media
2162 Broadway
New York, NY 10024-0621
e-mail: cs@insight-media.com
Internet: http://www.insight-media.com

This documentary traces the world history of punishment and describes execution by wild animals in ancient Rome, the torture of religious dissidents during the Inquisition, and cruel and unusual punishments that are pervasive in contemporary societies throughout the world. It considers the irony of society's resort to barbarism in its attempts to create and perpetuate humanity and justice.

QB VII
Type: DVD
Length: 5 hours
Date: 1974
Cost: $25.49
Source: Movies Unlimited
3015 Darnell Road
Philadelphia, PA 19154-4344

Telephone: (800) 668-4344
Internet: http://www.moviesunlimited.com

Ben Gazzara and a host of well-known stars seek justice against former Nazis who operated death camps during World War II. The designation QB VII refers to Queen's Bench VII, a courtroom in which most of the action occurs. This film is an excellent example of how justice is eventually obtained for those seeking retribution against their former abusers in Nazi death camps. Also this film functions as a comparative tool, permitting viewers to see how British courts operate somewhat differently from U.S. courts.

Rights of the Accused
Type: DVD
Length: 30 minutes
Date: 2002
Cost: $109
Source: Insight Media
2162 Broadway
New York, NY 10024-0621
e-mail: cs@insight-media.com
Internet: http://www.insight-media.com

This program discusses the U.S. Bill of Rights, focusing on how the Fourth, Fifth, Sixth, and Eighth Amendments deal specifically with the rights of criminal defendants. It explores the ongoing friction between the rights of the accused and the rights of society and victims of crime.

Runaway Jury
Type: DVD
Length: 127 minutes
Date: 2003
Cost: $12.74
Source: Movies Unlimited
3015 Darnell Road
Philadelphia, PA 19154-4344
Telephone: (800) 668–4344
Internet: http://www.moviesunlimited.com

Gene Hackman and John Cusack star in this film about the behind-the-scenes activities of attorneys for the plaintiff and defense as they do various things to win their case. The film focuses upon the jury in the case and how easily jury opinions can be changed by individual jurors, some of whom may be bribed or cajoled into working for the defense's attorney. An excellent portrayal of social dynamics in jury deliberations.

Shotgun Justice
Type: VHS
Length: 50 minutes
Date: 2001
Cost: $89
Source: Insight Media
2162 Broadway
New York, NY 10024-0621
e-mail: cs@insight-media.com
Internet: http://www.insight-media.com

This program examines the unusual case of Michael Pardue, who escaped from jail three times over two decades after being convicted for three 1973 murders. In 1995 a federal judge decided that Pardue's lawyer had inadequately defended him during the original murder trial and overturned those convictions, freeing Pardue from jail. A case of wrongful convictions is examined, and the reasons why Pardue was never charged with escaping from a jail in earlier years are also examined.

Solitary Confinement
Type: DVD
Length: 50 minutes
Date: 2004
Cost: $24.95
Source: A and E Television Networks
235 East 45th Street
New York, NY 10017
Telephone: (888) 423-1212
Internet: http://www.AandE.com

Today's penal system is in flux, with new theories of punishment and confinement and new technologies being devised and promoted. Supermax prisons cost more than $50,000 per cell, and it is becoming increasingly expensive to house long-term offenders. This documentary visits several facilities, including Pelican Bay in California and the Arizona State Penitentiary, where solitary confinement is used as a punishment. The documentary explores the pros and cons of solitary confinement, its rehabilitative and punitive value, and other factors.

A Son's Confession
Type: VHS
Length: 50 minutes
Date: 2000
Cost: $99
Source: Insight Media
2162 Broadway
New York, NY 10024-0621
e-mail: cs@insight-media.com
Internet: http://www.insight-media.com

This documentary is about the controversial case of Peter Reilly, who was convicted of killing his mother in 1973 when he was a teenager. It considers claims by Reilly that police officers forced him to confess to a crime he didn't commit, and it discusses how help from friends and celebrities who believed in Reilly's innocence resulted in a new trial in which the state dropped its prosecution. The program discusses several questions about police and prosecutorial methods of extracting confessions from innocent persons under coercive circumstances.

Sources of Law
Type: DVD
Length: 20 minutes
Date: 1980
Cost: $129
Source: Insight Media
2162 Broadway
New York, NY 10024-0621
e-mail: cs@insight-media.com
Internet: http://www.insight-media.com

This short documentary takes a historical look at the legal system of the United States, examining the Bill of Rights and earlier codes, such as the Code of Hammurabi. It explains the bases for the Bill of Rights amendments and the need for order in society. Also, it articulates the rights of citizens under the law and what society should expect by adopting a comprehensive codified legal code.

12 Angry Men
Type: DVD
Length: 92 minutes
Date: 1957
Cost: $19.95
Source: Movies Unlimited
3015 Darnell Road
Philadelphia, PA 19154-4344
Telephone: (800) 668-4344
Internet: http:www.moviesunlimited.com

Henry Fonda and a group of well-known actors are locked in a jury deliberation room in which they engage in powerful exchanges of opinion and arguments as they debate the guilt or innocence of a minority youth accused of murder. This film explores the deliberation process and highlights some of the types of situations that accompany many jury deliberations in the real world. The film is a powerful instructional aid for use in court procedure courses and criminal justice courses generally.

What Is Justice?
Type: VHS
Length: 30 minutes
Date: 1998
Cost: $109
Source: Insight Media
2162 Broadway
New York, NY 10024-0621
e-mail: cs@insight-media.com
Internet: http://www.insight-media.com

This film discusses the theoretical and philosophical underpinnings of justice in civil societies from a historical perspective. It examines the works of Aristotle, Plato, Marx, Rawls, and Nozick as they pertain to world legal systems and imposing the will of the people on society. Also, it discusses the different philosophies of justice and the meaning of justice for different cultures at different points in time.

You the Jury
Type: DVD
Length: 30 minutes

Date: 1995
Cost: $119
Source: Insight Media
2162 Broadway
New York, NY 10024-0621
e-mail: cs@insight-media.com
Internet: http://www.insight-media.com

Asking viewers to serve as jurors, legislative drafters, lawyers, and judges, this program presents the case of a teenager accused of buying stolen property. It features a law professor who explains the right to a jury trial, the confrontation clause, and the laws regarding search and seizure that might lead to a conviction.

Internet Sources

ABA Juvenile Justice Center
http://www.abanet.org/crimjust/juvjus/home.html

Abuse of Judicial Discretion
http://www.constitution.org/abus/discretion/judicial/judicial_discretion.htm

Administrative Office of the U.S. Courts
http://www.uncle-sam.com/uscourts.html,
http://www.uscourts.gov

American Arbitration Association
http://www.adr.org/index2.1.jsp

American Bar Association
http://www.abanet.org/crimjust/links.html

American Community Corrections Institute
http://www.accilifeskills.com

American Correctional Association
http://www.corrections.com/aca/index

American Probation and Parole Association
http://www.appa-net.org

American Psychological Association
http://www.apa.org

BI Incorporated
http://www.bi.com

Boot Camps
http://www.boot-camps-info.com

Boot Camps for Struggling Teens
http://www.juvenile-boot-camps.com

Building Blocks for Youth
http://www.buildingblocksforyouth.org/issues/girls/
resources.html

Bureau of Justice Statistics
http://www.ojp.usdoj.gov/bjs/correct.htm

Bureau of Justice Statistics Courts and Sentencing Statistics
http://www.ojp.usdoj.gov/bjs/stsent.htm

Center for Community Corrections
http://www.communitycorrectionsworks.org/aboutus

Center for Court Innovation
http://www.courtinnovation.org

Center for Restorative Justice
http://www.ssw.che/.umn.edu/rjp

Citizen Probation
http://www.citizenprobation.com

Citizens for Legal Responsibility
http://www.clr.org

Coalition for Federal Sentencing Reform
http://www.mn.sentencing.org

Corrections Corporation of America
http://www.correctionscorp.com

Corrections Industries Association
http://www.correctionalindustries.org

Council of Juvenile Correctional Administrators
http://www.corrections.com/cjca

Faith to Faith Friends
http://www.f2ff.com

Federal Judicial Center
http://www.fjc.gov

Gurley House Women's Recovery Center
http://www.thegurleyhouse.org

History of Federal Bureau of Prisons
http://www.bop.gov/lpapg/pahist.html

Home Confinement Program
http://thwp.uscourts.gov/homeconfinement.html

International Community Corrections Association
http://www.iccaweb.org

International Corrections and Prisons Association
http://www.icpa.ca/home.html

International Institute on Special-Needs Offenders
http://www.iisno.org.uk

ISCOS Halfway Houses
iscos.org.sq/halfway.html

Juvenile Intensive Probation Supervision
http://www.nal.usda.gov/pavnet/yf/yfjuvpro.htm

Juvenile Justice Reform Initiatives
http://www.ojjdp.ncjrs.org/pubs/reform/ch2_k.html

Legal Resource Center
http://www.crimelynx.com/research.html

National Association for Community Mediation
http://www.nafcm.org

National Association of Pretrial Services
http://www.napsa.org

National Association of Probation Executives
http://www.napchome.org

National Association of Social Workers
http://www.naswdc.org

National Corrections Corporation
http://www.nationalcorrections.com

National Council of Juvenile and Family Court Judges
http://www.ncjfcj.unr.edu

National Criminal Justice Reference Service
http://www.ncjrs.org

National Institute of Corrections
http://www.nicic.org

National Institute of Justice
http://www.ojp.usdoj.gov/nij

National Institute on Drug Abuse
http://www.nida.nih.gov

National State History of Halfway Houses
http://www.ni-cor.com/halfwayhouses.html

National Youth Court Center
http://www.youthcourt.net

Office of Juvenile Justice and Delinquency Prevention
http://www.ojjdp.ncjrs.org

Paraprofessionals
http://www.ptcwct.ptc.edu:8800/public/CRJ244OSM

Pretrial Procedures
http://www.uaa.alaska.edu/just/just110/courts2.html

Pretrial Services Resource Center
http://www.pretrial.org

Probation and Parole Compact Administrators Association
http://www.ppcaa.net

Recidivism of Adult Felons
http://www.auditor.leg.state.mn.us/ped/pedrep/
9701-sum.pdf

Recidivism of Adult Probationers
http://www.co.hennepin.mn.us/commcorr/reports/
RecidivismofAdultProbationers.htm

Reynolds Work Release Second Chance Program
http://www.wa.gov/doc/REYN02DSWRdescription.htm

Sentencing Advisory Panel
http://www.sentencing-advisory-panel.gov.uk

Sentencing Project
http://www.sentencingproject.org

Sex Offenders Treatment Program
http://www.auditor.leg.state.mn.us/sexoff.htm

Special Offenders and Special-Needs Offenders
http://www.shsu.edu/~icc_rjh/364f00.htm

Teen Boot Camp
http://www.teenbootcamps.com

Teen Court
http://www.teen-court.org

U.S. Courts
http://www.flmp.uscourts.gov/Presentence/presentence

U.S. Department of Justice
http://www.usdoj.gov/02organizations/02_1.html

U.S. Parole Commission
http://www.usdoj.gov/uspc/releasetxt.htm

U.S. Sentencing Commission
http://www.ussc.gov

Vera Institute of Justice
http://www.vera.org

Volunteers in Prevention, Probation, and Prisons, Inc.
http://www.comnet.org/vip

Volunteers of America
http://www.voa.org

Wilderness Programs, Inc.
http://www.wildernessprogramsetc.com

Youthful Offenders Parole Board
http://www.yopb.ca.gov

Glossary

acceptance of responsibility   A genuine admission or acknowledgment of wrongdoing. In federal presentence investigation reports, for example, convicted offenders may write an explanation and apology for the crime(s) they have committed. A provision that may be considered in deciding whether leniency should be extended to offenders during the sentencing phase of their processing.

aggravating circumstances   Elements of a crime that may intensify the severity of punishment, including bodily injury, death to the victim, or the brutality of the act.

alternative dispute resolution (ADR)   A procedure whereby a criminal case is redefined as a civil one and the case is decided by an impartial arbiter, where both parties agree to amicable settlement. Usually reserved for minor offenses.

bench parole, bench probation   Action by a court to permit convicted offenders to remain free in their communities under the jurisdiction of the sentencing judge only.

board of pardons   Special appointed boards in different jurisdictions that convene to hear requests from inmates to be pardoned or to receive executive clemency from governors.

board of parole   Any body of persons, usually appointed by the governor or chief executive officer of any jurisdiction, that convenes for the purpose of determining an inmate's early release. Each state and the federal government have a parole board. Most state parole boards are gubernatorial appointments. Parole boards vary in size from three-person panels to as many as ten to twelve members. No special qualifications are required for parole board membership.

classification, classification of prisoners   Inmate security designation based on psychological, social, and sociodemographic criteria and various types of instruments relating to one's potential dangerousness or risk posed to the public. It is used to categorize offenders according to the level of custody they require while incarcerated. It measures potential disruptiveness of prisoners and early release potential of inmates for parole consideration. Some offenders may be placed in particular vocational, educational, counseling, or other types of programming and treatment.

Code of Hammurabi (circa 1792–1750 BC) Babylon's first written criminal code. It was preceded by the Sumerian Code of Ur-Nammu. It was believed to be the first and most important codification of law, before the discovery of the Code of Lipit-Ishtar.

Code of Lipit-Ishtar (circa 1868–1857 BC) Subsequent code of laws devised in Sumer following the Code of Ur-Nammu.

community-based corrections facilities, community-based corrections programs, community corrections Locally operated services offering minimum-security, limited-release, and work-release alternatives to prisoners about to be paroled. These programs may also serve probationers.

community-based supervision Reintegrative programs operated publicly or privately to assist offenders by providing therapeutic, support, and supervision programs for criminals. Programs may include furloughs, probation, parole, community service, and restitution.

community-service orders Judicially imposed restitution for those convicted of committing crimes. Some form of work must be performed to satisfy restitution requirements.

Comprehensive Crime Control Act of 1984 A significant act that authorized the establishment of the U.S. Sentencing Commission, instituted sentencing guidelines, provided for the abolition of federal parole, and devised new guidelines and goals for federal corrections.

conditions of probation or parole, conditions of release on probation or parole The general (state-ordered) and special (court-ordered or board-ordered) limits imposed on offenders who are released either on probation or parole. General conditions tend to be fixed by statute; special conditions are mandated by the sentencing authority and take into consideration the background of the offender and circumstances surrounding the offense.

concurrent sentences, sentencing In multiple-conviction cases involving two or more crimes, sentences run in sequence rather than concurrently; two ten-year sentences would be served at the same time; offenders would serve a total of ten years in prison, serving both sentences simultaneously.

consecutive sentences, sentencing More than one sentence imposed on the same occasion to a convicted offender, with the sentences to be served one after another and not concurrently.

corporal punishment The infliction of pain on the body by any device or method as a form of punishment.

corrections The aggregate of programs, services, facilities, and organizations responsible for the management of people who have been accused or convicted of criminal offenses.

creative sentencing A broad class of punishments as alternatives to incarceration that are designed to fit the particular crimes. They may involve community service, restitution, fines, becoming involved in educational or vocational training programs, or becoming affiliated with other "good works" activity.

criminal history information Any background details of a person charged with a crime. The term refers to any legal actions, such as prior convictions, indictments, and arrests.

day reporting center A community correctional center where offenders report daily to comply with the conditions of their sentence, probation, or parole program.

defendant's sentencing memorandum A version of events leading to the conviction offense in the words of the offender. This memorandum may be submitted together with a victim impact statement.

diversion program One of several programs preceding a formal court adjudication of charges against defendants in which they participate in therapeutic, educational, and other helping programs.

electronic monitoring (EM), electronic monitoring devices The use of electronic devices (usually anklets or wristlets) that emit electronic signals to monitor offenders, probationers, and parolees. The purpose of their use is to monitor an offender's presence in the environment in which the offender is required to remain or to verify the offender's whereabouts.

extralegal factors Any element of a nonlegal nature. In determining whether law enforcement officers are influenced by particular factors when encountering juveniles on the streets, extralegal factors might include juvenile attitude, politeness, appearance, and dress. Legal factors might include age and specific prohibited acts observed by the officers.

fair sentencing Sentencing practices that incorporate fairness for both victims and offenders. Fairness is said to be achieved by implementing principles of proportionality, equity, social debt, and truth in sentencing.

felony probation A procedure of not requiring felons to serve time in jail or prison, usually because of prison overcrowding. It involves a conditional sentence in lieu of incarceration.

fixed indeterminate sentencing A sentencing scheme whereby a judge sentences offenders to a single prison term that is treated as the maximum sentence for all practical purposes. A parole board may determine an early release date for the offender.

good marks Credit obtained by prisoners in nineteenth-century England. Prisoners were given "marks" for participating in educational programs and other self-improvement activities.

"good time," "good-time" credits An amount of time deducted from the period of incarceration of a convicted offender, calculated as so many days per month on the basis of good behavior while incarcerated; credits earned by prisoners for good behavior. The system was introduced in the early 1800s by British penal authorities, including Alexander Maconochie and Sir Walter Crofton.

"good-time" laws Regulations that allow a reduction of a portion of a prisoner's sentence for good behavior while in prison.

habitual-criminal laws, habitual-offender statutes These statutes vary among states. They generally provide life imprisonment as a mandatory sentence for chronic offenders who have been convicted of three or more serious felonies within a specific time period.

habitual offender Any person who has been convicted of two or more felonies and may be sentenced under a habitual offender statute for an aggravated or longer prison term.

hard time A sentence served under conditions that create relatively severe discomfort. The term is used to describe actual imprisonment for a specified period.

indeterminate sentencing A sentencing scheme in which a period is set by judges between the earliest date for a parole decision and the latest date for completion of the sentence. In holding that the time necessary for treatment cannot be set exactly, the indeterminate sentence is closely associated with rehabilitation.

intensive supervised probation/parole (ISP) No specific guidelines exist across all jurisdictions, but ISP usually means lower caseloads for probation officers, fewer than ten clients per month, regular drug tests, and other intensive supervision measures.

intensive supervision program A probation or parole program in which the officer-offender ratio is low, offenders receive frequent visits from their officer-supervisors, and continuous communication is maintained by the supervising agency or authority.

jail as a condition of probation A sentence in which the judge imposes limited jail time to be served before commencement of probation.

judicial plea bargaining The recommended sentence by a judge who offers a specific sentence or fine in exchange for a guilty plea.

life sentence A judicially imposed term of imprisonment equal to the life of the sentenced offender.

life-without-parole (LWOP) A penalty imposed as the maximum punishment in states that do not have the death penalty. It provides for permanent incarceration of offenders in prisons without parole eligibility. Early release may be attained through accumulation of good-time credits.

mandatory minimum sentencing   A flat-time sentence that must be imposed such that a minimum amount of time must be served before an inmate becomes eligible for parole.

mandatory sentencing   Sentencing in which the court is required to impose an incarcerative sentence of a specified length, without the option for probation, suspended sentence, or immediate parole eligibility.

maximum sentence   Under law, the most severe sentence a judge can impose on a convicted offender.

mixed sentence   Two or more separate sentences imposed after an offender has been convicted of two or more crimes in the same adjudication proceeding.

objective parole criteria   General qualifying conditions that permit parole boards to make nonsubjective parole decisions without regard to an inmate's race, religion, gender, age, or socioeconomic status.

offender-based presentence investigation report   A presentence investigation report that seeks to understand an offender and the circumstances that led to the offense, and to evaluate the potential of the offender to become a law-abiding and productive citizen.

offense seriousness   Crimes with greater punishments associated with their commission; the degree of gravity of the conviction offense (for example, felonies are more serious than misdemeanors).

parole   Prerelease from prison short of serving a full sentence; the status of an offender conditionally released from a confinement facility prior to the expiration of the sentence and placed under the supervision of a parole agency.

parolee   A convicted offender who has been released from prison short of serving the full sentence originally imposed, and who usually must abide by conditions established by the parole board or paroling authority.

parole guidelines   Protocol to be followed in making parole release decisions. Most guidelines prescribe a presumptive term for each class of convicted inmate, depending on both offense and offender characteristics.

parole program   The specific conditions under which inmates are granted early release.

parole revocation   A two-stage proceeding that may result in a parolee's reincarceration in jail or prison. The first stage is a preliminary hearing to determine whether the parolee violated any specific parole condition. The second stage determines whether parole should be canceled and the offender reincarcerated.

plea bargaining, plea negotiation   A preconviction deal-making process between the state and the accused in which the defendant exchanges a plea of guilty or nolo contendere for a reduction in charges, a promise of sentencing leniency, or some other concession from full, maximum implementation of the conviction and sentencing authority of the court. Types of plea bargaining include implicit plea bargaining, charge reduction bargaining, sentence recommendation bargaining, and judicial plea bargaining.

predisposition investigation, predisposition report, predispositional investigation, predispositional report A report prepared by a juvenile intake officer to furnish a juvenile judge with background about a juvenile so that the judge can make a more informed sentencing decision. It is similar to a presentence investigation report.

prescriptive guidelines Sentencing guidelines in which the sentence values are determined on the basis of value judgments about appropriateness rather than on the basis of past practice.

presentence investigation An examination of a convicted offender by a probation officer, usually requested or ordered by the court, including a victim impact statement, prior arrest records, and the offender's employment and educational history.

presentence investigation report, presentence report (PSI) A report filed by a probation or parole officer appointed by the court containing background information, socioeconomic data, and demographic data relative to a defendant. Facts in the case are included. It is used to influence the sentence imposed by a judge and by a parole board considering an inmate for early release.

probatio "Test" (Latin); a period of proving, trial, or forgiveness.

probation An alternative sentence to incarceration in which the convict stays under the state's authority. It involves conditions and retention of authority by the sentencing court to modify the conditions of sentence or to resentence the offender if the offender violates the conditions. Such a sentence should not involve or require suspension of the imposition or execution of any other sentence.

punishment Any penalty imposed for committing delinquency or a crime.

recidivism The return to criminality, including rearrest, reconviction, and reincarceration of previously convicted felons or misdemeanants.

recidivism rate The proportion of offenders who, when released from probation or parole, commit further crimes.

recidivist Repeat offender.

restitution A stipulation by a court that offenders must compensate victims for their financial losses resulting from crime; compensation to a victim for psychological, physical, or financial loss. Restitution may be imposed as a part of an incarcerative sentence.

risk assessment, risk assessment device or instrument, risk prediction scale The process of forecasting one's likelihood of reoffending if released from prison on parole or placed on probation by a judge. Any instrument designed to predict or anticipate one's future behavior based on past circumstances or answers given to questions on questionnaires.

Salient Factor Score, SFS 76, SFS 81 A score used by parole boards and agencies to forecast an offender's risk to the public and future dangerousness; the numerical classification that predicts the probability of a parolee's success if parole is granted. The different versions (SFS 76, SFS 81) refer to the years in which they were devised.

seamless parole, seamless probation To provide continuity of care for inmates while they are confined, and to continue this care and treatment into their community life once they leave the prison environment. Such parole programs are often used with drug-dependent offenders. The program oversees and coordinates all interrelated state and private programs involved in substance abuse treatment for offenders, both inside and outside of prison. Case management and drug and alcohol testing are used, and the program ranges over 6 to 9 months inside prison, depending on offender needs and responses to provided services and treatments.

sentence A penalty imposed on a convicted person for a crime. Penalties may include incarceration, fine, both, or some other alternative.

sentence, flat A term of incarceration that must be served in its entirety without early release, sometimes called flat time; the actual amount of time served.

sentence, maximum The upper limit of time one must serve in incarceration.

sentence, minimum The least amount of time one must serve in incarceration before being freed.

sentence, suspended A period of time of incarceration imposed by a judge but the implementation of which is withheld temporarily while the person serves probation in lieu of incarceration.

sentencing The process of imposing a punishment on a defendant convicted of one or more crimes.

sentencing commission A group commissioned by the legislature to determine sentencing policy and usually to monitor implementation of that policy.

sentencing disparity Inconsistency in the sentencing of convicted offenders, in which those committing similar crimes under similar circumstances are given widely disparate sentences by the same judge, usually on the basis of gender, race, ethnicity, or socioeconomic factors.

sentencing guidelines Instruments developed by the federal government and various states to assist judges in assessing fair and consistent lengths of incarceration for various crimes and past criminal histories. Use of these guidelines is referred to as "presumptive sentencing" in some jurisdictions.

sentencing hearing An optional hearing held in many jurisdictions in which defendants and victims can hear the contents of presentence investigation reports prepared by probation officers. Defendants and victims may respond to a report orally, in writing, or both. The hearing precedes the sentence imposed by the judge.

sentencing memorandum A court decision that furnishes a ruling or finding and orders it to be implemented relative to convicted offenders. This document does not necessarily include reasons or a rationale for the sentence imposed.

Sentencing Project, The An organization headquartered in Washington, D.C., that promotes the development of sentencing alternatives. It publishes numerous reports, many indicating the inequitable and discriminatory treatment of minorities in the criminal-justice system.

Sentencing Reform Act of 1984 An act that provided federal judges and others with considerable discretionary power to provide alternative sentencing and other provisions in their sentencing of offenders.

shock probation The practice of sentencing offenders to prison or jail for a brief period, primarily to give them a taste, or "shock," of prison or jail life, and then releasing them into the custody of a probation or parole officer through a resentencing project.

split sentence A punishment imposed by a criminal court that consists of a term of confinement together with conditional release, such as probation.

split sentencing The procedure whereby a judge imposes a sentence of incarceration for a fixed period, followed by a probationary period of a fixed duration; similar to shock probation.

suspended sentence A jail or prison term that is delayed while the defendant undergoes a period of community treatment. If treatment is successful, the jail or prison sentence is terminated.

truth in sentencing, truth-in-sentencing laws Close correspondence between the sentence imposed and the sentence actually served; federal policy and admonition advocated in the Crime Bill of 1994.

unconditional diversion (standard diversion) program A diversion program requiring minimal or no contact with a probation department. It may include a minimum maintenance fee paid regularly for a specified period, such as one year. No treatment program is indicated.

unconditional release The final release of an offender from the jurisdiction of a correctional agency; also, a final release from the jurisdiction of a court.

United States Sentencing Guidelines Implemented by federal courts in November 1987, these guidelines obligated federal judges to impose presumptive sentences on all convicted offenders. The guidelines are based on offense seriousness and offender characteristics. Judges may depart from the guidelines only by justifying their departures in writing.

victim-impact statement Information or a version of events filed voluntarily by the victim of a crime, appended to the presentence investigation report as a supplement for judicial consideration in sentencing the offender. It describes injuries to victims resulting from the convicted offender's actions.

victim/offender mediation A meeting between a criminal and a person suffering loss or injury from that criminal whereby a third-party arbiter, such as a judge, attorney, or other neutral party, decides what is best for all parties. All parties must agree to the decision of the third-party arbiter. The technique is used for both juvenile and adult offenders.

Victim/Offender Reconciliation Project (VORP) A form of alternative dispute resolution, whereby a civil resolution is made by mutual consent between the victim and an offender. Objectives are to provide restitution to victims, hold offenders accountable for the crime committed, and reduce recidivism.

Index

About the Author

Dean John Champion is professor of criminal justice at Texas A&M International University, Laredo, Texas. Dr. Champion has taught at the University of Tennessee–Knoxville, California State University–Long Beach, and Minot State University. He received his Ph.D. from Purdue University and his B.S. and M.A. degrees from Brigham Young University. He completed several years of law school at the Nashville School of Law.

Dr. Champion has written more than thirty-seven texts and/or edited works and maintains memberships in eleven professional organizations. He is a lifetime member of the American Society of Criminology, Academy of Criminal Justice Sciences, and the American Sociological Association. He is a former editor of the Academy of Criminal Justice Sciences/Anderson Publishing Company Series on *Issues in Crime and Justice* and the *Journal of Crime and Justice,* and a contributing author for the *Encarta Encyclopedia 2000* for Microsoft. He has been a visiting scholar for the National Center for Juvenile Justice and is a former president of the Midwestern Criminal Justice Association. He has also designed or offered numerous online courses for the University of Phoenix, Excelsior University, the University of Alaska–Fairbanks, ITT Tech, and Texas A&M International University.

His published books include *Administration of Criminal Justice: Structure, Function, and Process* (2003, Prentice Hall); *Basic Statistics for Social Research* (1970, 1981, Macmillan); *Research Methods for Criminal Justice and Criminology, 3rd ed.* (1993, 2000, 2006, Prentice Hall); *The Juvenile Justice System: Delinquency, Processing, and the Law, 5th ed.* (1992, 1998, 2001, 2004, 2007, Prentice Hall); *Corrections in the United States: A Contemporary Perspective, 4th ed.* (1990, 1998, 2001, 2005, Prentice Hall); *Probation, Parole, and Community Corrections, 5th ed.* (1990, 1996, 1999, 2005, 2008, Prentice

Hall); and *Policing in the Community* (1996, with George Rush; Prentice Hall). Additional forthcoming books include *Leading U.S. Supreme Court Cases in Criminal Justice: Briefs and Key Terms, 4th ed.* (2009, Prentice Hall) and *Basic Statistics for Criminal Justice and Criminology: Social Science Applications, 3rd ed.* (2009, with Richard Hartley; Prentice Hall). Other books include *The U.S. Sentencing Guidelines* (1989, Praeger); *The American Dictionary of Criminal Justice: Key Terms and Leading U.S. Supreme Court Cases* (1997, 2001, 2005, Roxbury); *Felony Probation: Problems and Prospects* (1993, Praeger); *Police Misconduct in America* (2003, ABC-CLIO); *Sociology* (1980, with S. Kurth, D. Hastings, and D. Harris; Holt, Rinehart, and Winston); *Sociology of Organizations* (1975, McGraw-Hill); *Methods and Issues of Social Research* (1976, with J. Black; John Wiley Sons); *Criminal Justice in the United States* (1998, Wadsworth); *Measuring Offender Risk: A Sourcebook* (1994, Greenwood Press); *Transferring Juveniles to Criminal Courts* (1992, with G. Larry Mays; Praeger); and *Crime Prevention in America* (2007, Prentice Hall). His areas of specialization include juvenile justice, criminal justice administration, corrections, and statistics/methods.